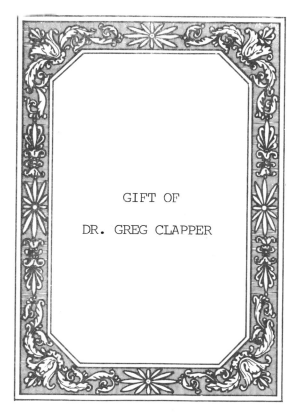

KNOWING AND
THE FUNCTION OF
REASON

KNOWING AND THE FUNCTION OF REASON

BY

RICHARD I. AARON

OXFORD
AT THE CLARENDON PRESS
1971

Oxford University Press, Ely House, London W. 1

GLASGOW NEW YORK TORONTO MELBOURNE WELLINGTON
CAPE TOWN SALISBURY IBADAN NAIROBI DAR ES SALAAM LUSAKA ADDIS ABABA
BOMBAY CALCUTTA MADRAS KARACHI LAHORE DACCA
KUALA LUMPUR SINGAPORE HONG KONG TOKYO

PRINTED IN GREAT BRITAIN
AT THE UNIVERSITY PRESS, OXFORD
BY VIVIAN RIDLER
PRINTER TO THE UNIVERSITY

CONTENTS

Introduction   vii

PART I THE CONSTRAINT OF KNOWLEDGE

I. Knowing and Being Sure 3

II. Unfailing Assurance 27

III. Certain Knowledge 49

IV. Illustrative Cases 66

PART II THE SPONTANEITY OF THOUGHT

V. Characteristics of Thinking: Preliminary Remarks 91

VI. The Use of Language 104

VII. Speech and Thought 123

VIII. The Spontaneity of Thought 147

PART III THE FUNCTION OF REASON

IX. The Function of Reason 175

X. Knowledge of What Is 188

XI. The Framework of Conceptual Thinking: Substance and Causality 209

XII. Consistency and the Laws of Thought 240

Conclusion 266

Index of Persons 273

Index of Subjects 275

INTRODUCTION

ONE of the earliest extant examinations of human knowledge is Plato's in the *Theaetetus* and at the opening of the dialogue he makes a point which deserves our attention. In discussing this matter, he argues, we ought to concern ourselves not primarily with what is known, with, for instance, the body of knowledge which any craftsman has (in carpentry, cobblering, medicine, and so on), but rather with the knowing. The question that is fundamental is not 'what the objects of knowledge are, nor yet how many sorts of knowledge there are. We did not want to count them, but to find out what the thing itself—knowledge—is.'[1] On this view a person who drew up a list of possible objects of knowledge would not be attending to the central problem of epistemology nor would one who listed the various crafts and sciences. The latter would be a useful exercise, but not the fundamental one in this field. So too the inquirer who set out the procedures of each craft and the methodologies of the various sciences—admittedly a praise-worthy achievement—would still be failing to grapple with the true problem. A catalogue of methodologies is no substitute for an account of human knowledge; the study of a particular method is a task for a specialist; a writer who is able to discuss adequately the methods employed in one discipline, say physics, is not likely to write with equal competence of, say, botany, not to mention so totally different a discipline as history. In any case the task of the philosopher, in Plato's view, is not with these methodologies. The questions Plato actually sets before himself in the *Theaetetus* are whether knowing can be identified with sense-perception; failing this, whether it is true judgement; or, failing this again, whether it is a true belief with adequate explanatory evidence. As it turns out he finds that none of these accounts is satisfactory and no theory emerges that he is prepared to accept, but what he does offer is a delimitation of the epistemologist's field.

[1] *Theaetetus* 146 e.

In what follows we need not discuss these matters in the language of Plato's dialogues, yet it is his central problem which we still need to discuss, even though we do so in a modern idiom. Now discussion within this field tends to concern itself today with the contrast between certain knowledge and belief that so-and-so is probable, and with the question whether we can claim that any knowledge whatsoever is certain. Certain knowledge is sometimes spoken of as knowledge 'in the strict sense'; if one knows in the strict sense one is certain or sure. But is it enough to say this? Can knowing in this strict sense be identified with being certain or being sure? Hardly, for if one knows in the strict sense one cannot be in error, but a person may be sure of something and yet be in error. Knowing, therefore, cannot be identified with being sure, though being sure is one requirement. What more is needed? What are the requisites of knowledge in the strict sense? One requisite, on the theory, is that one is sure. What are the other requisites?

I propose to begin the discussion of knowledge with an examination of this contemporary inquiry, hoping that a satisfactory account of knowing in the strict sense will emerge. It will then be necessary to widen the scope of this discussion, for other elements, in addition to knowing in the strict sense, are present in cognition and need to be understood. One element is that of thinking, and the question that at once arises is how thinking is related to knowing. It has been held, as we shall see, that knowing *is* thinking, but this is a position not easy to defend. There would seem to be obvious differences between them, though it is also true that by thinking one may extend one's knowledge. Certainly the study of thinking, and of its relation to knowledge, has its rightful place in epistemology and due attention must be paid to it. Further, our thinking is for the most part verbal—we must later consider the extent to which this is so—and consequently the nature of language has to be considered. In particular, we must consider the way in which language functions as an instrument of thought and how thought itself is influenced by its use of language.

A third task will remain when the examination of knowing

and thinking (and of the relationship between them) will have been completed, and this is to ascertain the nature of reason and its role in cognition. We shall argue that the existence of Reason, in the sense in which rationalists speak of it, need not be presupposed as a precondition of knowledge. This argument will involve us in a study of the *a priori* as an allegedly necessary precondition of human knowledge. It is held that Reason is the *a priori* source of our knowledge of such categories as substance and cause and of such principles as noncontradiction, identity, and excluded middle; but we shall question this and put forward a theory which will provide an alternative account of the function of reason.

This point leads to another. Objection may be made to the programme I have just outlined on the ground that it would appear to ignore the two traditional theories of knowledge, namely, rationalism and empiricism. We may accept for the moment the usual working definitions of these two theories that run somewhat as follows: Rationalism is the theory that man is endowed with a capacity or power of intellectual intuition or *nous* which enables him to apprehend the truth, this being the only way in which it can be apprehended. Empiricism, on the other hand, is the theory that human knowledge is acquired in sense-perception, or is derived from what is so acquired, and is verified by subsequent sense-perception, it being understood that what sense-perception reveals is never the full reality, so that the problem of correlating appearance and reality arises. These are the traditional theories and there is a strong assumption that anyone who sets out to give an account of human knowledge must do so in terms of either rationalism or empiricism. In addition these theories tend to be linked with metaphysical theories, rationalism with idealism and empiricism with positivism. So the philosopher is faced with two alternatives and two only; he has to choose between rationalism, and the metaphysic that goes along with it, and empiricism, and its accompanying metaphysic.

But this assumption seems to me mistaken, for it oversimplifies the issue. It would appear that any wholly rationalist or wholly empiricist theory of human knowledge is bound to be inadequate, whilst a straightforward amalgamation of the two would not be a coherent theory. It is admittedly not easy to free oneself from the tendency to make the above assumption, but the effort must be made. Needless to say the rationalisms and empiricisms of the past contain valuable elements which will be freely used in what follows. Yet the argument of this book is dominated by neither theory; in part it is the outcome of a dissatisfaction with the traditional rationalist and the traditional empiricist theories of human knowledge and it rejects the view that these are the only alternatives open to the inquirer.

PART ONE
THE CONSTRAINT OF
KNOWLEDGE

I

KNOWING AND BEING SURE

1. The word 'know' is used in widely different ways, but the epistemologist has always found his main interest in that use of it which involves a contrast between knowledge and opinion. In the wide sense of the term 'knowledge', opinion is itself a species of knowledge, but in the narrower sense knowledge is contrasted with opinion. If I say: 'The Labour party will win the next election', then that the Labour party will win the next election is a belief or opinion of mine, for which I do not claim certainty. Belief in this sense is contrasted with knowledge which is certain; the former is fallible, whilst the latter, it is claimed—for instance by Plato—is infallible. The question then arises what sort of knowledge is infallible knowledge. Has it a distinct kind of object? Is infallible knowledge the only knowledge? Or would opinion be knowledge if what was believed was true?

The traditional contrast requires further examination. In opining, it is claimed, my knowledge is fallible and I myself do not pretend to certainty; in knowing in the strict sense my knowledge is infallible and I am certain. But what are the relations between being certain and knowing? If I am certain do I then know in the strictest and narrowest sense of that term? Is certainty to be equated with infallibility? It can be argued that the Cartesian doctrine of *intuitus* does make the equation. On the other hand, most philosophers today would reject the view that if a man is certain he then *ipso facto* has knowledge.

The debate about this matter provides a good starting-point for reflection on knowledge. A person is certain or is sure that *p* (in this context we may identify being certain with being sure). This, it is argued, is no proof that he knows. For three conditions have to be satisfied before a man can be said to know.[1] In the first place, he must be sure; in the second, he must be able to produce evidence justifying his assurance; and in the third place, what he is sure of must be true. Being sure in itself is not enough. I may be sure that John is on the lawn, but I do not know this unless I can produce adequate evidence and unless, too, John *is* on the lawn. When the three conditions, or requirements are satisfied I may be said to know (and not merely be sure) that John is on the lawn. This theory was formulated in the thirties of this century, but it is grounded on much earlier thinking.

The theory, which may be termed the Three Condition Theory, at first seems convincing, but in what follows I wish to suggest that it is not as convincing as it at first appears, that it is indeed misleading, and that its neatness and apparent completeness make it the more dangerous. The argument implies that if one doubts whether A knows when he is sure that p one can then test A's claim to knowledge by the presence or absence of the other necessary conditions. But is this in fact possible? A is sure that p. I test his claim to knowledge by examining the evidence that would justify his being sure, or again by finding out whether p is or is not true. But this means that I myself become sure either that the evidence does (or does not) justify him or again that p is true. Yet what right have I to trust my own assurance if I doubt A's assurance when he is sure? I assume that I know when I am sure but I do not allow that this too is true of A. But how then can I justify my own position? This is the fundamental difficulty which the Three Condition Theory appears to ignore, and it is the matter to be investigated in the present chapter.

2. In considering the theory certain preliminary questions require attention. In the first place it will be obvious that it does not apply to knowing in some of the uses of that word. Thus, in so far as one can distinguish between 'knowing that'

---

[1] The use of the term 'condition' in the debate is frequent. As an example cf. A. J. Ayer, *The Problem of Knowledge*, p. 35, where he speaks of the three 'necessary and sufficient conditions for knowing that something is the case'.

and 'knowing how', the theory does not generally apply to knowing in the 'knowing how' sense. 'He knows how to grow dahlias.' Obviously the theory does not apply here; at the moment he may not even be thinking of dahlias, but he still knows how to grow them. Nor does it apply to 'He knows French.' If somebody were to speak in French he could answer; if he opened a French book he could read and understand it. But there is nothing here to which the Three Condition Theory can apply. If in translating he translates 'house' by 'maison' he then can be said to know that the French word for 'house' is 'maison' and the theory, it may be held, is in that case applicable. Generally speaking the theory cannot be said to be applicable to 'knowing how' statements, though there are uses of the phrase 'knowing how' to which it may be applicable. Consider these further examples: 'As soon as he read the letter he knew how deeply she had felt' and 'He knew how great the difficulties would be.' In these cases the theory could apply, but these statements are not 'knowing how' statements as usually understood.

Again, it is doubtful whether seeing a colour, tasting a taste, or hearing a noise can rightly be held to be an instance of knowing, though recognizing these on subsequent occasions would usually be thought to be so. Certainly seeing a shade of colour would be too primitive an experience to rank normally as an instance of knowledge to which the Three Condition Theory could appropriately apply. On the other hand were I to say: 'This is a buzzard' on the strength of sensory experience then this presumably would be a situation in which the theory did apply.

Thus the theory does not apply to any and every instance of knowing. It is still more obvious that it does not apply to every occasion on which the word 'knowing' is used. The point has been frequently made that whereas 'know' is used in statements that signify that a person knows so and so, for instance, 'He knows now that his father is dead', the word can be used too in ways very different from this. J. L. Austin was right when he said that such phrases as 'I know that . . .' have a performative or an illocutionary use, though it would be wrong to suggest that this was the invariable use. Thus in saying: 'I know that he is reliable' I may indeed want to draw attention to the fact that I do *know* that he is reliable and a hearer could sensibly consider whether I do know this and ask whether the above three conditions are satisfied. But much more often, as the tone of voice, the emphasis, the gestures, and the context go to show, I use the words in another way. At different times 'I know that he is reliable' is equivalent to (*a*) 'I agree that he is reliable', (*b*) 'I concede that he is reliable', (*c*) 'He is reliable and I emphasize that he is so', (*d*) 'Whatever others think I state categorically that he is reliable', and so on. On such occasions I do know that he is reliable, but I am not saying that I know this, though I do say: 'I know that he is reliable'; my purpose in using these words is different. So much is this so that 'I know that he is reliable' in other situations might even be equivalent to 'I don't know that he is reliable, but it is best that you believe it and so I affirm it categorically to make you believe it'. Indeed I might utter this sentence in such a tone of voice and with such hesitation that you will know that I do not really believe that he is reliable. It is odd, and yet true, that I can use the phrase 'I know that *p*' in a manner that will make it clear to my hearers that I do not know that *p* and do not want them to think that I do. The teacher says to her class of rowdy youngsters: 'I know you'll be quiet till I return.' She does not believe that they will, but she makes the appeal. 'I know you'll keep this to yourself', says one inveterate gossip to another. How difficult it is for a foreigner to catch all the varied and the minute differences in the uses of this one English word, 'know'. His dictionary, if it is a good one, will give him six or seven definitions of the word, yet no lexicographer can hope to make clear what the word can convey in all its uses in the living speech.

Now in the case of many of these uses there can be no question of applying the Three Condition Theory, and we are not concerned with them in this chapter. But when I say, for instance: 'Tom knows that the gates shut at five' I am very likely to mean (though this is not inevitable) that Tom is sure of this, and I can ask whether the evidence in favour of what he says is adequate and whether his statement is true. There are many ways in which Tom may have become sure. He may have seen the gates being shut on several occasions; he may have been told that it was the rule; or he may have inferred that they shut at five from what he has seen and heard. But whatever the means of acquiring the information, he is now quite sure about it and the question arises whether he knows. This, on the theory, is identical with the question whether the other conditions are satisfied.

3. Before proceeding further it would be of interest to consider a statement of Kant's, which is itself a summing up of considerable earlier doctrine. At the end of the first *Critique* in discussing the canon of pure reason Kant sets forward a distinction between opining (*Meinen*), believing (*Glauben*), and knowing (*Wissen*). 'The holding of something to be true (*das Fürwahrhalten*)', he says,[1] 'or the subjective validity of the judgement, in its relation to conviction (which is at the same time objectively valid), has the following three degrees: *opining, believing*, and *knowing*. Opining is such holding of a judgement as is consciously insufficient, not only objectively, but also subjectively. If our holding of the judgement be only subjectively sufficient and is at the same time taken as being objectively insufficient, we have what is termed *believing*. Lastly, when the holding of something to be true is sufficient both subjectively and objectively, it is *knowledge*. The subjective sufficiency is termed *conviction* (for myself), the objective sufficiency is termed *certainty* (for everyone). There is no call for me to spend further time on the explanation of such easily understood terms.'

We may compare this theory with the Three Condition Theory. Of statements that may possibly be taken to be true I find some subjectively insufficient, that is I am not sure that they are true. They are also objectively insufficient; by which Kant seems to mean (judging by the rest of this paragraph) that the

[1] A 822, B 850.

evidence that would convince not only myself but everyone else is lacking. This is opining, and in opining the evidence is convincing neither to myself nor to anyone else. Suppose, however, that I do find the evidence sufficient, I am then believing; though the fact that I find the evidence sufficient is not proof that it is sufficient. When lastly the evidence is sufficient both subjectively and objectively then I know; I myself have conviction (*Überzeugung*) and all share the certainty (*Gewissheit für Jedermann*). Objective sufficiency in this case seems to mean, first, that the evidence is adequate, second, that all accept it as adequate.

Opining, believing, and knowing are said to be degrees in the holding of something to be true (*das Fürwahrhalten*). Kant is limiting his field; if nothing is held to be true in, for example, claiming to know how to swim or how to speak French, or in seeing a colour, or in any other experience, then it is outside the present field of study. Again, I may be conscious of another's goodness and reliability and this is knowledge of a sort, but it is not the knowing in question here unless I 'hold something to be true'. This touches on the greatest difference between Kant's formulation and that of the Three Condition Theory, for the third of the latter's conditions, that *p* must be true, is absent in Kant's formulation. All that he says is that whether one opines, believes, or knows one must then be opining, believing, or knowing something which is held to be true.

On the other hand Kant recognizes in this division what the moderns insist upon but the ancients sometimes ignored. It is not enough to pose the problem of knowledge in terms of knowing and opining, of certainty and probability. To do so is to turn away from the acutest problem in human epistemology, for a man may be convinced and subjectively certain and yet not be knowing. In Kant's language, in addition to *Meinen* and *Wissen* there is *Glauben* or, in the modern expression, one may be quite sure of *p*, and not merely opine that *p* is probable, and yet fail to know. Kant recognizes this, the conviction may be a 'subjective' phenomenon only. It needs testing. Kant asks that the evidence on which the conviction rests should be adequate. And for him the evidence is adequate if it is such that all accept it. For Kant, then, I know that p when I am convinced or sure that p and when the evidence is adequate for all; these are the two conditions of knowledge.

4. Unlike Kant the modern theory sets down three conditions, and I propose in the rest of this chapter to consider each in turn.

(i) *Being sure*. Somebody says that he knows that p. The first condition that has to be satisfied, on this theory, is that he is sure. If he claims to know but is not sure this is not knowledge. If so much were accepted, it would follow that to say: 'He knows that the table is mahogany but is not sure of this' would be to contradict oneself.

Clearly, this is the very restricted use of the word 'know' already referred to. For what has just been said would not be true, for instance, of so-called dispositional knowledge. In the latter case he might know how and yet not be sure that he knew how. 'Do you know how to ride a bicycle?' 'I'm not sure that I know how, for I haven't been on one for many years.' Yet he mounts the bicycle and rides away safely. He knew how all along, we say, but he wasn't sure that he knew how. A slightly different case is that of repeating lines of a poem one has learnt by heart. 'Can you recite *The Daffodils*?' 'I knew it once, but I am not sure now.' Yet he recites it through correctly, showing that he knew it all the time.

Whilst these are instances of knowing, they are not instances for which being sure is said to be a condition. So, too, being sure is not a necessary condition for believing or opining (unless we say we are sure in the believing or opining that p is probably true—but this is another matter). Again, there is the mass of hearsay knowledge of some of which I may be quite sure, and of some not so sure. I am quite sure that Greenland is to the north of Britain, but not sure at this moment that Mozart was buried in a pauper's grave. I feel fairly sure that I have read that Mozart was so buried but should have to look it up to be sure.

The theorist who seeks to defend the Three Condition Theory is not concerned with these cases and he is not concerned with much that goes by the name of 'knowledge'. He concentrates on the cases in which one is sure, and he argues that being sure is a necessary condition in these cases and not an irrelevant feature. He would not be disturbed if I said: 'I thought I knew that Mozart had a pauper's burial—but now that you ask me I'm not completely sure of this.' On the other hand he would be seriously disturbed if I said: 'I know that this is my right hand but I am not sure óf this.'

Professor Woozley, however, has drawn our attention to those queer pathological states in which people will say that they know that p but yet do not feel sure. 'I know that I have locked the door but cannot be sure.' 'I know that my hands are clean for I have just washed them, but I cannot be sure and must wash them again.' The existence of such states as these, it may be said, gives a basis for refuting the thesis that to know that p invariably involves feeling sure that p. So the Three Condition Theory fails. Yet in the case considered we speak both of knowing and of being sure in an abnormal sense. It is difficult to enter into the frame of mind of the obsessed person who knows that he has washed his hands or locked the door and yet is not sure. It would be foolish to ask whether this is 'really' knowledge and 'really' being sure. But supporters of the Three Condition Theory might well argue that such cases are not instances of the knowing and of the being sure to which their theory applied. They will still maintain that knowing that p in their sense of these terms involves being sure.[1]

Suppose we agree to accept their view for the time being—if only to keep the Three Condition Theory alive. There then looms up a still more formidable difficulty. We are creatures who err and who are conscious of our fallibility. But can fallible creatures ever be sure? Shall we not always feel some degree of uncertainty in view of our liability to error? But if we are never sure then, on the theory, we never know.

[1] For further examples of a knowing that is not accompanied by being sure cf. Colin Radford, 'Knowledge—by Examples', *Analysis*, October 1966, 1–11.

Now, as has been frequently remarked, this is a philosophic doubt. It does not bother ordinary people, and it bothers the philosopher only in his study. In his study, however, he argues that in view of his consciousness of his fallibility he should be content with probability only, for nothing more is possible for him in his state. But against this argument two counter-arguments may be propounded. First, if doubt rules out certainty it also rules out probability and with equal force, since the assertion that p is probable is the assertion of the certainty of the probability of p. If this is valid then reflection on error would lead us to doubt whether even probable knowledge is possible.

More to the point, however, is the second argument aimed directly at philosophical scepticism. It is only too obvious that man is a fallible creature, but the sceptic who concludes in the light of this that no one can ever be sure is ignoring another fact, namely, that men are sure about many things. This may be paradoxical; but it is true, none the less, that fallible man is in fact frequently sure. Since this is so, it is wrong to rest one's argument totally on human fallibility and forget human assurance; in an inquiry into human knowledge both factors must be taken into consideration. Moreover, to say that a man is fallible is not to say that he always errs; it is not even to say that he sometimes errs. What is said is that he may err.

If this second argument be accepted, and it is a strong argument, then it is not in order for us to deny that a man can be sure on the ground that he is a fallible creature. On the other hand, it is in order for us to ask 'Is A sure that p?' and to deny that he knows p if he is not. If he is sure it does not follow that he knows, but, in the sense of the word 'knows' in which it is being used here, it is correct to say that there is no knowing without being sure. It is not enough to guess that p, or to have a hunch, or to think it likely to be true and be fairly sure of this. Even though p is in fact true and even though the evidence is such that others are convinced, unless A himself is sure he does not know. In the present sense of the word, knowing is not correct guessing, nor is it the judgement that p is probably true, even when p is true. Let us agree that being sure is the first condition, the first requisite, of knowing.

5. (ii) *Having a right to be sure*. One may be sure and yet not know; being sure is not enough. People have been completely convinced of many things in the past and have been subsequently shown to be in error. If A says he is sure that p, it does not follow that he knows that p. He must produce his credentials. Has he adequate evidence?

In discussing this question two minor points need to be cleared up at the outset. First, as G. J. Warnock has pointed out, in one sense the question whether A has a right to be sure never arises. Obviously, A has a right to be sure of anything he pleases. Why not? If a person is sure that his friend is reliable he has the right to be sure and he would continue to have this right even though the friend turned out to be unreliable. People have been sure of queer things, but they had every right to be even when they were wrong. At the same time one can reasonably ask, whilst acknowledging A's right to be sure, what his reasons are for saying that he is sure. He, explicitly or implicitly, claims to know that p, in being sure of p, but it does not follow that p is true because he is sure. It is quite sensible to ask A for his evidence for the truth of p.

In the second place, it was argued above that 'if A says he is sure that p it does not follow that he knows that p'. But this too may be misleading. For A must not only *say* that he is sure that p but *be* sure, for of course he may say this when not sure. He may pretend that he is sure or he may lie. Moreover, one may use 'I'm sure' in sentences that are not meant to convey that one is sure. 'I'm sure you're right' usually means 'I agree with you.' 'I'm sure that you will behave yourselves' from the harassed teacher can mean 'I know you're most unlikely to behave yourselves, but for goodness' sake try.'

Clearly, the question is not whether saying that one is sure is enough but whether being sure is enough, and the answer of the Three Condition Theory is that it is not enough. There must be evidence justifying one's claim to knowledge. A says he is sure that the box contains a ring. *B* asks for the evidence. *A* opens the box and says: 'See for yourself' and *B* sees the ring within it. The evidence justifies the claim. But this latter statement too is ambiguous. Granting for the moment that we know what evidence is and what justifying is, do we mean that *A* must have the evidence before him when he is sure? Supposing that through laziness, or because he does not think it necessary, or because no one is there to listen, *A* does not make clear to himself what the evidence is, but yet could state it if called upon to do so. Is this enough? Presumably it would be enough and the second condition would be met. On the other hand, some upholders of the theory might refuse to agree that *A* knows unless he has the evidence fully before him and unless he has consciously adjudged the evidence adequate.

At present we need not follow this point. A more important matter concerns the assumption that there always is evidence to justify knowledge. Anyone who is sceptical whether *A* really knows that *p* will want to inspect the evidence. But is the knowledge always such that evidence is available? I know that I have a headache now. What is my evidence? Could I say that my feeling the pain is my evidence? But this seems absurd, presumably because feeling the pain and knowing that I have it cannot be held apart in such a way that the former can be held to be evidence. In any case, if this were the evidence, I couldn't appeal to it to still your doubts that I have a headache, for you could not experience my pain. When, therefore, I say I am sure that I now have a headache and you query this, it is no good asking for evidence. All I can do is to repeat that I have the pain, and that I am as sure of this as I can be of anything. If it be insisted that wherever there is genuine knowledge not only is one sure but one's right to be sure can be shown, that is to say, adequate evidence can be brought forward, then one would have to say that knowing that one has a headache is not an instance of genuine knowledge. But this seems foolish.[1]

---

[1] It seems even more foolish to argue that, since I do not normally *say*: 'I know that I have a headache', it follows that I do not know that I have a headache.

Let us now consider the case of alleged knowledge where evidence can be brought forward. The evidence, says the theorist, must be adequate before we can agree that A has a right to be sure. Now what is adequate evidence? Indeed what is evidence? The word is associated strongly with law-court procedure. Evidence is information that is given either to establish, or to go some way towards establishing, the factual point at issue. The judge has to come to a decision, the evidence helps him to come to that decision. Sometimes the evidence submitted is sufficient to settle the issue, sometimes it is not. When it is not then the judge has to decide on the best available evidence. In such a context evidence is adequate if it enables the judge to come to a decision. But this needs amplification. For first, the evidence may be only enough to enable him to arrive at a probable judgement. On the other hand, it may convince the judge, it may settle the issue for him and in that case to say that the evidence is adequate is to say that it is issue-settling evidence. Even within the legal context the term 'adequate' may convey these two meanings and it is necessary to distinguish between them.

I am not attempting here to set forward *the* definition of evidence or of adequate evidence, if there is one definition; it would seem that the meaning of 'evidence' and 'adequate evidence' varies from context to context. I merely seek to understand what the theorist has in mind when he tells us that A must produce adequate evidence. In the context of the Three Condition Theory what is meant clearly is that A must produce issue-settling evidence, for we are not in this case thinking of judging that so and so is probably the case. A is sure; if he thought that p was probable only he would not be sure. The theorist requires that A's evidence should really settle the issue, and this alone would be adequate evidence for him. It follows that if the available evidence is not issue-settling it lacks adequacy in this context. Adequate evidence convinces, and if A can produce convincing evidence then he meets the second condition.

But convinces whom? Presumably it convinces the inquirer

who asks whether A really knows when he says he is sure. A is convinced, but he has to produce evidence and go on producing evidence till the inquirer B says (if ever he does say this): 'You need go no further. What you've said now proves the point. I am convinced that you are right.' In other words the convincing (and so the adequate) evidence is evidence that will enable B to be sure that p. But if this is the theory it is a very strange one. A is sure and convinced that p, but he does not know that p unless the evidence is adequate, and the evidence is adequate when B is sure and convinced. Yet why should B's conviction be a condition of A's knowledge?

6. As thus set forth the theory amounts to an absurdity, but before concluding that it is absurd, we should consider a possible alternative interpretation. When the theorist says that A must produce adequate evidence he may not be wanting to say simply that A must convince B, that he knows if he does convince B and does not know if he fails to convince B. Could we revert to Kant's distinction between subjective conviction and knowledge? Neither A's subjective conviction nor B's is knowledge, for knowledge must be 'objectively sufficient', that is to say, certain for all. If we accept this interpretation, however, a further question arises immediately: Whom are we to mean by 'all'? If it is necessary to wait till literally everybody is certain that p we shall have to wait a long time. Do we mean the majority of the community to which we belong? It is true that we find much comfort in the agreement and concurrence of others. Since advance in knowledge is so much of a social achievement and since we learn so much in any case from others, it is encouraging to know that others agree that p. 'Well, everybody says so' is a common way of clinching an argument. Nevertheless, a community, as well as an individual, may be in error. If the community is less prone to error than the individual, it is not infallible. The certainty of all, in this sense, cannot be the final criterion by which to judge the individual's conviction.

The argument thus rejected, however, may be put in slightly

different terms. In any specific inquiry, it may be said, there exists a body of accepted knowledge and an agreed procedure for the enlargement of this knowledge. Now it is quite legitimate to ask whether the individual has taken into account the accepted knowledge and whether he has proceeded in accordance with the agreed techniques in attempting to add to his knowledge. Consider a physicist defending a new position of whose truth he has become convinced. He will try to show how his new position is linked with the body of generally accepted facts in physics and he will use the acknowledged techniques in doing so. He may thus hope to convince other physicists and to show thereby that he was not mistaken. Supposing that someone, who is either ignorant of, or who ignores, the accepted body of knowledge, has become convinced of a certain conclusion in physics and has reached this conclusion by methods which physicists in the past have found dangerous, it is natural that physicists in such a situation mistrust his conviction and regard his evidence as inadequate. The individual conviction will find it difficult to stand in the face of the conviction of all.

On this view, a conclusion, in any inquiry, is 'certain for all' and 'objective', if it is part of the accepted knowledge in the field, or if it has been gained by taking the accepted knowledge into account and by passing forward to further knowledge in accordance with the agreed method of procedure. Generally speaking, this view is correct and the extent to which progress in scientific inquiries is a communal rather than an individual achievement must be acknowledged. But this in no way diminishes the importance of the individual insight and individual judgement, and it is with these that we have primarily to do in this chapter.

Suppose a physicist A claims to know that p and says he is sure of it. This, we say, is not enough. His fellow physicists will look to his premises and his method. They may judge that his conclusion is not in accord with generally accepted doctrine. Their disapprobation will cause A to think again and to reconsider the claim that he is making. Yet whilst this is true it is also true that this appeal to the generally accepted methods and to the body of knowledge already gained will not finally settle the issue. This is not evidence adequate to refute p. For the generally accepted body of knowledge may in this particular prove to be wrong. Objectivity is not to be attained by counting heads. A may be correct in insisting that p even if all others disagree. Conversely, even if it be the case that what he says is in line with the universally accepted doctrine, and even if he has proceeded in accordance with the 'correct' procedures, it does not follow that what he says is true. Thus the agreement or disagreement of others is evidence, but of itself it is not adequate evidence.

Agreement with accepted procedure may suggest, however, still another line of objective justification. If one considers not the demands of the specific inquiry but of thought in general, it may be argued that there is in every case a specific logical procedure, and if A can be shown to have failed to follow it then he has no right to be sure that p. Whether one is seeking to establish a conclusion by deductive reasoning, or a general principle by some form of inductive reasoning, or finally a proof of some contingent proposition, there are, it is said, logically correct procedures. If it can be shown that in reaching a conclusion A has committed a logical fallacy then A has no right to be sure that p. Now this must at once be admitted, and A, we assume, will admit it too if the fallacy is pointed out to him. Perhaps, because of his wishes and hopes, he may take some time to see that it is a fallacy, but when he does there is then no choice; he has to admit that he has no right to be sure that p, and we, who have observed the fallacy in the argument purporting to establish p, agree that he is in error. If we say that this is 'objective' proof we have identified the 'objective' with the 'rational', where the 'rational' is that which is consistent with logical rule. This argument seems acceptable, given what it assumes. In particular, it assumes that the objective can be identified with the rational, and it assumes a theory of the rational. These matters will need to be considered later.

We are now, it will be noted, taking it for granted that p is established by argument, and that if this argument is proved fallacious p can no longer be sustained. But p may not be established by argument, nor may it be possible to bring forward arguments to justify it. Moreover, when arguments can be brought forward, it would be agreed that A's claim to know that p would not be established by simply showing that his argument establishing p was free from fallacies. Valid inference is proof only if the premisses are true. So more would be needed than simply to show that A's argument was logically flawless; it would be essential as well to show that the premisses are true. Admittedly it might be argued that certain statements, for instance 'John is or is not on the lawn', are true logically or true formally, that is, true by the meaning of the terms, and it might even be claimed that here is completely objective truth freed from all subjectivity. At this stage I do not wish to consider the nature of logical truth, but one point is at once obvious. If logical truths of the above kind were the sole completely objective truths and if completely adequate evidence could consist only of logical truths, then objective truth and adequate evidence would never be found in the cognition of the factual. Yet when A claims to know that p, p is rarely a logically necessary truth, assuming that there are such truths. So, except on the rare occasions when p is a logically necessary truth, it would be impossible to produce adequate evidence to justify A's claim to know. But this is a conclusion with which few would be happy.

7. Before bringing the examination of the second of the three conditions to an end I should like to consider briefly some of the interesting modifications which Roderick M. Chisholm makes of the general theory we have just been discussing.[1] They are to be found in his two books, *Perceiving*, 1957, and *Theory of Knowledge*, 1966. Instead of formulating the three elements as (1) A is sure of p, (2) A can produce evidence justifying his

---

[1] In the discussion I had much in mind the contributions of Norman Malcolm (*Mind*, January 1942 and April 1952), A. D. Woozley (*Theory of Knowledge* and *Proc. Arist. Soc.*, 1953), L. E. Thomas (*Mind*, July 1955), A. J. Ayer (*The Problem of Knowledge*, 1956), and the symposium on 'Claims to Knowledge' (*Proc. Arist. Soc.*, Supp., 1962) in which G. J. Warnock and L. J. Cohen were the symposiasts.

assurance, and (3) p is true, he formulates them thus, (1) A accepts p, (2) A has adequate evidence for p, and (3) p is true.[1] These three elements must be present if A is to be said to know that p. The new analysis, he thinks, has the advantage that it covers belief as well as certain knowledge, for instance, it covers the knowledge of the judge who accepts p without claiming that p is completely certain. If we wish to speak of certainty then a further demand must be met, namely, that there be no proposition q such that q is more worthy of A's belief than p.[2]

Since he has in mind knowledge in this wider sense he rejects the phrase 'is sure' or 'feels sure' used by the other writers we have considered and substitutes for it the word 'accepts'. But the question then arises whether his analysis of certain knowledge suffers as a consequence. When the judge considers the evidence and, without making any claim to certainty, concludes that p, he may appropriately be said to 'accept' the opinion that, for instance, the accused was guilty of the crime. But if 'accept' may be regarded as the appropriate word in this situation, is it the correct word when speaking of certain knowledge? Chisholm thinks it is, if we also add that there is no proposition (or hypothesis) q which is more worthy of A's belief than p. Still, if our state were one of 'accepting', even granting the additional modification, should we be certain? The view of the other writers is that there is no certain knowledge without assurance. One must be sure; accepting is not enough, and being sure is not the same thing as accepting.

The writers referred to might object to Chisholm's modifications in a further respect. Chisholm says: ' "S knows that h is true" means (i) S accepts h (ii) S has adequate evidence for h and (iii) h is true.' This is knowing in the broad sense. But if we speak of S being certain then, Chisholm says, ' "S is certain that h is true" means (i) S knows that h is true [and this means (i), (ii), and (iii) above] and (ii) there is no hypothesis i such that i is more worthy of S's belief than h.' To this it might be objected, first, that i could be more worthy of S's belief than h

---

[1] *Perceiving*, p. 16.   [2] Ibid., p. 19.

and still be probable only. Secondly, on Chisholm's analysis, S is certain that h if (i), (ii), and (iii) above and if there is no hypothesis i such that i is more worthy of S's belief than h. But is it not also necessary that S should *be sure* that there is no hypothesis i more worthy of his belief than h? The analysis makes no provision for this essential item.

Chisholm's avoidance of the phrase 'being sure' marks his desire to avoid subjectivity in his account of knowledge, but the other writers, who do use it, seek to avoid this danger too. This is why the demand is made for the satisfaction of the other two conditions. Yet, as things turn out, their demand for 'adequate evidence' does not in fact save them from subjectivity, since 'adequate evidence' is apparently convincing or issue-settling evidence, that is, evidence which makes one sure. Does Chisholm's account of adequate evidence secure objectivity?

The account is stated in the following terms:[1] ' "S has adequate evidence for h" means that it would be unreasonable for S to accept non-h.' Further: ' "It would be *unreasonable* for S to accept h" means that non-h is more worthy of S's belief than h.' That is to say, to have adequate evidence in support of p (or h) would be to show that it is reasonable to accept p and that it would be unreasonable to accept non-p. But why would this be unreasonable? Because, says Chisholm, p is more worthy of our belief. We may not accept p but it makes sense to say that we ought to. Adequate evidence, therefore, is not something dependent on one's whim or mood at the moment; it is what is reasonable to accept, what is worthy of acceptance. The question then is as to the further analysis of the phrase 'p is more worthy of A's belief than q.' Chisholm speaks of it here[2] as something to be accepted without seeking to define it; it is 'an undefined epistemic locution'. In a further discussion of it in a later chapter[3] he thinks it should be regarded as a conviction, analogous to a conviction in the moral field. He acknowledges some doubt whether such a value judgement can ever be said to be true or false. Thus in the final analysis knowledge rests on an assessment of what is and is not worthy of belief, but the assessment may be such that we cannot speak of it as true or false.

In his *Theory of Knowledge* Chisholm develops the same general thesis but makes further interesting emendations. He here formulates his definitions of 'know' in terms of 'evident': '*S* knows at *t* that *h* is true, provided: (1) *S* believes *h* at *t*; (2) *h* is true; and (3) *h* is evident at *t* for *S*.'[1] He has already explained that 'a proposition *h* may be said to be *evident* for a subject *S* provided (1) that *h* is reasonable for *S* and (2) that there is no proposition *i* such that it is more reasonable for *S* to believe *i* than it is for him to believe *h*.'[2] Thus 'evident' is defined in terms of 'reasonable' and 'more reasonable' and the more reasonable is what a rational being whose 'concerns are purely intellectual' would choose. It is noteworthy too that *S* now 'believes' rather than 'accepts'.[3]

This further formulation however is still not free of difficulties.[4] The question which immediately concerns us in this chapter is whether it clears up the problems about evidence. 'Know' is to be defined in terms of 'evident' and 'evident' in terms of 'more reasonable', and the 'more reasonable' is what the rational person would choose. This is not very satisfactory, the last statement might even be held to beg the question. But Chisholm is justified in seeking one concept, in this group of concepts, in terms of which the others can be explained. Yet what may be questioned in his approach is the assumption that the concept of knowing is definable in terms of another concept or concepts, if we can find that concept. The converse may be the truth, that 'know' itself is the ultimate in terms of which the 'more reasonable' and the 'more worthy to be believed' etc. can be defined. There is much in Chisholm's discussion and that of the other writers mentioned to suggest that this alternative may be a more promising approach.

[1] *Theory of Knowledge*, p. 23.
[2] Ibid., p. 22.
[3] '*S* believes that *p*' has during the last decade been fairly generally substituted for the original '*S* is sure that *p*' in the statement of the theory. I shall return to this point later in Ch. 3, section 22, when considering the more recent discussions of the theory.
[4] Chisholm himself discusses one of these difficulties in the footnote to p. 23.

8. We may sum up the discussion of the second condition. The original Three Condition Theory is concerned not with knowledge in the wide sense in which Professor Chisholm speaks of it, that is, as including believing and opining, but in the narrow sense, and no knowledge is knowledge in this sense unless the knower is sure. But his being sure is not enough, he must also be able to justify his claim to know by producing adequate evidence if he is asked to do so. This he finds difficult to do. For, on the one hand, there seem to be instances of knowing in respect of which no justifying evidence can be brought forward. Unless the word 'knowing' is defined in such a way as to omit much that generally goes by that name, for instance knowledge that one has a headache, then in some cases no evidence other than, for example, the speaker's saying that he has a headache, can be adduced. On the other hand, in those cases where evidence can be brought forward, adequate evidence seems to be defined in subjective terms as evidence acceptable by A and by all others. A is sure that p. His assurance is justified if he can convince B, C, and all others. A is sure that there is a ring in the box and when it is opened we all see it. Again we all see, in another sense of the word 'see', that certain statements brought forward by A, which we grant to be true, entail the further statement which A has been all along affirming as something of which he is sure. So A is justified; he has a right to be sure. Yet the sceptic's question remains. Does the fact that others are sure that p, or even that all are sure, give A the right to be sure? May they not all be in error?

The difficulty can be set out in the following terms: If we say that in knowing (in the narrow sense) we must be sure, then knowing that the evidence is adequate in the case of another's claim to know is itself an instance of being sure, whatever else it be. And if we doubt the other's assurance why should we not also doubt our own? Obviously, we should wish to find an objective and impersonal justification of the claim to know, but if this justification is also a knowing and if knowing is being sure then, it would appear, no wholly impersonal justification is possible.

9. (iii) '*And* p *is true.*' Certainly. It is a contradiction to say: '*A* knows that there are men on Mars, but there are no men on Mars.' *A* is sure that there are men on Mars, the evidence appears adequate to him and to all others. Yet unless in fact there are men on Mars he does not know. This is unimpeachable.

Suppose it be objected, none the less, that the truth of *p* cannot be a condition of knowledge. There is no difference, it might be said, between knowing that *p* and knowing that *p* is true. If we do know that *p* we do know that *p* is true. But in that case can we speak of knowing that *p* is true as *a* condition of knowledge?

In answer, the condition in question is not that we know that *p* is true but that *p* is true. It is the latter which is taken by the theory to be a condition, and this meets the above objection. But does it meet another related objection? Granted that *p* is true is a necessary condition of knowing that *p*, can we use this to test *A*'s claim to knowledge? The exponents of the Three Condition Theory do not aim merely at describing knowing; they also think their theory provides means of checking whether *A* knows that *p* when he is sure that *p*. One test is the adequacy of the evidence, and we have seen the difficulties in applying this test. The other is whether *p* is true. But it is one thing to say that *A* does not know that *p* unless *p* is true, and another that this provides us with a criterion whereby we may test *A*'s claim to knowledge.

It is good to look at Kant's position again in the passage quoted earlier. If one is sure that *p* one does hold *p* to be true; *p* is *das Fürwahrhalten*. Admittedly, one may *say* that one is sure and not hold that *p* is true, or one may be in one of the queer pathological states in which one feels sure and yet doubts whether *p* is true. But these are not the states which are being considered here. What Kant is thinking of is being sure that *p* where it is identical with being sure that *p* is true. Now it would be quite sensible to ask someone whether he was sure in the Kantian sense. The teacher *says* she is sure the class will be quiet, but the way in which she says it and her actions make it clear that she does not take this to be true. It would make

sense to ask a person who asserts that he is sure: 'Are you or
are you not taking p to be true?' But if we are considering the
case in which being sure that p is being sure that p is true we
cannot hold these two apart in such a way that we can sensibly
ask: 'You are sure that p, but are you sure that p is true?' On
the other hand, it would be sensible, even where p is taken to
be true, to ask: 'But may you not be in error?'

Consider the case then in which A's being sure that p is
being sure that p is true. B wishes to test whether A does know
that p, and after examination becomes himself convinced that
p is true. Others too become convinced that p is true and so
conclude that A did know. But note that what is now established is not that p is true, but that all are convinced that p is
true. But no conviction, we are agreed, is beyond suspicion, and
there is consequently no proof here that when A is sure that p
is true then p is true. If A really knows that p then p is true; in
theory this does provide a test whether A knows, namely to
show that p is true. But this is a test we cannot apply, for what
happens, at the best, is that we ourselves become sure that
p is true. Yet this itself needs further testing, though no further
testing seems possible. So the third condition does not provide
us with a test that can be applied.

It comes to this. If one *knows* that p then p is true, but it is
not possible to justify the claim to knowledge by any appeal to
the fact that p is true. For the appeal could only be to the
conviction that p is true. But, if it be the claimant's conviction,
this is what is doubted; if it be the conviction of any one else,
this too can be doubted. If the convictions of others confirm
ours we find comfort and gain a pragmatic satisfaction. But
all of them together do not prove that p is true. Kant, who was
prepared to test subjective conviction by the agreement of all,
does not propose a further test, namely, whether p is or is not
true, and on this last point he is surely right as against those who
see in the third condition a test that can be used to show that A
does or does not know.

10. We may now conclude the discussion of the whole theory.

In one sense of the word 'knowing', and this perhaps the most important, if A knows that p, then A is sure, the evidence is adequate, and p is true. There are other senses of the word, some of them differing greatly from the above, others only slightly. An instance of the latter is the following: If A knows that p, then A is sure that p is true. No mention of evidence is present because, in this case, no evidence is possible, so that we cannot ask whether the evidence is or is not adequate. Some philosophers would say that this is not 'really' knowing but they would then be dogmatizing, possibly assuming that there is only one sense of the word 'know' when in fact there are many.

The analysis offered by the Three Condition Theory of the knowing with which it is concerned is correct. These characteristics do belong to knowing in that sense. But when these characteristics are regarded as necessary and sufficient conditions of knowledge error may creep in, for inevitably the conditions come to be regarded as tests. In particular the second and third conditions are taken to be means of testing whether when one is sure one is then knowing. One can, it is true, question A on the evidence upon which he bases his assurance and one may convince him that it was wrong for him to be sure. But this means that he is now sure, as we are, that he was formerly in error. It is still an appeal to our common assurance. It is no test of that assurance. If his being sure that p is no guarantee that A knows that p, so his being sure later that non-p is also no guarantee that A knows that non-p. Nor will the conviction of B, C, and D, or even the conviction of all, be a guarantee. So, too, the third condition cannot be used as an objective test of whether a person knows when he is sure, for it can never be applied. Thus though we accept the analysis of the Three Condition Theory we do not accept the interpretation of that analysis that makes the second and third conditions tests of the claim to knowledge.

From the examination of this theory two points emerge with striking force. The first is the recognition that being sure cannot be identified with knowing; the second is the centrality none the less of being sure.

Now the problem of human knowledge has to do primarily with the tension created within this situation; it is a situation in which a man may be sure and yet not know. Other kinds of knowing interest the epistemologist and other considerations, logical, psychological, and even physiological. Their study is important and necessary; but the central problem must not be ignored. Whatever the defects in the presentation of the Three Condition Theory, its fundamental teaching is correct. It bids us take being sure seriously, but at the same time refuses to identify it with knowing.

II

UNFAILING ASSURANCE

11. If one knows one is sure; it would be easy to fall into the error of identifying knowing with being sure. But that this would be a grave error our ordinary language shows. One may contrast the two sentences 'I was sure, but I was wrong' and 'I knew, but I was wrong.' The former sentence is to be found in ordinary use, but not the latter. 'I said that I knew, but I was wrong' is a sentence that might well be used, but not 'I knew, but I was wrong.'

Recognizing the deep difference between being sure and knowing one may nevertheless ask whether there ever exist circumstances in which it would be as incorrect to say: 'I was sure, but I was wrong' as it is to say: 'I knew, but I was wrong.' Suppose, for instance, that I was sure that p and suppose that p was a statement which could never turn out to be false and I knew this, then I should never be in a position to say: 'I was sure that p, but I was wrong.' In such a case to be sure that p would be to know that p; the assurance would never fail me and the knowledge would be infallible. But is there such assurance?

The answer of traditional rationalism is that there is. The human mind, it is claimed, is able to grasp truths by reason once and for all. One is sure of these truths and to be sure is to know. This is the thesis I wish to examine in the present chapter.

12. It is recognized that complete and unfailing assurance is claimed in fields other than that of rational apprehension of truth. Indeed the contrast has been made frequently between the sure grasp of non-intellectual cognition and the fumbling efforts of the intellect. Thus the instinctive behaviour of animals and insects is said to possess a sureness of operation (resting on precise, infallible knowledge) usually absent from

intelligent behaviour. And in human relationships there is talk of a 'knowledge of the heart' as when a mother is said to have a knowledge of her child that never fails. Infallibility is claimed too for religious pronouncements, but here the ground is different. Statements are put forward which form part of the dogma of a religious body; these are held to be infallible because they are revealed. The believer is sure; yet he has not discovered these truths for himself but accepts them on divine authority, which being divine is infallible. Statements of natural, as opposed to revealed, religion are not usually held to be infallible; if ever they were it would be on rationalist grounds. Finally, claims to infallibility are sometimes made in respect to religious experience, and this knowledge is then said to be of a like order to the mother's knowledge of her child or of a person's knowledge of his closest friend.

Unfailing assurance has been claimed for two further kinds of knowledge which should be mentioned here. I refer in the first place to sensory knowledge. Philosophers who have contended that sensing is infallible usually distinguish between 'sensing' and 'perceiving'. Just seeing a brown patch, for instance, is 'bare sensation', but recognizing that what is before me is the brown surface of a table is said to be 'perception'. Few would claim that perception in this sense is infallible knowledge; the possibilities of error are too obvious. But 'bare sensation' is sometimes claimed to be infallible. We see what we do see and there cannot possibly be error.

Yet not all would accept the view that 'bare sensing' is an instance of infallible knowledge; indeed not all would accept the distinction between 'bare sensing' and 'perception'. Can sensing ever be 'bare'? If the slightest element of recognition is involved there may be error, as would generally be conceded. If there is assertion, even if one merely tells oneself, 'This is a brown patch', error again is possible. It may none the less be insisted that 'bare sensing' occurs with no element in it of recognition or assertion. If it does there is presumably no place for error in it. The further question arises however whether we can rightly designate such bare sensing 'knowledge'? This is an interesting problem, but not one we need pursue here. If one were asked: 'Do men ever know anything with infallible certainty?' it would be odd to reply: 'Yes, they have infallible knowledge in bare sensing.'

The other case to which reference must be made is of greater importance. It is that of the enjoyment (if this is the proper term) of one's own experiences. I see something before me and I say: 'This is a table.' Error may occur in the identification. But there can be no error, it is said, in my consciousness of this experience. This is infallible knowledge. To examine this claim fully we should first need a close analysis of the knowledge involved. Until it is completed we are in no position to repudiate the claim. On the contrary, the evidence for infallible knowledge in this context is strong. Consider being sure itself. Not only am I sure but I am conscious that I am sure; I claim to know that I am sure and this knowledge can be differentiated from the being sure. For though I must admit that when I am sure I may be in error, it is difficult to see how it is possible that my present knowledge that I now am sure can ever turn out to have been erroneous. And yet is there more here than being sure that I am sure? And if there is not, can the being sure be identified with knowledge? Supposing, however, that we were prepared for the moment to accept this as an instance of infallible knowledge, we might still feel uneasy about putting it forward as an instance. To the question: 'Do we know anything with infallible certainty?' we might hesitate to reply: 'Yes, we are aware of our own experiences of feeling pain, of striving to do something, of being sure and so on.' The hesitation may be due to the fact that we tend to regard knowledge of the objective world, the world other than the subject knowing, as the knowledge that matters. Yet knowledge of ourselves may play a more important role even in our knowledge of the objective world than we are sometimes disposed to think. For the present, however, let us move forward to consider the traditional rationalist account of infallible knowledge, which is a knowledge primarily of the objective world.

13. Traditionally the doctrine of infallible knowledge is bound up with that of intellectual intuition and this is an intuition not of the subjective, nor of one's own experience, but of the objective world. It is true that as the theory developed in the rationalist school emphasis on knowledge of the subject became greater, as will be clear from a consideration of Leibniz's position, but traditionally the theory had little to do with the subject and much with the object. The *episteme* (which Plato contrasts in the *Republic* with *doxa*), the 'active *nous*' of Aristotle, the 'active intellect' of Aquinas, were held to provide infallible knowledge of eternal, universal, objective truth.

Not that the intuitionists ever claimed that all human knowledge was intuitive; the distinction that Plato made between intuitive knowledge and opinion or belief was always present. It was recognized too that opinion could carry with it a high degree of certainty even if it was not wholly certain. Nevertheless, central to their doctrine was the view that some knowledge was infallible, and that human beings were capable of such knowledge.

It would be profitable at this point to examine some of the more celebrated statements having to do with this theory. Perhaps the clearest and most explicit statement is that of Descartes in the *Regulae* and we may first examine this. It would then be useful to turn to Aristotle's teaching on the place of *nous* in intellectual inquiry generally. Finally, we may briefly consider how the rationalist, intuitionist theory is modified in the thought of the seventeenth and eighteenth centuries, with the emergence of modern science.

Descartes distinguishes *intuitus*, which is the term he uses for intellectual intuition, sharply from sensory intuition and from imagination. In the third section of the *Regulae*[1] he explains how *intuitus* is 'not the fluctuating testimony of the sense, nor the misleading judgement that proceeds from the blundering constructions of imagination, but the pure intellectual cognizing of which an unclouded and attentive mind is capable; a cognizing so ready and so distinct that we are wholly freed

[1] *Regulae ad Directionem Ingenii*, Regula III.

from doubt about that which we thus intellectually apprehend'. In intuitive knowing the mind is fully awake, unclouded, wholly attentive, and entirely free from doubt.

Intuitive knowledge is for Descartes the supreme activity of the human mind. But to say this, and no more, would be to misinterpret the Cartesian position, for though in one sense the mind is at the height of its activity in intuiting, in another sense it is passive. It is receptive, receiving what it cannot but receive. There are Augustinian strands in Descartes's thought, and sometimes the stress on illumination becomes the most prominent feature of his epistemology, as is evident, for instance, from the letter to the Marquis of Newcastle in 1648. He there remarks that the fact that we gain indubitable knowledge is 'proof of the capacity of our souls to receive from God intuitive knowledge. Intuitive knowledge is an illumination of the spirit by which it sees in God's light the things that it pleases Him to discover by a direct impression of the divine clarity upon our understanding, which in this context is in no way to be considered as an agent, but solely as the recipient of the rays of Divinity.' In this striking passage it is not the activity of the mind which he stresses, but its passivity; the understanding is viewed more as a recipient than as an agent. Yet Descartes is not always in this Augustinian mood. In the *Regulae* and in the *Principia* it is the mind's full activity in intuitive knowledge which is emphasized. There may even be a certain tension at this point in Descartes's thought but it never amounts to a contradiction, for intuitive knowledge on Descartes's view, though it can only occur when the mind is active and attentive, is none the less always a discovery of what the mind must accept. Locke, it seems to me, owes his intuitionism to Descartes and in his description of intuition in iv. ii. 1 of the *Essay* he brings out this feature of Descartes's teaching very clearly. 'This part of knowledge', he says, 'is irresistible and, like bright sunshine, forces itself immediately to be perceived as soon as ever the mind turns its view that way; and leaves no room for hesitation, doubt or examination, but the mind is presently filled with the clear light of it. It is on this intuition that depends all the certainty and evidence of all our knowledge.' Intuitive knowledge then in Descartes's sense can be gained only by a mind fully activated, but the knowledge, none the less, is an illumination, even a constraint. It is the reception of the infallibly certain by a fully active mind. Furthermore, intuitive knowledge is distinctive not merely on the subjective side; its object too is distinct. The knowing is 'pure' and that which is known must be 'simple'. Only that which is through and through clear and distinct, only a 'simple nature' lacking all inward complexity (clear) and cut off from everything else (distinct), can possibly be an object of intellectual intuition. Hence for Descartes the epistemological ideal is the pure intuition of the sheer simple. In the light of this it is easy to appreciate his insistence on the resolution of complexes into simples.[1]

But if this is Descartes's ideal it is likely to be a troublesome one, as will be clear on a moment's reflection. What is intuited is a number of unrelated 'simple natures', each known with clarity and certainty, but each closed within itself and atomic. As the argument of the *Regulae* proceeds it becomes obvious, however, that it is not possible for Descartes to maintain this position. For, if one stood consistently by the ideal of the pure intuition of the sheer simple, how could one find room for that other element which Descartes judges to be an equally essential item in human knowledge, namely *deductio*? Deduction, at least, presupposes relationships. It is not strange that we find Descartes speaking less of 'simple natures' and more of 'simple notions' or 'simple ideas' as he advances in his argument. He speaks too, of 'simple propositions' and neither Descartes nor anyone else would want to say that a proposition, however simple, is lacking in related parts.

14. This Cartesian ideal of a knowledge consisting entirely of pure intuitions of sheer simples is clearly far removed from the human condition. Descartes himself was well aware of this; the

---

[1] In its light one may better understand too the rationalist theory of analysis as a resolving of the complex 'till we come to the primitives'.

ideal is set forth in the *Regulae* only, and even in that work, it may be said, the account of *deductio* is not wholly consistent with it. Human knowledge for the most part is gained through sense-perception, through communication with others, and through processes of inference. If there exist intuitive elements in human knowledge they are to be looked for therefore within knowledge of this kind. Aristotle, whilst believing that intellectual intuition (or *nous*) played an essential role in the achievement of knowledge, is also clear that it is to be thought of in the context of sense-perception and inference. Since his influence on subsequent thought is so great it might be well to draw attention to one or two points in his teaching.

Speaking generally, Aristotle makes less of the distinction between sense-perception and intuition (that is to say, *aesthesis* and *nous*) than does Plato. Indeed in *Ethics* vi. 11 (1143ʰ5–6) we have a passage—in which *aesthesis* admittedly is moral sense rather than sense-perception—wherein the two are apparently identified. This is unusual, but there are other passages relating the two closely,[1] and others in which sense-perception seems to have noctic as well as aesthetic features[2] and in which the view that *aesthesis* and *nous* are two independent cognizings seems not to be adhered to. None the less, Aristotle's general position is that *aesthesis* is a 'discriminative capacity' shared by all the animal creation,[3] but that in addition there has been bestowed on men the faculty of *nous* which he refers to on more than one occasion as 'a divine element', particularly when it is fully active, not merely 'receiving' the object but actively 'possessing' it.[4]

The book which perhaps best reveals Aristotle's thoughts on the role of intellectual intuition or intuitive reason in the gaining of knowledge is the *Posterior Analytics*. Here he is dealing with argument, which he terms scientific, that is argument which advances logically from pre-existent knowledge to further knowledge. The pre-existent knowledge is

---

[1] Cf. Aristotle's account of our knowledge of individual things in *De Anima* iii. 6 and again *An. Post.* 88ᵃ5–8.

[2] Cf. *De Anima* 418ᵃ20–3, 430ᵇ5–6, and *An. Post.* ii. 19.

[3] *An. Post.* 99ᵇ33–5.   [4] Cf. *Metaphysics* 1072ᵇ18–24.

something itself demonstrated, so that the conclusion of one argument becomes the premiss of another. But this cannot always be the case, for if it were we should be involved in an infinite regress of arguments. Accordingly, in every discipline there are basic truths, 'those elements in it the existence of which cannot be proved'; some of these are peculiar to the discipline, for instance 'the definitions of line and straight', whilst others are common to many disciplines, for instance 'take equals from equals and equals remain'.[1] The question then is: How do we know these basic truths which are not demonstrated by scientific reasoning?

Aristotle's answer is that we know them by intuition. But what is interesting in his answer is that the intuition in question is a species of intuitive induction. He expressly teaches that we do not know them innately, for it cannot be the case that we know such fundamental truths as these and yet 'fail to notice them'.[2] So they have been acquired. But how? We begin to gain knowledge in sense-perception. On the basis of what we perceive and of our memories of what we perceived in the past we are able to predict future occurrence and set forward general scientific truths. What is universal first emerges in a rudimentary way, but soon in a way which makes scientific reasoning possible.[3] Now the basic truths and primary premisses of the scientific disciplines are themselves suggested in experience. 'It is clear that we must get to know the primary premisses by induction.' They are suggested by sense-perception but they are not known in sense-perception. On the contrary, these basic truths are the truths we know with the greatest certainty, and sense-perception would not give this certainty. 'Now of the thinking states by which we grasp truth, some are unfailingly true, others admit of error—opinion, for instance, and calculation, whereas scientific knowing and intuition are always true.' The basic truths are not themselves known by scientific reasoning, yet they are of certainty true. 'From these considerations it follows that there will be no scientific knowledge of the primary premisses, and since except intuition

[1] Cf. *An. Post.* 76ᵃ30–ᵇ23.   [2] Ibid. 99ᵇ27.   [3] Ibid. 99–101.

nothing can be truer than scientific knowledge, it will be intuition that apprehends the primary premisses.'[1] Thus the basic truths, for instance 'take equals from equals and equals remain', are known intuitively. Aristotle's reference to induction should not lead us to suppose that the end-product is not an intuition, an infallible intuition at that. But Aristotle is aiming to break down the isolation of intuition in cognition; he holds that the final intuition may be suggested in sensory experience; it may be an intuitive induction. If we do know these basic truths we know them intuitively and we cannot be wrong about them, yet sense-experience may already suggest them.

The most basic of all truths is the law of non-contradiction. We may conclude these comments on Aristotle's position by referring to his account of this law, particularly in the *Metaphysics*. Here, he thinks, is the principle presupposed in all thought, for no thinking can occur unless it is based on non-contradiction. Since this is so it itself cannot be proved in thought; that is to say, it cannot be shown to follow from a premiss or premisses. It *can* be shown that to deny it significantly one would have to assume its truth; further, that to deny it is to wipe out all distinctions, so that all things, a warship, a wall, and a man, would be identical. 'If all contradictory statements are true of the same thing at the same time, clearly all things will be one.'[2]

But this is no rational proof or demonstration of it and no rational proof is possible of this law which itself makes rational proof possible. Yet, according to Aristotle, we are completely certain of it; it is not an assumption, neither is it a hypothesis which may turn out to be false. 'For a principle which every one must have who knows anything about being, is not a hypothesis. . . . Evidently then such a principle is the most certain of all; which principle this is, we proceed to say. It is, that the same attribute cannot at the same time belong and not belong to the same subject in the same respect.'[3] As stated the

[1] Ibid. 100[b]10–13.   [2] *Metaphysics* 1007[b]18–19.
[3] Ibid. 1005[b]15–20.

law holds of things of which attributes can be predicated, but Aristotle proceeds at once to show that it holds equally well of opinions and beliefs.

This discussion of the *Metaphysics* might suggest another line of argument, namely, that the principle of non-contradiction must be true, for otherwise science, thought, and even action, would be impossible. The argument is not unlike Kant's in those passages of the *Critique* in which he 'deduces' his categories. But to stress this feature would be wrong, for Aristotle is clear that the principle is not demonstrated, nor is it 'deduced' in the Kantian sense. It is intuited by *nous* and known with complete certainty. Thus an intuitive element pervades reasoning; its presence is what guarantees the truth of scientific reasoning. On this point Aristotle is as firm as Plato. In spite of the differences which exist between the two philosophers, there is also a close kinship, particularly in their epistemology. Both equally stress the necessity, the certainty, and utter reliability, of intellectual intuition. Aristotle is more concerned to show its presence in discursive thinking and how the intellectual truth may be suggested in sense-experience, but these points too are not wholly absent from the teaching of Plato.

15. The fortunes of the intuitionist school, thus founded, have varied in the course of the centuries. In the modern age the empiricism of modern science has blunted the force of intuitionism. There is no more interesting passage in the writings of epistemologists than that in which Locke, still retaining Aristotle's sense of the word 'scientific', concludes regretfully that scientific knowledge of the physical world is not possible. The scientific knowledge which Aristotle had talked about, for instance in the *Posterior Analytics*, as 'not possible through the act of perception', was certain, exact, and universal. Locke remarks: 'And therefore I am apt to doubt, that how far soever human industry may advance useful and experimental philosophy in physical things, scientifical will still be out of our reach; because we want perfect and adequate ideas of those very bodies which are nearest to us and most under our

command.'[1] We proceed inductively and make generalizations, but this induction is not that intuitive induction of Aristotle that reveals the true universal and reveals it 'perfectly and adequately'. 'Philosophy in physical things' is not an exact science; it is of the greatest use, but only as providing probability; it does not give certainty.

It is a measure of the strength of intuitionism in his day that Locke does not conclude from this that there exists no intellectual intuition; on the contrary, he tells us that knowledge, in the most exact sense of the word, is intuitive.[2] Nor is it a mere ideal; in one field we do gain completely certain and infallible knowledge by intuition. A distinction, he holds, must be made between 'ideas whose archetypes are without them', an example being the idea of a physical object, and 'ideas which are their own archetypes'; and though intuitive knowledge is not possible if our ideas are of the first kind it is possible if they are 'their own archetypes'. Thus we intuit with complete certainty that the interior angles of a triangle are equal to two right angles. For we have only to attend to the ideas themselves to perceive this intuitively, and the existence or non-existence of triangular figures in the world of physical objects is irrelevant.

That Locke found it necessary to make this distinction is of the very highest epistemological significance, for he is, clearly, feeling his way towards the later distinction between synthetic and analytic knowledge, and he looked to the latter for intuitive knowledge and complete assurance, having failed to find it in the new physical science of his day.[3] Within the field of 'ideas which are their own archetypes' a wholly intuitive knowledge remains possible; for its truths are truths of reason. Leibniz in the *Monadology* (§ 33) gives classic utterance

---

[1] *Essay*, IV. iii. 26. [2] Ibid. IV. ii.
[3] Not that the concept of working with that which is its own archetype is identical with the concept of analytical thinking. There is at least a difference of emphasis. Locke is concerned first and foremost with the development of thought in a field where one has not to be constantly looking over one's shoulder at what one is experiencing. It is interesting to speculate on the possible consequences had the concept of 'being its own archetype' been emphasized in subsequent philosophical speculation rather than the concept of 'being analytic'.

to this doctrine. 'The truths of reason', he says, 'are necessary and their opposite is impossible and those of fact are contingent and their opposite is possible. When a truth is necessary, we can find the reason by analysis, resolving it into simpler ideas and truths till we come to the primitives.'[1] There can be no question of error here; the intuition of the truth of reason is wholly infallible. Thus intellectual intuitionism is saved, even if the battle is lost on the empirical front. At least it is saved till the conventionalist begins to ask questions about analytic knowledge itself—but at the moment we need not consider these further questions.

It was not only to analytic knowledge that the rationalist turned in face of the growing empiricism, he concerned himself too with self-knowledge, a knowledge that had for him some of the marks of intuition. I am quite sure I now have a pain, am angry, or am thinking out a problem. The mind's reflection upon itself is a knowledge which is not derived from sense-experience. In spite of this it tells us something about all existences and not merely about our own, for the rationalist argues that in knowing ourselves we know too what it is to exist or to be, we know what it is to be a unity, a cause, and so on. Thus some of the fundamental categories of being are known in self-knowledge. Leibniz in the passage in which he criticizes empiricism for ignoring the *intellectus* brings out this very point. 'You oppose to me', he says,[2] 'this axiom received by the philosophers, that there is nothing in the soul which does not come from the senses. But you must except the soul itself and its affections. *Nihil est in intellectu quod non fuerit in sensu,* excipe: *nisi ipse intellectus.* Now the soul comprises being, substance, unity, identity, cause, perception, reason, and many other notions which the senses cannot give.' ['Or l'âme renferme l'être, la substance, l'un, le même, la cause, la perception, le raisonnement, et quantité d'autres notions, que les sens ne sauraient donner.'] Leibniz's emphasis here, it will be seen,

---

[1] Resolving the complex into the primitives, but also showing thereby that the subject in the statement stating the truth contains the predicate necessarily.

[2] *Nouveaux Essais,* II. i. 2.

is not on the *nisi ipse intellectus* solely but on the fact, as he sees it, that this non-empirical knowledge of the mind is knowledge, too, of certain parts of the fundamental structure of the universe. In so far as one knows oneself one knows a part of existence and of its structure and this knowledge, henceforth, is an ingredient in one's total knowledge of the world and can be used, for instance, to interpret what we learn empirically of the physical world. But if we hold that these basic categories are known intuitively in our intuition of our selves, the question arises whether our notion of intuition is not now changing from the clear and distinct intellectual intuition of Descartes's *intuitus* to something vaguer; for the knowledge of being, substance, unity, identity, cause, and the rest, manifestly lacks the requisite transparent clarity of Cartesian *intuitus* and is 'clouded'. So though this is non-empirical knowledge (if the empirical is conceived as solely that which is derived from sense-perception) and non-deductive, it is no longer Cartesian *intuitus*.

We must return to these points later. They show how intuitionism was modified in the face of the rapid development of empirical science. Throughout, however, its core remains the same, the assertion that an assurance is possible for human beings which is unfailing and a knowledge that is infallible. Sensible 'intuition', the *anschauung* of the concrete particulars, is not reliable, but there is an intellectual intuition of the universal which is wholly reliable and beyond all doubt. Under the pressure of empiricism the tendency manifested itself to think of intuition as working in the field not of fact but of logic. This led to the distinction between truths of fact and truths of reason; a distinction which emerged from rationalist thought but which was found useful too by those empiricist and positivist writers who were equally anxious to find somewhere a safe anchorage for human knowledge. Thus rationalist and empiricist combined to establish the dichotomy of factual and logical knowledge, the former being the realm of probability the latter of infallible certainty and necessity. Yet it is important to recall that in traditional intuitionism not only the logical, but some part of the factual too, in its most universal features, is known intuitively and infallibly.

16. We have now considered some of the arguments used to support the theory of intellectual intuition. If the theory were true certain items of knowledge would be infallible so that, in the case of these items, being sure would be knowing. Unfortunately, there are grave objections to the theory. First, there is opposition to the Cartesian linear intuito-deductive theory, particularly as an account of mathematics. Secondly, there is doubt about the occurrence of Cartesian intuitive knowledge generally. Thirdly, axiomatic and conventionalist theories of knowledge make it unnecessary to suppose that the heart of deduction is, as Descartes would hold, the intuition of an implication. Lastly, objection can be made to the Cartesian theory on the ground that it ignores the social aspect of human knowledge in stressing individual intuition. We may consider these points in what follows.

Seventeenth and eighteenth century thinkers were clear that the science which best illustrated the workings of intellectual intuition was mathematics. The basic principles were intuited; theorems could be deduced with the help of these principles and further theorems from the first theorems; the deduction itself was a series of intuitions of implications, each intuition making possible the passage to the next step. Unless our memory of the steps involved failed us—the memory was admitted to be fallible—the mathematical system could be built up without error, for the intuitions themselves were wholly infallible.

Now it is obvious that mathematicians do not today think of their discipline in this way. We may consider geometry, which was once regarded as the classic instance of this ideal intuito-deductive procedure. Doubt was expressed, however, whether Euclidean geometry was quite as rigorous as the intellectual intuitionists supposed it to be, and by the nineteenth century it was acknowledged that the basic principles of this geometry were not intuited as eternal truths, that indeed some of them, for instance the Principle of Continuity,[1] were only introduced as the building of the system proceeded, and then not as intuited truths but as principles necessary for the further construction of the system. Moreover, some of the principles postulated could not be demonstrated to be cogent with the system. The most celebrated example was that of the postulate of parallels (Postulate 5). Euclid postulates that through a given point not more than one parallel can be drawn to a given straight line.[2] Now on his system it can be demonstrated as a theorem that at least one parallel can be so drawn, but not that only one. The latter is postulated but not demonstrated. Successive geometers attempted to demonstrate it but failed in the attempt.

Reflection on this failure, and attempts to demonstrate the principle by the method of absurdity, led to the setting up of non-Euclidean geometries. This development was possible, however, only in so far as the geometrician had ceased to think in classical intuitionist terms of the basic principles of geometry. Contrary to classical theory the geometrician was now held to be free to set down arbitrarily his own basic principles, and then draw whatever conclusions he could within a system so based. This did not rule out the possibility of a system of geometry whose basic principles and principles of procedure were intellectually intuited, but it did show that neither Euclidean geometry nor any one of the alternative geometries was a geometry of this kind.

One cannot then look to the modern geometer for a defence of classical intellectual intuitionism. Nor do those who today inquire into the foundations of mathematics defend the theory. The so-called 'Intuitionists' amongst these inquirers are certainly not intuitionists in the classical sense; for the intuitionism in their theory is more sensory and imaginative than intellectual.[3] The fundamental notion in their theory, as with

---

[1] Cf. T. L. Heath, *The Thirteen Books of Euclid's Elements*, 1908, vol. i, pp. 234–5.
[2] For Euclid's statement of the postulate and what it involves cf. T. L. Heath, op. cit. i. 202 ff.
[3] The intuition of space cannot be assumed to be classical intellectual intuition. It belongs to *Anschauung*, to sensory knowledge, though in what precise way we need

other theories, is constructionalism, and if one speaks of mathematics primarily in constructionalist terms one is not then speaking of it in terms of intellectual intuitionism. Moreover, the occurrence of paradoxes, such as Russell's paradox, even in mathematical logic makes it at once impossible to believe that we discover by intellectual intuition, once and for all, the basic, unchangeable principles of this logic. We seem rather to be constructing a scheme for which we can never claim finality, since the occurrence of inconsistencies within the scheme, and of deep antinomies which make a revision necessary, is apparently always possible.

Thus, if Descartes could turn to mathematics and claim to find in it the very exemplar of intellectual, intuitional knowledge, few today would look to this quarter for the justification of classical intuitionism. Whatever account of mathematics emerges from the contemporary scrutiny we are unlikely to see a return to the traditional rationalist theory.

17. But it is not the intuitionist theory as applied to mathematics alone that has been questioned. The whole conception of intuitive knowledge in every field needs re-examination. This is not the place to consider the criticism of the intuitive theory in morals made during this century, but much of this has been penetrating and has helped to increase doubt about intuition. Further, it is not the popular, looser use of the term that is now suspect. We do speak loosely of 'having an intuition'. The heroine in the novel the first time she sees the villain has an intuition that he is a bad lot. Such claims to intuitive knowledge do not worry us. But man, it is said, is a rational creature and has rational intuitions of what is true everywhere and for all time. To a rational being certain things are self-evident, the intuitive is the self-evident. Yet the critics are sceptical today of this very concept of self-evidence and are not prepared to

not here consider. Even if one supposes it to be *a priori*, it is still very different from the intellectual intuitionism we have been speaking of. The work of the latter, on the classical theory, may in fact be hindered by the appeal to what is seen and by the substitution of sensible illustration for intellectual proof.

take the view that the self-evident must always be true. For it happens frequently that the self-evident is merely that with which we are completely and wholly familiar. We talk of rational insight, when in fact we are determined by habit and custom. Again, we sometimes claim to know a principle to be intuitively true, but later, when our experience is widened, come to doubt its truth, particularly in the new circumstances in which we find ourselves. The principle is self-evident as long as our experience is narrow, but with greater experience it loses its self-evidence. As we reflect upon this phenomenon even the most basic self-evident principles become suspect in so far as universal applicability is claimed for them.

But, possibly, we should not identify the intuitive with the self-evident. It would be safer to think of it in terms of rational insight. An example is the apprehension of implications in a deductive argument. Here, it may be claimed, is infallible knowledge essential for the development of any deductive argument; certain premisses are seen to imply certain conclusions and such seeing or insight is precisely what is meant by intellectual intuition. Now inference is the primary concern of the logician, but he is concerned with the structure of the inference rather than with its epistemological character. The consequence is that the question whether we intuit the implication or not is from his point of view a trivial question; what really matters is the formal structure, $p \supset q$, p, $\therefore q$. The intuitionist may answer that what is trivial to the logician need not be trivial to the epistemologist. We are examining ways of knowing, he will say; hence it is foolish to fasten on logical form solely. Certainly no deduction can occur unless the premisses imply the conclusion, but certainly too no inference will be made unless someone intuits the implication. In logic the second point does not concern us; in epistemology it is of crucial importance.

Yet if this were granted to the intuitionist, it would not free him from his difficulties. For the real question here is not whether the intuiting is trivial, but whether it occurs at all. An alternative account of deductive inference is possible for which the intuition of implications is not necessary and this account, it has been held, is more consonant with the thought of today.

This alternative account proceeds as follows: Premisses are statements in a language; the language has its syntax and rules. The syntax and the rules are learnt in learning the language and if we know how to use the language they are wholly familiar to us. So much is this the case that it is not essential consciously to recall them in using them, just as a person may speak his language perfectly and yet find it difficult to state the grammatical rules which he is following correctly at the time. Now the syntax covers the formation of the sentences in the language and also the transformation of these sentences, and to deduce from premisses in a specific language is to proceed according to the syntactical rules of transformation. In the language of *Principia Mathematica*, for instance, it would be to proceed in accordance with the principles of tautology, addition, permutation, association, and summation, together with the recognition that what is implied by a true proposition is true and that whatever can be asserted about any proposition can be asserted about any given proposition. Deduction is moving forward from the premisses in accordance with these rules. The movement may be described, if we choose so to describe it, as inevitable and necessary. But nowhere does it involve an intuitive apprehension of an implication. The necessity is not something grasped by intellectual intuition, it is the outcome of the fact that the rules permit one to proceed in this way and in no other.

It may be argued that the language of *Principia Mathematica* is an artificial language as contrasted with living languages, such as English or French. But since it is more precise, it will be answered, a study of it more truly shows the nature of deduction. Certainly too some of the rules of the language may apply beyond the system formulated in the language, although, if they do, this is quite irrelevant to the system itself. In any case there is no necessity for the rules to apply beyond the system. They apply within the system because the system is so constructed. For what is being proposed is an axiomatic theory of reasoning, and in this theory no intellectual intuition is presupposed even in its account of deduction.

This is the alternative position and it appears to be supported by much evidence; certainly it would be rash today to reject the axiomatic theory out of hand, and yet it is a theory which shakes intuitionism in the Cartesian sense to its very foundations. To accept the alternative theory, however, we should have to be satisfied that recourse is never had in it to intuition by stealth, that there are no apprehensions of implications so familiar to us that we are hardly conscious of the intuition involved, and no intuited basic principles which are not axioms in the conventionalist sense. For if tolerance means complete freedom in the choice of axioms in the case of each system, then in principle there can be no non-conventional axioms.

Yet when the thinker allows, say, the principle of non-contradiction to regulate his system-making, is the principle then a mere conventionalist axiom? It may be argued that he freely chooses even this basic principle and that in theory he is free to decide not to choose it. But can non-contradiction be thought of as an axiom conventionally chosen? Aristotle held that things (and thoughts) cannot contradict themselves and that we know this intuitively. Do the conventionalists too in practice assume this and does this mean that their conventionalism is self-contradictory from the start?

The problem of our knowledge of non-contradiction is one that must be considered more fully later.[1] But even if it were the case that implicit in axiomatic theory is the principle of non-contradiction, and that this is not a principle that can be regarded as an axiom that is postulated for a specific system and decided upon by the system-maker, the main burden of the conventionalist's criticism of the intuitionist theory of deduction still remains. For it can still be maintained that conventionalism gives an alternative theory of deduction to the intuitionism which affirms that the core of deduction is the intuition of the implication. If there is a real alternative here then intuitionism is certainly shaken, even though it might still be felt that the

[1] Cf. Chapter XII below.

conventionalist theory has within it some elements which do not seem to be explicable in conventionalist terms.

18. We may now pass forward to consider a further charge laid against the intuitionist theory. The knowledge with which it is concerned, it is said, is remote and almost academic, its theory of knowledge consequently rarely applies to human knowledge. Our everyday knowledge, by which we live, consists of perceivings, hearsay knowledge, probabilities, loose inductions, and so on—none of which is intuitive in the sense in question. If there are any intellectual intuitions in scientific knowledge, they are few as contrasted with what is not intellectual intuition. Generalizing from observations, making inductions, setting forward hypotheses for testing and verifying and such procedures, seem to have little to do with intellectual intuition. The intuitionist's model fits neither the knowledge of every day nor the precise knowledge of the natural sciences, and, as has been seen, an alternative theory to intuitionism can be given even of pure deductive inquiry. It is true that it may be argued that there are non-precise intuitions behind all these procedures, and that these are not merely sensory intuitions or *anschauungen*. For instance, it is frequently suggested that the insights of scientists into new hypotheses are intuitional and that the bases even of logic and mathematics are vague intuited notions. This may be so, but it is obvious that the classical theory of intellectual intuition cannot be saved by reference to these non-precise intuitions.

Objection can be made to the intuitionist epistemology, too, on the ground that it puts all its emphasis on the effort of the individual and appears to ignore the extent to which knowledge is a social product. The advancement of knowledge, it will be said, is primarily a social rather than an individual phenomenon. This, however, as it stands, is not a particularly damaging criticism. Granted the importance of co-operation in the attainment of human knowledge, the actual advance may still be, and frequently is, the consequence of one individual's insight. Team work does not rule out private intuition. But the critic may be arguing too that human knowledge is social since it is inevitably the enlarging of a system constructed by many generations of men, and in this sense cannot possibly be the work of one, and that since this is so intuitionism must be judged inadequate. Moreover, a criticism of intuitionism implicit in the coherence theory of the Hegelians applies once it be agreed that all knowledge is systematic. An item of knowledge can be true or false only in the context of the system; and if the system of knowledge is incomplete, as it is in the case of human knowledge, then no assertion of truth is absolute and none infallible. This account of knowledge would seem to rule out entirely the intuitionist theory that the basis of knowledge is an infallible, intellectual intuition of fundamental truths by the individual.

19. To sum up the argument of this chapter. It began with the question: Can knowing that p ever be identified with being sure that p? It was argued that only in one set of circumstances would that be possible. If I were sure that p and if p was a statement that could never turn out to be false and I knew this, then to be sure would be to know.

The intuitionists claim that there is knowledge of this kind. Certain statements can be known to be true by intellectual intuition and the knowledge is infallible and known to be such. It needs no confirmation outside itself; it is self-guaranteeing and is 'its own criterion'. This must not be interpreted to mean that the statement p is true *because* we know it. The most ardent rationalist never advocated anything as foolish as this. But rationalists did claim that men could know the truth of certain statements in such a way that, in respect to such statements, they could never find themselves in the position of having to admit 'I was sure that p but I was wrong.'

Can this claim be justified? The argument of the present chapter leaves us doubting. We do not doubt the occurrence of 'intuitions' in various senses of the term; but we do doubt the occurrence of intuitions in the rationalist sense. Nor do we deny that some of the arguments brought forward against rationalist intuitionism are themselves uncertain, or that the critics fail to provide a completely convincing refutation. But the cumulative effect of their many-sided arguments makes acceptance of intellectual intuitionism today difficult. To this extent, it is not possible to return a sure affirmative to the question whether there is infallible, intellectual knowledge such that to be sure that p in this case is to know that p.

III

CERTAIN KNOWLEDGE

20. Much of our knowledge pretends to nothing more than probability. We guess, have hunches, and believe on such evidence as is available, and for the time being we take what we believe to be true without, however, claiming certainty for our beliefs. If we are wise we go on testing our beliefs, searching for further evidence that will confirm or refute them. A great deal of our knowledge clearly is of this kind and it has been held that all of it is so. This view, however, does not allow for human certitude; it seems perverse to say that we are never certain of anything, for the evidence is clear that we are frequently certain of many things. When then, in the face of the evidence to the contrary, writers affirm that all human knowledge is of what is probable they apparently assume that the certainties we are now talking of are not certainties. Why do they assume this? Presumably because they think of certainty in terms of the absolute certainty of traditional rationalism. They assume that the alternatives before the epistemologist today are two and two only, either to say that all human knowledge is of what is probable or to admit that the absolutely certain knowledge of the rationalists is possible. Faced with these alternatives the theorist, in view of his doubts about the possibility of absolutely certain knowledge, is prone to accept the view that all human knowledge is of what is probable, although he may do so with some hesitation since he would then appear to be breaking the fundamental rule in all these matters, namely, that due regard should be paid to the evidence.

But the view that these two alternatives exhaust the possibilities is surely erroneous; the choice before the epistemologist is not simply between probabilism on the one hand and Cartesianism on the other. This could only be supposed to be the case on a superficial analysis of human knowledge and on a failure to take note of the certainties of which human beings are capable. Accordingly the task here is to attempt an analysis of human certitude, making clear its main characteristics. It will then be necessary to consider its relationship to absolute certainty and to absolute truth. These are the matters that must concern us in this chapter.

21. We may begin by considering whether anything now remains of intellectual intuitionism. The intuitionists held that we are sure of several items of knowledge, completely sure as opposed to opining or guessing, or even being reasonably sure. They then proceeded to say that in these cases being sure is knowing infallibly. In view of modern criticism it must be conceded that the second point is dubitable; for even in the instances the intuitionists had most frequently in mind it is not established that we know that p in such a way that p will never turn out to be false.

But what of the first part of the intuitionist thesis, that we are completely sure of several items of knowledge? This seems to be true even if the second part be doubted. If it is true it would then appear to follow that what remains of intellectual intuitionism in modern epistemological theory is the doctrine of complete assurance; what is suspect is that of unfailing assurance.

This view of the situation is confirmed by the Three Condition Theory. According to this theory the first condition of knowledge is that the knower is sure. The term 'knowledge' is being consciously used in the narrow or strict sense; the theory in no way rules out the existence of knowledge of what is probable where the knower is not sure, but this is not its immediate concern. Strictly speaking a person knows, on this theory, only if he is sure. Other conditions must be satisfied too and, as it happens, the theorist is more interested in these other conditions than in the first. This is because the main purpose of the theory is to show that being sure is not enough and it seeks to make clear what more is needed. Yet it starts by asserting the need for being sure, and it assumes that this is a condition which can be, and frequently is, satisfied. Critics may object that the conditions of knowledge on this theory can never be met because the first condition is never met, because we are never completely sure. This is conceivable, but the theorist is clearly untroubled by this possibility. He begins by supposing that we are frequently sure and completely sure.

It would be interesting to speculate why this assumption is so readily made by the philosophers who advocate this theory. It might be argued, for instance, that they are still under the influence of G. E. Moore and of the so-called Oxford Realists in the immediate past, or of traditional Aristotelian intellectual intuitionism and of Cartesianism. But the theorists we now have in mind would not admit any specific debt to intuitionism, for they think intuitionism as such to be a false doctrine, and certainly they do not consciously borrow from it. No, they have rather discovered in their own experience that one can be completely sure, and they have no hesitation in beginning with this discovery. In so far as they do begin in this way, however, they reaffirm one vitally important item in the intuitionist doctrine, namely, that some part of our knowledge is completely certain and that probabilism is to be rejected. This much remains of the intuitionism of the past.

22. Now the assumption made by the supporters of the Three Condition Theory that the basic requirement in knowing is being sure is one made by many others as well, and the question which must now be faced is whether the assumption is justified. I may say at once that I think it is, if we are still speaking of knowledge in the sense of certain knowledge, and that the assumption is justified by experience. But there are two lines of objection to this view and before proceeding further these need to be examined.

The first of the two objections mentioned is made on the ground that being sure is an irrelevancy in the discussion of knowledge. For what, it will be asked, has the presence or absence of a feeling of conviction to do with knowledge? Waves of conviction which come and go signify little cognitively. Now this may be so, though they are still cognitive experiences however faltering and transient. But when, for instance, the theorists of the Three Condition Theory speak of being sure as one element in knowledge they are not then usually thinking of momentary convictions of this kind. I am sure now that a bird is singing outside the window, and I am sure that $7+5 = 12$. It is straining language to speak of 'momentary waves of conviction' in this context, but this is the context that matters.

But the critics may mean that being sure is irrelevant in another sense, it is logically irrelevant. They do not deny that we do have the experience of being sure, but argue that if the logical validity and cogency of what is claimed to be a piece of knowledge is questioned then whether we are sure or not in the process of gaining the alleged knowledge is quite irrelevant. This must be admitted, but we have also agreed that what is logically irrelevant need not be epistemologically irrelevant. It is dangerous so to confound epistemology with logic that features central to epistemology are neglected. Such a feature is the experience of being sure. I agree with the view that being sure is basic in any theory of knowledge, even though it be shown to be irrelevant in logic.

A second objection to the view that being sure is basic to knowledge will come from the probabilist. Human beings, he argues, are never sure of anything: theirs is opinion and certainty is beyond them. This objection rests on the insight that human beings are not capable of infallible knowledge. But it fails because it does not recognize the all-important distinction between being sure and knowing infallibly. For though, as is emphasized throughout this book, human beings are fallible creatures, they are nevertheless quite sure about many items of knowledge. I am now quite sure that I am sitting here writing these words, and I cannot accept any suggestion that this piece of knowledge is of what is probable only. It is difficult to believe too that the probabilist himself is never sure of anything. Is it the case then that, being obsessed by man's general fallibility, he either ignores his own being sure or seeks to explain it away as illusory, since, he would argue, only an infallible being can be 'really' sure? But if he is sure that he is, say, now sitting at his desk then it seems to me he is really sure of this.

It is interesting in this connection to note that some of the most recent discussions of the Three Condition Theory tend to be in probabilist terms, and this for the above-mentioned reason. The tendency seems unfortunate since the acknowledgement of human certitude is essential for a correct epistemology, and since the difference between knowing with certainty and opining without being certain needs to be stressed. But in these most recent speculations[1] this difference tends to be blurred. They have to do with A's believing that p rather than A's being sure that p. What are the grounds on which A judges that p? Are they good grounds? Do they justify the belief? The discussion is lively and valuable, but it is different in character from one which commences by assuming that one of the conditions of knowledge is being sure. Being centred on belief it tends to ignore certitude. The conclusions of one of the most recent contributions, that of William W. Rozeboom,[2] are significant. It is possible that not all the other contributors to the debate would agree with him, but Rozeboom's conclusion is that believing (with various degrees of certainty but never total certainty) is worthy of study and that the question 'How strongly should A believe p?' is a legitimate question. By contrast knowing with certainty is 'so impossibly idealized that no real life episode ever satisfies it'. We may, if we choose, retain the name 'knowledge' for 'true beliefs at the theoretical limit of absolute conviction and perfect infallibility so long as we appreciate that this ideal is never instantiated', but such knowledge, he thinks, 'is no longer of serious philosophical concern'. I should argue that what has happened here is as

---

[1] They have been carried forward for the most part in *Analysis*. E. L. Gettier's article, 'Is Justified True Belief Knowledge?', in 1963 began the discussion, and this was followed by articles by Michael Clark, Ernest Sosa, Saunders and Champawat, Keith Lehrer, and Rozeboom.

[2] 'Why I know so much more than you do', *American Phil. Quart.*, 1967, 281–90.

follows. It is assumed that human cognition is a form of believing, with a higher or lower degree of assurance, and the assumption leads to the conclusion that the true cognitive contrast is between believing and an absolute knowing which is infallible. It is then thought obvious that human beings attain the former cognition but not the latter. But this does not seem to me to be the true picture. I am inclined to agree that 'no real life episode ever satisfies' the concept of absolute infallible knowledge; but I also wish to assert and to insist that human beings are frequently quite sure or quite certain that p, and that to ignore this certainty is to miss the central point in the argument about human knowledge.

It should be mentioned here that other arguments have been put forward from time to time in favour of the view that the probabilist's position cannot be sustained. It is argued that on this theory probabilism itself could only be probable and might be false. More to the point, it is argued further, that to know that something is probable is to be certain that it is probable, so that probability presupposes certainty. I do not know of any statement of these arguments which is completely convincing and prefer to rest the argument against the probabilist theory on the fact that one is sure, and on the probabilist's failure to distinguish between being sure and knowing infallibly. If it be granted that we are at times sure, then the evidence would certainly permit us to say that we are sometimes sure that, of two statements p and h, p is more probable than h. But this is different from saying that to know that something is probable is to be sure that it is probable.

23. Is it possible now to bring out more clearly the nature of being sure or being certain? Or are we in the position in which Oxford Realists found themselves when trying to describe knowing. Knowing, they said, is knowing, and nothing more can be said. Are we confined to saying that being sure *is* being sure, that we are all acquainted with this experience and there is no more to be said? If we did try to say something more than this, what sort of

description could we offer? It is unlikely that it would be in behaviourist terms. Are there observable actions or looks or gesticulations which are always present when one is sure and which are sufficiently different from other actions to enable us, by means of them, to differentiate this state from other states? Hardly. Or again, could we consider the utterance of certain phrases to be the distinguishing behaviour? For instance, we might say that to be sure is reducible, for our present purposes, just to the utterance 'I am sure that . . .', 'I am certain that . . .', or any equivalent phrase. But this would not take us very far. For it will be recalled that we use such phrases as these not only to say that we are sure but also to emphasize a point, to concede one, and so on. As has been seen, people even use these phrases when, as the context shows, they are not sure but, on the contrary, uncertain. It would be obviously mistaken to identify being sure with the mere utterance of one of these phrases. It is, consequently, not at all easy to determine what behaviourist terms there are in which being sure could be described.

But the fact that we cannot speak of being sure in behaviourist terms does not mean that we cannot describe it in language which others will understand. To English-speaking peoples 'being sure' is a significant locution and we realize from what people say that they use this phrase in much the same way as we do. We also assume that their experience of being sure is roughly the same as ours. We shall consider later what is involved in this situation. Thus there is no difficulty in describing features of the experience in language which others understand. And in particular I wish to mention here three of its characteristics which seem to have considerable epistemological significance.

In the first place, being sure is, in a special sense, personal and individual. No one else can be sure for me. This does not mean that I am uninfluenced by the convictions of others and certainly not that I do not learn from others. Much of what I am sure of I have learnt from others, but I am now convinced of its truth and this conviction is something personal to me. It is more than taking for granted on the authority of others. I do accept a great deal from others in this way, although I may not then be sure of these items of knowledge. But if I am sure, then at that moment it makes no difference whether others are sure too; I do not need the support of others and, even if others deny what I am sure of, at the moment it makes no difference. Most emphatically being sure that p does not wait upon universal agreement about p, nor even upon the agreement of those in my immediate circle. I may be sure that p even though everyone around me is sure that p is false.

In the second place, if one is sure that p then the issue is, for the time being, settled. The experience has a finality which leaves no room for doubt. If my state is still one of doubting, if I question whether I really know, then I am not sure. The intuitionist was right in claiming that being sure was issue-settling; where one hesitates to follow him is in his further claim that it settles the issue for all time. We can be sure at the present moment that the statement p is true, but later we may come to doubt this, and may even become sure that p is false, thus settling the issue once again, but in another way. Being issue-settling the experience possesses a finality, and since this finality is not possessed by other kinds of cognitive experience the characteristic provides a clear and definite distinguishing criterion. Believing without being sure, estimating, guessing, assuming, taking for granted, may all be said to be instances of knowing in a wide sense, but none of them is issue-settling.

We have to distinguish between issue-settling in the present sense and coming to a decision. The latter may also settle the issue, though not in the same sense. A judge comes to a decision about a case and settles it legally, but he may yet not be completely sure that the decision is the correct one to make. In one sense he settles the issue, but he lacks the issue-settling conviction in the other sense. Speaking generally, one needs to differentiate sharply between being sure and making a decision. One does make decisions; sometimes one is sure in making them and sometimes one has doubts. When one is sure another factor has entered and, whereas the main characteristic of deciding is the choosing freely between alternatives, in so far as one is finally sure there is no choice. In the case of deciding without being sure, as when one decides after examining all the available evidence that probably hypothesis h is true, it may be argued that choice is free to the end. On the other hand, even in this case it might be said that one is sure, and cannot but be sure, that h is probable in this context and so one is sure of something even in deciding that h is probably true. Certainly, where the deciding ends in being sure the knowledge cannot then be wholly described in terms of free choice between alternatives. Reflection upon this matter leads to the conclusion that any account of knowledge wholly in terms of decision-making must be inadequate.

The third characteristic to which I wish to refer is that of constraint. The knower is constrained. To recall Locke's words, 'this part of knowledge [i.e. intuition] is irresistible and like bright sunshine forces itself immediately to be perceived as soon as ever the mind turns its view that way'. This is analogy and not to be taken too literally. Nor should the reference to the immediacy of the experience be taken literally, for a man may spend months and years following up various clues before he finally becomes sure that p. Yet just as bright sunshine forces itself upon the senses so too he is constrained to accept.

In being sure one is constrained and to that extent is not free. Yet one is not passive either. Possibly the active–passive terminology fails us in this context. Knowing is not something that simply happens to a passive mind, just as a passive lump of clay is moulded by the sculptor; knowing is accepting. As the traditional rationalists taught, it is the alert and attentive mind that is sure. The passive clay analogy is far from the mark; it would be better to compare the state of mind in being sure with the 'Here stand I, I can no other' predicament, though the latter, perhaps, presents the condition in too emphatic and dramatic a way. Yet it brings out the sense in which a free agent, without losing his freedom, is none the less under compulsion. So an active mind in being sure is, though active, also constrained. This is a third characteristic of being sure.

24. It is interesting to observe the connection between the notion of constraint and that of objectivity. The contrast between the objective and the subjective is ambiguous; but here is one ground (of many) on which the distinction rests. If we are constrained what constrains us is objective; on the other hand, what we freely conjure up ourselves is subjective. The distinction is found at all epistemological levels. Berkeley, it will be recalled, distinguishes on this ground between subjective images and objective sensations. 'When in broad daylight I open my eyes, it is not in my power to . . . determine what particular objects shall present themselves to my view.'[1] We are constrained to see the objects and this is taken to mean that they have an objectivity that images do not have. In much the same way it is felt that if we are sure and *must* accept, what we then accept is objective and independent of us.

A contrast is assumed between the subjectivity (and the unreality) of, for instance, a day-dream and the objectivity (and reality) of the world which I am constrained to accept. In a day-dream one is fancy-free; not that all constraint, perhaps, is absent but there is at least a partial freeing of oneself from it. But then one jerks oneself out of the dream, accepts the constraint of knowledge and 'faces the real as it is'.[2]

To digress for a moment, there may be room for a constraint theory of dreaming, though one hesitates to add one more theory of dreams to the many that now exist. It would have to do with some dreams only, namely, with those which occur when we are about to awake. Physiologists can now trace the more or less wakeful periods in sleep, and experiments carried out suggest that much of our dreaming occurs during these periods. Now a feature of dreams is their incongruity; the expected temporal and spatial relations are absent, as are the familiar social relationships, and the oddest incoherences

---

[1] *Principles*, § 29.
[2] We speak here of the constraint of knowledge, but of course there are other constraints. There are constraints in dreams themselves, for instance the constraint and compulsion of the nightmare. There is no suggestion here that only in being sure are we constrained. The constraint of knowledge is one of many other constraints.

occur. Is it feasible that the dream, as we wake, is, as it were, a rudimentary process of sorting things out, of bringing present stimulations into line with waking experience, of getting the world into focus again? Order must overcome disorder, the familiar be restored and the incongruities made congruent. As we awake the knowledge guiding our daily life takes over, and in the memory of the dream we have this brief but fascinating glimpse of the strange restoration.[1] Part of this restoration lies in taking upon ourselves once more the constraint and discipline imposed upon us by our understanding and knowledge of the world in which we live, both physical and social. We take up again the yoke of knowledge, that is to say, the constraint of the objective.

How far this theory of dreams will work I leave the reader to determine. He will at any rate recognize the distinction on which it is based between the subjectivity of free imagining and the objectivity of the knowledge that constrains us.

25. But to return to the main argument. Being sure is a personal experience, issue-settling and constraining; as such it is a key factor in knowledge. There are other factors, for instance, gathering the evidence, making generalizations and testing them, using deductive arguments. It is also understood that we do not always reach certainty but may have to be content with probability. Nevertheless, being sure is of central significance for epistemology, and that in two respects. On the one hand it is of the first importance that men can in fact be sure; the criticism that men are never really sure or never fully sure is refuted by the evidence. Rationalists and intuitionists in the past took this to be true and made it the foundation of their epistemology. It is equally true today. Yet while this is granted, it also remains true that being sure is an experience of a fallible creature who remains fallible even when he is sure. That

---

[1] As we are in the process of waking when dreaming these dreams it is easier to speak of remembering them. Norman Malcolm in *Dreaming* has shown the difficulties in the view that we remember dreams which occur in deep sleep. Perhaps the question that arises is whether such dreams ever do occur. Do *all* dreams occur at the more wakeful periods?

this too is true falsifies the rationalist doctrine of absolute infallibility. Thus the experience is highly significant for epistemology in this further sense that it enables, and indeed compels, us to maintain, at one and the same time, two propositions, first that one can be completely sure and have no doubts, and, second, that throughout one is a fallible creature.

Any theory of human knowledge, as I see it, must rest on these two propositions. This means that it cannot be Cartesian on the one hand or probabilist on the other, for both these theories over-simplify the issues. They fail to recognize the possibility of two kinds of *certain* knowledge, in addition to opining or believing, the two being (1) certain knowledge which is infallible and (2) certain knowledge which is none the less fallible. Now 'fallible certain knowledge' would appear to some to be a contradiction in terms and, obviously, if one begins by holding knowledge, by definition, to be infallible then 'fallible knowledge' (not to mention 'fallible certain knowledge') is a contradiction in terms. Yet, should we define 'knowledge' in these terms? Here is a fact about human cognition, that the man who knows is a fallible creature. In such a case it is not wise to define the word 'knowledge' in such a way that we can never speak of a human being knowing without thereby contradicting ourselves.

It would be useful to find appropriate names for the two sorts of certain knowledge. It is customary to speak of infallible knowledge as 'absolute' and this might suggest that fallible knowledge should be termed 'relative'. But this latter term would not do, since it might imply that the second sort of certainty is only relatively certain, and this would be misleading since it is completely certain. It would be misleading too to call it prima facie certain knowledge, for this would suggest that it was not in truth certain but only appeared to be certain. Some more neutral adjective is required and I suggest we call the fallible certain knowledge *primal* knowledge and the infallible *absolute* knowledge.

We should then recognize three sorts of knowledge, belief

about what is probable, primal knowledge, and absolute knowledge. Now to which of these three does being sure belong? For the most part being sure is primal knowledge; in the next section we may consider whether it is ever absolute knowledge. But this at least is clear. If I do acquire absolute knowledge I cannot be in error, but if I acquire primal knowledge and am quite sure I may yet be in error. Primal knowledge is fallible, though, to repeat a point, to say that a person may err is not to say that he does err.

26. Once these distinctions are made, the next question that arises is whether human beings ever do acquire what we now term absolute knowledge. Now it is easier to answer this question, given the difference between absolute and primal certain knowledge. For if probability and absolute certainty were the only alternatives the conviction that not all human knowledge is of the probable would lead one, somewhat unwillingly perhaps, to defend the view that human knowledge can be absolute. But if the possibility of a knowledge which is certain and yet fallible be acknowledged, the pressure upon one then to concede the existence of absolute knowledge would not be so great. I am quite sure now that there is a bird singing outside this open window, but I should not want to claim that this was infallible knowledge, and I should not wish to claim this of any piece of empirical knowledge. What of more formal knowledge? What of pure logical deduction? I am quite capable of erring in the deductions I make. Descartes himself advised frequent revisions of such deductions. And how many revisions are necessary to give me absolute knowledge? Still Descartes would have insisted that there was a core of infallible knowledge in logical deduction, namely, the intuition of the implication. But, as we have seen, whether any intuition of this kind is in fact present in deduction can be queried. On the other hand, knowledge of the principle of non-contradiction is regarded fairly generally as an instance of absolute and infallible knowledge. But, even in this case, as we shall see, doubts arise with the further study of the principle. We cannot

assume without further question that the knowledge of this principle is absolute.

It is not easy to find any instance of human certainty which is absolute, as opposed to primal, knowledge. Is there possibly an *a priori* argument to prove none the less that we do acquire absolute knowledge? We might conjure up an argument analogous to the ontological argument in some of its forms. We have the notion of infallible knowledge, for the contrast between fallible and infallible knowledge is significant to us; but it can only be our consciousness of infallibility which gives us the standard whereby we are able to know that the fallible is fallible. So fallible knowledge presupposes infallible knowledge. In answer, we certainly do have the notion of infallible knowledge. But must we know something infallibly before we can have this notion? In our present situation we feel completely sure of many things, though we sometimes find later that we were in error even though we were sure. But we know from experience what it is to be certain, and there is nothing to prevent us from imagining a situation in which we are, first, certain and, second, never in error. This would provide us with the notion of completely certain, infallible knowledge, even though we have never had such knowledge.

What we do have is certain knowledge, completely certain, for when we are sure we are completely sure. If then it turned out that we were in fact beings capable of infallible knowledge the degree of assurance enjoyed by us could not possibly be greater than we enjoy at present. Hence it is easy to assume that being sure is itself infallible knowledge. The assumption is not justified, yet the error does not lie in a difference in the degree of assurance, but solely in the fact that the assurance in primal knowledge may still turn out to be misplaced, whereas in absolute knowledge this cannot be the case.

Now the evidence suggests, strongly, that absolute knowledge, though it can be conceived, cannot be gained by human beings. And if this is so the criticism made earlier of the Three Condition Theory can be set out in new terms. *B* questions *A*'s right to be sure and asks for evidence. When he is given the evidence he concludes, say, that A has the right to be sure. But B's knowledge is primal, as is A's, and if C confirms the finding of A and B he still has no absolute knowledge. That they all agree does not make their knowledge absolute. But the assumption of the Three Condition Theory is that we can absolutely and finally determine whether A has the right to be sure, and this, we now see, is to be doubted.

One point remains to be made in this analysis of being sure. It might be felt that it engenders scepticism, since we conclude that when we are completely sure and completely convinced we may yet be in error. Still it would be wrong to find here a source of scepticism alone, for it is also true that we are sure and that we do know, though the knowledge is not infallible. The importance of the positive side in fact far outweighs that of the negative. The scepticism is not such as to make us conclude that man cannot know, for he does know and is quite sure; what we doubt, and must doubt, is whether at any time he gains absolute, infallible knowledge.

27. If it be agreed that a distinction must be made between primal and absolute knowledge what effect will this doctrine have on one's theory of truth? Truth, it is said, is What Is. This does not take us very far, but at least it means that to say that a statement is true is to say that it states what is the case. The statement 'John is on the lawn' is true if, and only if, John is on the lawn. It is on this theory of truth that the Three Condition Theory rests. A knows only if what he is sure about is the case. He may be sure, and he may have evidence that convinces him and convinces everybody else, and yet if things are not as he is sure they are he does not know.

Now on this theory what is is absolutely—there is no question of its not being what it is. Further if we know it we know it as it is, once and for all. Knowledge of it, if it occurs at all, is itself absolute and infallible. In such a situation it would follow that whether A does or does not know that p can only be determined if someone knows that p is true and knows it absolutely; unless this is possible no final judgement can be made on A's claim. But now, since absolute knowledge appears to be beyond our reach, this *is* impossible, and the Three Condition Theory collapses. It is not to be wondered at that Kant did not include this third condition in his list.

The position then seems to be the following. When I am sure of something I am completely sure, and completely sure of it as being absolutely true. I thus think or conceive absolute knowledge. The question that remains, however, is whether I ever attain it, for on the analysis of knowledge presented in this chapter there is considerable doubt whether I ever do. Hence the dilemma. On the one hand, a statement is true if and only if it states the case. On the other hand, I can discover what is the case but, apparently, the discovery is invariably primal knowledge. It is completely sure but at the same time fallible. Thus I have primal knowledge that what I state is the case, but to establish absolute truth I need absolute knowledge. And yet I speak of knowing that p is true and being quite sure of this. What sort of truth is this? It would appear that just as we need to distinguish between primal knowledge and absolute know-ledge so too we have to distinguish between primal truth and absolute truth. What we want is absolute truth but what we get is a fallible person's truth, that is, primal truth. If I say that p is true what I want to say is that p is absolutely true; when I am sure I am sure that p is true absolutely; and yet I am fallible. Further, though we all agree on the truth, it is still primal; no amount of agreement about primal truth will make it absolute truth. Thus the argument seems to be pointing towards a distinction between primal truth and absolute truth.

We have been speaking in terms of the theory that what is true is what is. There are also relativist theories of truth, for which truth is not discovered but rather made. It is quite in accord with these theories to speak of p as being true relatively, p is true *for me*, true within one system that I am creating but not another. But these theories provide no way out in the present argument. For the distinguishing feature of the theory which is emerging in this book is the high significance and centrality of being sure, and being sure carries with it complete assurance; at the same time it is fallible and so not absolute knowledge but rather primal. Still the notion of absolute truth dominates the theory and gives no room for relativism.

IV

ILLUSTRATIVE CASES

28. The main implications and consequences of the Three Condition Theory have now been worked out. Concentration upon this theory has confined our study to a narrow field and it will be necessary to take a wider view. Before we do so, however, it would be well to look in some detail at certain illustrative cases of being sure.

What are we sure of? In the first place, we are sure of much in our moral life. It is true that we find ourselves lost and frequently bewildered about what we ought and ought not to do, on the other hand there are numerous occasions when we have no hesitation and no doubt. But in this book I do not propose to discuss moral knowledge. Further, we are sure of logical (and mathematical) conclusions, but I wish, too, to postpone discussion of this topic to a later occasion. What I should like to consider in this chapter are certain matters we are sure of at the factual level, and in particular three items of outstanding importance at this level. We are sure of our own existence, of the existence of others, and of the existence of physical things. I am here sitting before this table, my friend is there, and the table is between us. I say I am sure of these things, but what precisely does being sure mean in these contexts and what am I sure of? Let us consider each case in turn.

29. *Being sure that I am here.* I am sure that I am here. The subject to which the 'I' refers exists. But what is this I? What do I affirm when I say with so much assurance that I exist and am sitting here now?

For instance, am I affirming that I exist as body and mind? Do I exist as an embodied mind? The notion of an embodied mind is a notoriously difficult notion. It seems hardly correct to suppose that a man must first make clear to himself what it is to be an embodied mind before he can say that he himself exists. Am I then affirming that I as a person exist, and am now sitting here? But the notion of person, too, is difficult. It has legal and moral overtones; only a person it may be said can be morally responsible. Have I then first to clear up the problem of moral responsibility before I can say that I am sitting here? These approaches to the problem do not seem too promising.

It might be more helpful to begin by asking how one would try to defend the statement 'I am here' if pressed by a sceptic. 'Are you really there?' The answer would hardly be in terms of embodied mind or personality; it is much more likely to take the form: 'Well, here are my hands and feet and you can see them as well as I can. You hear me talk. You can touch me and find me a solid body taking a certain amount of room. Isn't this enough to prove to you that I am here?'

The critic might consent but add: 'Yes, I can see, hear, and feel you, but that at most could only prove that you are here as a body. When you say that you exist you are not merely saying that your body exists.' No, this is true, but it is also true that part of what I mean is that I exist as a body; I have only to look—or so I assume—in order to see that my body exists. That this perhaps evinces too great faith in the evidence of the senses need not concern us for the moment, and we may accept the argument. But if this is part of what I mean it is certainly not the whole. What more do I mean? That I am a mind? When I say that I exist do I mean that I exist as body and mind?

Body *and* mind. What is the force of the 'and'? Does it, for instance, signify a conjunction of two substances? Must I accept the two-substance theory before I can assert significantly that I exist? Obviously not, for even if the theory were true, knowledge of it could not be said to be a necessary prerequisite for the significant assertion that I am sure that I myself exist. This assurance is not one that metaphysicians of this school of thought alone can possess. If, on the other hand, the two-substance theory is rejected, it is not necessary for me, before I can be sure of my own existence, to decide between two forms of metaphysical monism, the idealist and the materialist. Fortunately, too, it is not necessary for me to explain how I can say (and what I mean by saying) that my body is the whole of me, but so too is my mind; or again how, if I am both mind and body, mind and body are not parts of me in the way in which my head is one part of my body and my foot another.

30. These are metaphysical problems and it is not necessary to solve them before one can say that one is sure that one exists. Nevertheless, it is true that when I say that I exist, I do invariably suppose that I am 'more than body' in at least one sense, and it will be good to get this sense clear. I say to the critic: 'You see me sitting here, I am at least as real as the table. But I am different from the table too, and the difference lies in this that I have certain experiences which, I assume, the table does not have, that is, mental experiences.' It is in this sense that I am more than body. The critic, however, may well reply that I am now begging the question. How is this phrase 'mental experience' to be interpreted? We had best take up the challenge.

A good procedure in seeking to answer the question is to observe the language we use, since it shows the difference between speaking of physical objects and speaking of objects that are not merely physical. In speaking of the latter one has to fall back upon a class of sentences which are unique. For want of a better name I call them psi-sentences.[1] Their distinguishing mark is this, that to use them significantly, and not merely parrot-wise, or to understand them when another uses them, one has usually had to have experiences of the sort mentioned in the sentences. When I say 'I have a pain' or 'I feel tired' these sentences are significant to you because you have felt a pain and you have felt tired. Of course, the observation of my physical behaviour, for instance wincing and writhing, if such occurs, would give you some information

[1] 'Dispensing with Mind', *Proc. Arist. Soc.*, 1951–2, 225–43.

about my state, but a deeper understanding of what is happening to me is possible for you because you too have experienced pain. Most sentences beginning with 'I' are psi-sentences, but not all. 'I am six foot tall' is not one, neither is 'I am in the kitchen'. Sentences vary according to the context. For instance, in the case of 'I know that the book is on the shelf', if I use the 'I know' for emphasis or again to concede a point, then the sentence is not a psi-sentence, but if I use it to refer to the experience of knowing then it is. On the other hand 'I feel sick', 'I do enjoy this sort of music', 'I pondered over the problem', are all likely to be psi-sentences. Further, many sentences not beginning with 'I' are usually psi-sentences, for instance, 'Henry decided to leave', 'Mary felt hurt'. Nor do their subject terms always refer to human beings. 'The dog felt a pain', 'The flower enjoys the air it breathes', are psi-sentences, though the attribution of such experiences to dogs and to flowers may be questioned. In primitive societies and in children's tales even inanimate things may be thought of as animated, so that one uses psi-sentences to refer to them also. 'The wind grew angrier and angrier.'

A behaviourist may wish to ignore the distinction set out here between psi-sentences and non-psi-sentences since it is of no significance for his theory. He may seek to reduce psi-sentences into non-psi-sentences and, up to a point, within limitations, may succeed in doing so. For instance, for 'He is in pain' he substitutes 'He winces'; for 'He feels embarrassed' he substitutes 'He blushes', and so on. We must admit too that a person who had never himself felt pain could *in theory*[1] have a concept of pain, that is of behavioural pain, as long as he has seen others wince, writhe, make certain grimaces, etc. and as long as he has been taught that the correct description of this condition in English is 'He is in pain'. Henceforward, we may suppose, he uses the phrase 'in pain' significantly and understands it when used by others; he also recognizes the condition

---

[1] I emphasize the words 'in theory', for in fact I am a being who has felt pain and further, in the world of persons as I know it, there are no persons who have never felt pain.

when he sees it. But he has never himself felt a pain and so this element is absent from his concept of pain. We may contrast the use of 'He feels a pain' by the person who had himself felt a pain. In his case, 'He feels a pain' cannot be reduced without loss of meaning to 'He winces'. There is indeed a profound difference between the meaning of the two sentences, the former being what I have called a psi-sentence and the latter a non-psi-sentence. The behaviourist finds no use for this distinction in his studies, but this is not to deny that it exists.

There may be objection to this distinction from the opposite, the subjectivist, side. It may be argued that any and every statement we make is a psi-sentence, for implicit if not explicit in all such statements is a clause 'I am sure that . . .', 'I believe that . . .', 'I guess that . . .', and so on. The sentences then are all psi-sentences, since I can understand the significance of, for instance, 'I believe that p' only if I myself have had the experience of believing. A like point could be made by an extreme empiricist whose empiricism is driving him to sub-jectivism. All sentences must be reducible to basic sentences such as 'I now see a red patch' and each of these is a psi-sentence only significant to a person who has himself had the experience of seeing, hearing, touching, tasting, or smelling.

But such gross subjectivism as this is difficult to accept. The sentence 'John is on the lawn' does not mean what 'I know (or I believe) that John is on the lawn' means. The latter does refer to the knower and would be classed with psi-sentences but the former does not. It tells us that John is on the lawn (and whether anyone knows or believes this fact is irrelevant). The issue is further confused by references to the performative uses of the word 'know'. The 'I know that . . .' may be used not to say that I know but merely, for instance, to emphasize a statement. If someone contradicts me, I say: 'I *know* that John is on the lawn.' In this case, it is argued, 'John is on the lawn' and 'I know that John is on the lawn' mean the same thing. But even if this be admitted, it gives no support to the view that the statement 'John is on the lawn' always means the same as 'I know that John is on the lawn', in all the latter's varied uses. There is no argument here for the theory that every statement made is either an explicit or an implicit psi-sentence.

In spite of possible objections then from behaviourists and subjectivists I conclude that a distinction can be made between psi-sentences and non-psi-sentences, and that whilst a limited reduction of psi-sentences into non-psi-sentences is possible there can be no question of reducing all psi-sentences into non-psi-sentences nor all of the latter into psi-sentences. Now once we have established this distinction, then what might be called a minimum explanation of the contrast between body and mind can be given, and this enables us to proffer a preliminary answer to the question: 'What am I saying exists when I say "I am sure that I am here, sitting at the table" ?' First, it is agreed, I assert the existence of a body which can be seen and touched. But I assert more. I assert that I exist as mind as well as body, and this means (as a minimum) that I exist as a being having experiences that can only be talked of significantly in psi-sentences.

When I, being awake, say that I exist sitting here at this moment I mean as a minimum (1) that I can now see and touch myself and that others can see and touch me (so that they exist as well as myself), and (2) that I have experiences that can only be talked of in psi-sentences. Having established this foundation for a theory I can explain that in addition I take myself to be a physical object in space, and to be a physical object one must be more than a mere *visibile* or *tangibile*. Later in this chapter it will be necessary to consider what it is to be a physical object. I mean too that, as physical and as mental, I am a being lasting through time, and am conscious of this. This is my body, the same body that I looked at five minutes ago, and it is the same I who look now as looked five minutes ago, and can now remember looking; it is my body, my looking, and my remembering. Nor can one continue with these first essentials alone, for when I say I am sure I now exist I mean too that I exist along with others, that I, who am a member of a family, have a job, work with my colleagues, and enjoy a full human life, exist. As a minimum, however, we may agree that what I am sure of is my existence as a being persisting in space through time who can be seen and touched and who has experiences that can only be spoken of in psi-sentences.

31. *Being sure that my friend is sitting opposite me.* Just as I am sure that I exist, sitting in this chair, so I am sure too that my friend is sitting there on the other side of the table. I am sure of the existence of another being who is, like myself, body and mind in the minimal sense explained. The problem here is often posed: 'How do we know that other *minds* exist?', yet we are dealing with beings who are bodies as well as minds, and the problem is made more difficult if we speak in terms of minds only.

But let us begin by considering some of the answers given to the question 'How do we know that other minds exist?' First, we are said to know that other minds exist by analogy. This traditional argument can be set out in the following terms. Certain of the bodies which surround me behave in a manner resembling that in which my own body behaves. My own body's behaviour is prompted and controlled by my mind, and I conclude that the behaviour of these other bodies is prompted and controlled by a mind resembling my own. Thus by analogy I infer that other minds exist as well as my own.

The unsatisfactoriness of this argument is obvious. It supposes that I must have a knowledge of my own mind and of my own behaviour and of the relations and correlations between my behaviour and my mind before I can know of the existence of the other mind, and that I then, observing a like behaviour in others, can infer the existence of other minds. But the supposition is to be queried. For, first, is it the case that I do have this extensive knowledge of my own mind and of its relations to my behaviour before I begin to know other minds? Surely, it would be agreed that a person knows more of how others behave, for instance, when angry, than of how he himself behaves when he is angry. It seems quite unreasonable to argue that I must be aware of my own behaviour when angry first before I can infer from another's behaviour that he is angry.

But next consider a case in which it might be easier to hold that I do argue from what has happened to me. I cut my finger, I feel a pain, and the finger bleeds. My neighbour cuts his finger, I see the blood and I conclude by analogy that he has a pain like mine. Now analogical reasoning at best is never completely safe. Its general form is as follows: A and B are two situations in which a b c d occur, e also occurs in A, therefore it is likely that e will occur in B. Or, again, A and B are two substances having the qualities a b c d, A has also e and so B is likely to have e. Applied to our present case, the argument would run: Since I experienced a pain when my finger was cut and I saw it bleed then the next time my finger is cut and bleeds I shall again feel a pain. This argument is not particularly strong, but it would be agreed that it is much stronger than the actual argument under consideration here, namely, since I experienced a pain when my finger was cut and I observed the blood, then on seeing a finger other than my own cut and bleeding I conclude by analogy that *another* mind exists and is feeling a pain. Obviously this is weak, and we cannot rest our assurance that another exists on such an argument.

Dissatisfaction with the argument from analogy led to the suggestion that we somehow know other minds without inferring the knowledge. Cook Wilson gave classic utterance to this point of view in his *Statement and Inference* (p. 853). 'If we think of the existence of our friends,' he says, 'it is the "direct knowledge" which we want; merely inferential knowledge seems a poor affair. To most men it would be as surprising as unwelcome to hear it could not be directly known whether there were such existences as their friends, and that it was only a matter of (probable) empirical argument and inference from facts which are directly known. And even if we convince ourselves on reflection that this is really the case, our actions prove that we have a confidence in the existence of our friends which can't be derived from an empirical argument (which can never be certain), for a man will risk his life for his friend. We don't want merely inferred friends.'

We certainly don't, and the suggestion that our friend's existence is merely an inference, and a probable inference at that, is wholly unsatisfactory to us. Yet what knowledge, other than inferential knowledge, have we? Have we 'direct' knowledge of our friend's mental life? To say so would conflict with the view that mental experiences are private. I am never (we usually suppose) directly conscious of anyone's experience other than my own. What of telepathy? Is there amongst close friends—Cook Wilson is speaking of friends—some bond, some sympathy, so deep that it provides a direct knowledge of the other? In view of the evidence available it would be foolish to deny outright the possibility of telepathic knowledge, yet it would be also unwise to think that telepathy provides the solution of our problem. For, in the first place, telepathy normally is not the direct experience of another's mental experience. It consists rather in becoming aware of something which another is experiencing at that time, although one is not aware that the other is experiencing it. As H. H. Price has said, it is like catching a fever. In the second place, telepathic experiences are comparatively rare,[1] yet consciousness of the existence of our friends is not rare, and we are conscious too of the existence of strangers where the telepathic link would be presumably weaker.

Thus telepathy cannot be the direct knowledge of others which we seek. We are all quite sure that others exist; if we were not, we could not reject solipsism as emphatically as we do. What then is the nature of the assurance? It must be something very familiar and universally shared, but it is difficult to say what it is.

32. Now the difficulty, it seems to me, is acute simply because we set out our problem in terms of knowledge of other *minds*.

[1] The possibility must not be ruled out that vague telepathic experiences, so vague as not to be recognized as telepathic, occur oftener than we suppose, and help us in the communication of thought. But no one would claim that vague telepathic experiences of this kind explain our assurance of our friends' existence.

For what we are sure of is the existence of other people. What I am sure of at the present moment is the existence of my friend sitting there on the other side of the table—body and mind (if one chooses to say so) but certainly not mind in isolation.

And the basis and foundation for this knowledge, I should claim, is sense-perception. Why am I sure that my friend exists there now? Why would it be absurd to say he does not exist? Because I see him and if I leant forward I could touch him. I know that he exists in the same way as I know that my hand exists or that the table exists.

'That means you know that his body exists.' But this is a misleading way of putting the point, for I know that *he* exists. A child knows that his friend is there, in the same room as himself, although he may not yet have recognized the distinction between body and mind. He will come later to know that his friend is mind and body as he himself is mind and body, but he does not know him now as body in contrast to mind, for these distinctions are yet to come. I, an adult, am sure of my own existence as mind and body; I am sure of my friend's existence as mind and body too; but the child may not know his friends in this way.

The familiar experience then which is the foundation of my knowledge of another is sense-perception and the assurance in its most primitive form is perceptual assurance. Obviously, other factors enter as soon as I begin to extend my knowledge. It is very necessary to distinguish between two questions here; first, how I come to know that others exist and, second, how I deepen my knowledge of another person. We have been dealing with the first question, and we have seen that when it is posed in this form: 'How am I sure of the existence of another mind?' the question is baffling; but if it be posed: 'How am I sure of the existence of my friend sitting opposite me?' the answer is plain, that I see him. If I *then* ask how I deepen my knowledge of him, how I come to understand more of his life, mental as well as physical, the answer can be more easily given.

Our friends reveal themselves to us by what they do, by their actions, gestures, facial expressions, and more than all by what they say. A very young child finds a response in certain of the bodies around it which it does not find in others and differentiates on this basis. Some of these bodies satisfy its needs, others do not, and it learns where to turn for the satisfaction of those needs. It comes to understand (by watching others) that in order to achieve x it has to do y. When it finds itself with others, possibly other children, in a frightening situation, it is frightened but observes too the frightened look of the other children. After a time when it sees that look, even if it is not frightened itself, it knows that the other child is frightened. Moreover, the other child *says* that it is frightened.

I do not wish at this point to be drawn into the discussion of linguistic problems. But if it is asked how an experience as private as this, namely being frightened, can none the less be described in a language which another understands, the ambiguity of the terms 'public' and 'private' in this context should be borne in mind. It is true that my fear experience is private, but it is also true that the same situation turns out to be frightening to many; the fear situation can be shared and it is not nonsense to talk of our having the same or a common fear. This consideration lessens the difficulty in understanding how a private experience can be talked of publicly. In respect of certain aspects of the experience a private experience may be public enough to be shared. This does not rule out the possibility that some experiences are so private that they cannot be described in a public language. I have a life of my own which no one else shares.

But to return to the main argument. When an adult is sure that his friend is sitting opposite him what is the nature of his assurance? Primarily, I argue, it is perceptual. But, as in the case of his assurance of his own existence so in being sure that his friend exists, he is conscious of his friend's existence not only as a physical being but as one, too, who has experiences which can only be spoken of in psi-sentences. His friend exists not as body alone, and certainly not as mind alone, but as one who is both physical and mental. Being sure that his friend exists he deepens his knowledge of him by observing his behaviour and interpreting it, and particularly by conversing with him. He has thus built up a considerable knowledge of his friend, and it is the existence of this rich, complex being that he is now sure of as he sits opposite him.

33. *Being sure that there is a table here.* I am not only sure of my own existence and of that of my friend, I am also sure of the existence of this table. What I am sure of in this case is the existence of a physical object. Now in being sure of my friend's existence and of my own I am already sure of the existence of physical objects, for he and I are such objects even if we are also minds. In the case of the table I am sure of something which is merely physical. It is accordingly necessary to enter here more fully into what we mean when we speak of being sure of the existence of a physical object. When I say of the table that it is merely physical the force of the 'merely' can be brought out by saying (in the language of the preceding paragraphs) that no psi-sentences are necessary to describe it. But in saying this certain reservations must be made. For it may be that some of our description of the world of physical objects may contain sentences which reveal themselves on analysis to be psi-sentences. An instance that comes to mind is any sentence attributing causal efficacy to physical objects, for it is possible, on some interpretations, that a sentence which contains such words as 'causes', 'produces', and the like, is a psi-sentence, even if we are not conscious of this in using it. The question remains, however, whether such interpretations are correct. I propose to examine the particular case of causality later. In the meantime I shall assume, without prejudice to any future discussions, that no psi-sentences are necessary to describe the physical table.

What am I sure of then when I am sure of the existence of a physical object? I am sure of an object's existence, having length, breadth, and depth; it has weight or mass; it lasts through a certain amount of time. Further, it exists independently of me who now observe it; even if I have had a hand in fashioning and shaping it—as may well be the case in the instance of the table—yet it now exists as independently of me as does the rock or the hillside I see in the distance.

34. This is what I mean when I speak of a physical object. Yet to speak in this way, it may be said, is, in view of considerable philosophical criticism over many years, to speak naïvely. Powerful arguments have been adduced purporting to show that we cannot be sure that physical objects in this sense do exist. But the strange thing about these arguments is that though we are acquainted with them, we not only continue to believe that the table exists as a physical body in the sense given, but are quite sure of this. How does it come about that these philosophical arguments do not shake our conviction? In other cases, where evidence is produced casting doubt on our convictions, if we feel the evidence has weight we cease to be sure. Do we feel that the evidence in the case of these philosophical arguments lacks weight? How is it that we are unaffected by them?

This phenomenon has been frequently commented upon in past discussion. Hume noted it; he sets out the arguments which lead inevitably to the conclusion that we cannot be sure that physical objects exist. Yet the moment he leaves his study he finds that his doubts at once disappear. Hume takes this to be confirmation of his own central doctrine that custom, and not reason, is king of our life. We are used to a world of physical objects, and arguments casting doubt on the existence of such a world do not change our beliefs.

It would be unwise to reject Hume's explanation of the phenomenon in its entirety, for custom and habit are certainly strong and normally prevail. Yet they do not always prevail; given sufficient evidence we can be convinced that a particular belief habitually accepted by us is none the less false and we give it up. Why does this not happen in the present case? Is the evidence after all inadequate? To answer we must consider the arguments set forward. Now it is obvious that the senses sometimes deceive us, but one does not normally for this reason deny the existence of physical objects. But the seeming contradictions in sense-perception, with the facts of illusion and hallucination, have led philosophers to make a distinction between what is sensed and what exists physically. What is sensed has been variously described as idea, impression, sense-datum, sense-phenomenon, sensum, and so on;[1] we may use the symbol s to refer to it, and the symbol p to refer to the physical object. On this theory, in the case of vision, I see s, but through seeing s I come to know something about p. It is also assumed that I have no other way of coming to know anything about p.

Considerable additional evidence is brought forward to support this suggestion of a dualism between the sensum and the physical object, and I may refer to some of these further arguments. (1) Seeing whatever we do see is an end-product of a process. In the case of seeing a table, for instance, light rays affect the retina, impulses move along the nerves from retina to brain where, both in the lower brain and in the cortex, complicated organizational processes occur. The outcome of these processes is that I see the *visibile*, s. Now it is arguable that this is the physical object p, that in spite of the complication of processes the final result is that I see the physical object. This is possible. It is possible further that s in this situation is an exact replica of p even if it is not p. But both these hypotheses are highly dubitable. It seems more in accordance with the evidence to distinguish between s and p and, further, not to expect s to be an exact replica of p. (2) This conclusion is reinforced by arguments from the changes induced in sense-perception by drugs, such as mescaline. Even though the physical object remains the same, and even though there is no change in the light so that the initial stimulus on the retina may be adjudged to be roughly similar, the drug produces physiological changes which apparently account for the changes in what is seen. But if this leads us to conclude that s_d, what is seen after taking the drug, is neither p nor a replica

---

[1] Some writers use the medieval term 'intention' in this context. I have avoided it because of the ease with which it is confused with 'intension'. On intentionality cf. below, § 40.

of p, can we still assert with assurance that what is seen under normal conditions, s, is either p or an exact replica of p? (3) In sense-perception the percipient is not a passive recipient—on the contrary he is active in filling gaps in his experience and extrapolating. He may not be always conscious of this activity (some of it may even be physiological), but if it occurs at all then s seems to be in part something brought about by the percipient, in part a creation of his. If this is the case it may still be a source of information about p, but it can hardly be identified with p. (4) Just as what a person sees in laboratory experiments varies according to the way in which he is prepared or 'set' by the psychologist, so our experiences and our desires 'set' each one of us. One's past experiences, as well as present desires and interests, affect one's present sensory experiences. (5) Mention might be made, finally, of the argument from the time taken by the physico-physiological processes involved in sense-perception. In the case of objects in our immediate neighbourhood the time taken to carry through these processes is so slight as to be negligible. But in, for instance, the seeing of distant stars the passage of light rays from the physical object to the eye may take thousands of years. The star may well have ceased to be by the time the rays from it strike my eyes. Surely, it is said, in such a case what I see is not the star itself, s is not p, nor is it a representation of p as it now is, for p no longer exists.

35. Now these are strong arguments in favour of a dualist theory of sense-perception, and others may be adduced. It is not surprising that so many physiologists and psychologists have concluded that the dualist account of sense-perception is inevitable. What is surprising is that the consequence is not more generally faced that if we can only know of the existence of p through the senses and that if what we sense is s which is not p, then we cannot be sure that p exists. Yet psychologists and physiologists, with few, if any, exceptions, make it manifest in what they say and write that they continue to be sure that physical objects do exist. Philosophers and epistemologists, on

the other hand, seem more conscious of the difficulty. Not only are they worried by the problem of the ontological status of *s*; they are even more worried by the argument that once it be granted that what we are aware of is *s*, and that we can only know of *p* through *s*, we are then in a position in which it is not possible to prove that the physical object exists, if anyone wants to doubt this.

To hold that *esse* is *percipi* would, it is true, restore a monism, for what existed then in the case of seeing would be what is seen. But the subjectivism of this position makes it unacceptable to most philosophers. Equally unacceptable is the phenomenalism which asserts that on viewing certain phenomena we may be inclined to infer the existence of physical objects, though (i) we can never be sure of their existence and (ii) we deal directly with phenomena which are not physical objects. This leads to scepticism. The phenomena at most suggest the possibility of physical existence, but we can never be sure that such objects do exist. Nor can we find a solution in the suggestion that beginning with phenomena we may reach a point at which, on account of regularities in experience and the consensus of many opinions, we may reasonably cease to *speak* of phenomena, sense-impressions, and appearances, and speak instead of physical things. We cannot find a solution on these lines because the difference between *s* and *p* is not a verbal difference; to suppose that it is, is to ignore the problem that led to the dualism and no solution is possible on these lines.

On the one hand, then, is dualism strongly backed by evidence; on the other is the assurance of the existence of physical objects, an assurance that is not at all affected by the strength of the evidence for the dualism. How can this situation be resolved? How can I grant that things are not always what they appear to be, that the senses deceive me, that there are contradictions, illusions, and hallucinations, and yet firmly assert, as something I am as sure of as I am of anything, that this table here exists and exists as a physical object independent of me? Am I just being obstinate and blind, refusing to consider the evidence? Is it, as Hume suggests, that I am so accustomed to the belief that the world around me is a world of physical objects that I ignore the arguments which suggest that it is not so? Yet the fact is that I do not ignore the arguments; on the contrary I have examined them and approached them with an open mind; none the less I remain quite convinced that a world of physical objects exists around me.

36. The truth is that one cannot read these arguments without sensing their inadequacy. When one seeks to make this inadequacy explicit one finds its explanation in a certain over-simplification in perceptual analysis. In an effort to think and speak precisely the critics concentrate on what they take to be the salient features and these features they isolate. We must begin with the sensum, they say, and then explain as best we can our knowledge of the physical world, unless we become sceptical of the very existence of that world.

But to begin with the sensum is to begin with an abstraction. Concretely, we begin with a human being seeing, hearing, touching, tasting, or smelling. Man is not a *tabula rasa*—no analogy could be more unfortunate—but a being capable of sensory experience. Further, he is a being stimulated and influenced by something other than himself; he is a perceiver perceiving in a world that is affecting him, and were it not affecting him he would not perceive. Now the critic, unless he is very careful, also assumes this. If he begins to speak for instance, of 'sense-impressions' or 'stimulus and response' the assumption is then made explicit. But he assumes it even though he makes no use of these terms.

Yet, it may be asked, need this always be the case? Is it so impossible for him to begin with mere sensa and steadfastly refuse to introduce the notion of a physical world? In answer, in the first place it would still be true that he would be assuming the existence of a sentient being. Secondly, he would, presumably, not wish to identify sensa with images. For if he identified them then he would be responsible for the sensa, just as we assume that he is responsible for his images. In that case his brand of sensum theory would seem to imply a solipsism.

He only would exist; and this is certainly not what he wishes to say. Berkeley, as was mentioned earlier,[1] when faced with the possibility that solipsism might be the outcome of his philosophy was most anxious to retain the distinction between sensation and image. These are, in his view, basically different, for I am constrained to sense the former whereas I myself imagine the images and am free to imagine them or not imagine them. Sensations, however, are independent of me. There is a world independent of me, which in Berkeley's case is an ideal world, since *esse* is *percipi*; it consists of Mind and its ideas. But this Mind is not my mind, it is 'external' to me, that is to say, other than me and independent of me, and yet influencing me in providing me with sensations. Thus, granted the determination to avoid solipsism, then, presupposed in all theories of sense-perception, realist and idealist alike, is the existence of a sentient being on the one hand and of a world external to this being on the other.

It is because we feel that the sceptical, philosophical arguments ignore this basic truth that we reject them, and here too lies the justification for our doing so. We reject further the doctrine that we begin with sensa, if by this is meant, as the empiricists held, that we begin with so many 'simple ideas' out of which we construct a 'complex idea', for instance, constructing the idea of table out of the simple ideas, brown, hard, rectangular, and so on. We reject the view that our first knowledge of the external world and of physical objects comes about in this way. On the contrary, we seem to be as speedily aware of the whole object as we are of any of its qualities. Indeed, in some cases, it is remarkable how we miss the sensa and only see the whole object. In looking at a portrait of a person I am very likely to see the whole face before I see the lines, the shading, and the texture which, it would be usual to suppose, make up part of the sensa. The same is true of seeing physical objects such as tables and chairs. It may be that for some special reasons I do first spot, say, the shading, but this is not normal. A painter or a draftsman makes it his special concern

[1] § 24 above.

to study these features, and we may never have been consciously aware of their presence until he points them out to us, and are surprised that they are there when he does so. There seems little support for the view that physical objects are constructs of ours out of sensa.[1]

37. We are sure of the existence of a world around us containing such objects as the table. But now it is still necessary to ask how the contradictions, illusions, and hallucinations of sense-perception occur, and how they affect our knowledge. Normally, we attribute these occurrences to changes in the physical and physiological conditions, or again to changes of psychological set or motivation. After reflection we learn how to allow for the changes, for instance, we know how to allow for perspective or for changing light. In the case of hallucinations the subject 'sees' what is not there. The old man looks out of the window at an empty street, but he says that he sees it full of children playing. He does not realize that this is hallucination, but others do and attribute it to his senility. Any injury to the brain, through disease or accident or again through the action of drugs, may produce hallucinations. If we are to accept the view of Dr. Penfield and Dr. Roberts, some of these experiences may well be a kind of re-experiencing. In their book *Speech and Brain Mechanisms* (Princeton Univ. Press, 1959) they show how the electrical stimulation of a specific part of the brain may cause the patient to 'see', as if it were now occurring, something which in fact he saw long ago. If such experiences can be educed by electrical stimulation of parts of the brain, it is possible that illness, damage to the brain, senility and so on can also educe them. The occurrence of such hallucinations as these, 'seeing' what is not now there, would in such a case throw no doubt on the existence of the physical world and physical objects. For though the children the old man 'sees' are not now in fact before him, they were before

---

[1] The argument of the above paragraph is in line with certain contemporary psychological teachings, cf., for instance, J. J. Gibson, *Perception in the Visual World*, 1952, and *The Senses considered as Perceptual Systems*, 1968.

him if he is re-seeing what he saw years earlier. The objects existed in the past (whether they exist now or not); just as the tree I saw in Kew, and now remember, existed there as a physical object. The odd thing is that the old man 'sees' the children as if they were now in the street, but the theory put forward by Penfield and Roberts may begin to explain how this comes about. This particular explanation, however, may not succeed with hallucinations of other kinds. But we expect some explanation of this sort and the expectation is so strong that our assurance of the existence of physical objects is unshaken by the occurrence of hallucination.

Nor do errors of interpolation and extrapolation shake our assurance. It is obvious that we do add to the evidence given us in sense-perception and we do it largely in the light of past experience. Sometimes we fall into error, concluding, for instance, that what is before us is an instance of x, whereas it turns out on further inspection to be an instance of y. We think that the object coming round the corner but not yet in sight is a bus, but it turns out to be a lorry. May this not be the sort of error which occurs too if I say on seeing a spot of light that a star exists, meaning a physical body like the sun travelling in space and radiating heat, when this star has ceased to exist? I have not taken into account, as I should have done, the passage of time since the light ray left the star. But there is nothing here to shake my conviction that physical objects exist. In this case the star did exist even if it now no longer exists.

If I say I am sure that this table before me exists, I do not mean that I am also sure that it has the qualities which it now appears to have. I may doubt whether it has these qualities whilst still being completely sure that it exists. When I see an object I see it from an angle, in a certain light and so on, and I know that I have to take into account the circumstances in which I see it. The child, possibly, is sure that the moon it sees is the size of a Japanese lantern, but the adult is sure that its size is not what it now appears to be. Nothing in the foregoing pages contradicts the principle that things are not always what they appear to be. But this, it will be said, is to admit a dualism.

Certainly it is to admit that the physical object which has, say, the quality of being green in ordinary daylight may appear to be yellowish-green in another light and that this may lead to contradictions and to error about its normal colour. But if admitting this is to admit a dualism it is not one which engenders doubt about the existence of the physical object. We do not admit that there exists a difference between s and p of such a nature that experiencing s we may yet justifiably doubt the very existence of p. We are sure of the existence of the table and the philosophic arguments that have been put forward from time to time purporting to show that we ought to feel doubtful about its existence do not in fact disturb our assurance. Why this is so has now been made clear.

38. To conclude then, here are three instances of being sure. I am sure that I myself exist, that my friend sitting opposite me exists, and that the table between us exists. There are further problems about existence, about existence in general and about the existence of each of the three entities mentioned, which have not been considered. Our concern has been to find reliable instances of being sure, and these are three.[1]

The three instances, as we have seen, are instances of perceptual assurance, but in the case of my assurance of my own existence and that of my friend I am sure not only of the existence of physical objects but also of persons having a mental life. Further, these are assurances about objects present here and now, but this must not be taken to signify that I can be sure only in speaking of what is now present. I can be quite sure that John was on the lawn an hour ago. An archaeologist may be quite sure that the pyramids were built by men, that they are not natural objects. He may be wrong but he is quite sure. He is as sure of this as he is that his friend is sitting opposite him.

In the three cases considered, though *what* we are sure of in each case differs, the assurance itself does not differ in kind

---

[1] The argument of this chapter will be developed further in Chapter X below, when the distinction between knowing and thinking will have been made clear.

from one case to the other. This is an important point for theory of knowledge. It has just been said that a person who is sure that the pyramids were man-made is as sure of this as he is that his friend is sitting opposite him. So too I am equally sure that the table exists, my friend exists, and I exist. But some may question whether this view can be sustained, particularly in the case of my assurance of myself. Am I really, it may be asked, as sure that the table exists, or that my friend exists, as I am that I myself exist? We may answer that, if there is any doubt in one's mind, however slight, about the existence of the table or of one's friend, then one is not sure. But, it will be said, supposing there are no doubts, my assurance of my own existence still differs from the assurance of the existence of a physical object or even of another person. I have an intuition of myself—whereas I do not claim to have an intuition of the existence of the table—and the intuition is infallible. The archaeologist is quite sure that the pyramids are man-made and yet he may be wrong. A person can be sure that the table exists and yet he may be wrong. But can he be sure that he himself exists and yet be wrong?

The question is whether we have in our knowledge of our own existence an assurance that is different in the sense that it is infallible. But is the notion of 'knowing oneself' sufficiently clear for us to claim infallibility in our knowledge of ourselves? We have seen earlier that it seems impossible to think of error in the case in which a person is conscious of, or enjoys, an experience. But does this justify the assertion that he knows infallibly that *he* exists? Hardly. Nor can we argue that one would be contradicting oneself if one said: 'He is sure he now exists, but he is wrong.' For a novelist, for instance, could say this of one of his characters. To this it might be answered that at least *I* cannot say; 'I am sure I now exist, but it may be that I do not.' Agreed, but then I cannot say: 'I am sure that the table exists, but it may not.' In both cases I am sure and have no doubts. When I am sure, I am sure; it is a total experience; and it is such in my being sure that the table exists as well as that I exist. My assurance that I exist cannot be distinguished from my assurance that the table exists in being more sure, or in being a deeper sort of assurance. I have no ground for making any such distinction.

To be sure is to be constrained, to submit oneself totally, and this is true whatever one is sure about. Whether doubts arise later or not, at the moment there is none. The assurance and the certainty are absolute. I have no doubt whatsoever that the table is here now, just as my friend is here, and just as I am here. But, if we are to understand human knowledge, it is also necessary to add that, whilst the assurance is absolute, the knowledge is primal and is not itself absolute.[1]

---

[1] I thank Dr. Owen R. Jones, a colleague at Aberystwyth, for discussing the material of Chapters I–IV with me. I found these discussions most helpful.

PART TWO

THE SPONTANEITY OF
THOUGHT

V

CHARACTERISTICS OF THINKING: PRELIMINARY REMARKS

39. We have been concentrating on one feature of the theory of knowledge, admittedly an important and central feature, but certainly not the whole of the theory. We have now to take a broader view. We could return to discuss again certain problems already touched upon in the previous pages but not developed, for instance, those of evidence and of probability, not to mention the problem of truth itself. But the most helpful procedure at the present moment, it seems to me, is to consider the relation between knowing and thinking and the role of thinking in the gaining of knowledge.

First, a word about the many uses of the term 'thinking'. It is usual to distinguish it from feeling in the sense of feeling a pain[1] and again from willing and desiring. Normally the term is used to cover reasoning, conceiving, imagining, perhaps day-dreaming, though rarely dreaming proper. If I now go over in memory the events of yesterday this would usually be regarded as thinking, but just remembering the shade of colour I saw in a picture yesterday would not. Certainly seeing, hearing, or sensing would not be described as thinking, nor intellectual 'seeing' or intuition nor, again, being sure. Further, it has to be conceded that thinking takes place at different levels and it would be incorrect, for instance, to confine the term to strict logical reasoning. We cannot at this stage too say that all thinking must be verbal. Nor can we take it for granted that only men think; for animals seem capable of thinking. It would be arbitrary to define thinking as a faculty pertaining to human beings only and to confine it to verbal thinking.

[1] Though 'I feel that . . .' is sometimes scarcely distinguishable from 'I think that . . .'.

40. We shall not here in these preliminary remarks attempt any precise definition of thinking, but shall seek instead to set out its main characteristics so as to differentiate it. It is sometimes argued today that thinking (using the term in this context in a very wide sense) does possess a unique differentiating characteristic, namely, intentionality. It would be good to begin by examining this doctrine, pointing out the insight of real importance which it contains.

The 'intention' we speak of here is not to be confused with the intention of the agent in action or with 'intension' (as contrasted with 'extension') in logic, though a discussion of intention in the present sense may be found necessary in the discussion of the intention of an agent and again of logical intension. Interest in the present doctrine was aroused mainly by Chisholm's study and development (in *Perceiving*, ch. 11) of a point made by Brentano in his *Psychologie vom empirischen Standpunkte* (1874). In the second book of that work Brentano is examining the nature not so much of thinking but of psychical phenomena in general, and he opens with a chapter on the difference between the physical and the psychical. Is there any one characteristic shared by all psychical phenomena that is absent from all physical phenoma? He replies that there is, namely, the intentional inexistence of the object on which the psychical event is directed. Every mental event is directed on an object, but this word 'object' is used here in a sense different from the usual sense, as when we speak of the table as an object. In the sense in which the latter exists the former does not exist. It is said to have immanent inexistence, and though it is an object it is 'not to be understood as a reality' (*worunter hier nicht eine Realität zu verstehen ist*).[1]

Out of this suggestion arose, amongst Brentano's disciples and readers, a theory postulating a third realm which is not real as the physical and the psychical realms are real, but which

---

[1] *Psychologie*, Leipzig, 1874, vol. i, p. 115. In a note on this page Brentano links the doctrine with Aristotle, Philo, Augustine, Anselm, and Aquinas. *Intentio* suggests representation, but Brentano's aim is not to put forward a representationalist theory but to stress the singularity of the object, when it is that upon which the thinking, or whatever it be, is directed.

is yet the place of possibilities, propositions, mathematical and logical principles, and so on. This theory contributed to the growth of formalism in the first half of this century, and its polemic against 'psychologism' was a significant item in that growth. But it is doubtful whether in 1874 Brentano intended his words to be interpreted in this way. Later, certainly, he emphatically repudiates the theory. Writing to Anton Marty in 1905 Brentano says: 'If, in our thought, we contemplate a horse, our thought has as its immanent object not a "contemplated horse" but a *horse*. And strictly speaking only the horse —not the "contemplated horse"—can be called an object. But the object need not exist. The person thinking may have something as the object of his thought even though that thing does not exist.'[1] It is difficult now to decide what precisely Brentano taught in his lectures in the sixties and seventies and what he said in 1905 may not have been identical with his teaching thirty years earlier. But the essential element in his doctrine which he adheres to throughout—and which need not be developed on either Meinong's or Husserl's lines—seems to be as follows: When one thinks of something (and if one is thinking one is always thinking of something) then this something may or may not exist, and if one is just interested in how a thought must have an object the question of the real existence or non-existence of the object can for the time being be disregarded. In this sense the object need not be a real entity.

Now Brentano may have meant much more than this by his doctrine of intentional inexistence, but this is a kernel which has considerable significance. He found in intentionality a differentiating characteristic of psychical phenomena, enabling him to distinguish such phenomena from physical phenomena. The problem for us in opening a discussion of thinking is whether we find here a unique differentiating characteristic of thinking. Brentano himself would not have regarded the

---

[1] *The True and the Evident*, Eng. edn. 1966, edited by R. M. Chisholm, pp. 77–8. This book is a collection of Brentano's papers and letters collected by Oscar Kraus to illustrate Brentano's theory of knowledge.

characteristic of intentionality as uniquely characterizing thinking, though it would be *a* characteristic of thinking. But it is *the* characteristic of all psychical phenomena, of which thinking is one phenomenon.

When we probe further into this minimal doctrine difficulties arise which are not easily overcome. One feature which is stressed is that any and every psychical phenomenon is directed on an object and that this is at least part basis of the distinction made between it and the physical. Yet there may well be a 'directing upon' in the physical world itself as when for instance a stream of water is directed upon a rock when no human agency is involved. It this be admitted, the feature in question cannot be taken to be a ground for distinguishing between the psychical and the physical. In the second place, and more important, is it not essential that we already understand the difference between the psychical and the physical before we are able to grasp the doctrine that all psychical phenomena have this characteristic? If Brentano meant, as he may well have done, that, being already familiar with the distinction, we now proffer a further criterion by which to distinguish between psychical and physical, it would be easier to accept his doctrine, though difficulties would still remain. But the view that the recognition of intentionality is necessary prior to making this distinction cannot be defended. It seems obvious that only a person already acquainted with the difference between the psychical and the physical could grasp the doctrine of intentionality. One must first know what thinking, desiring, etc. are before coming to see that the objects of thinking, desiring, etc. are intentional. The basic factor in our knowledge of the distinction between the psychological and the physical is our consciousness of our own thinking, desiring, feeling pain, etc. The fact that we speak of these experiences with one another presupposes, first, that others have experiences like ours and, secondly, that all of us have learnt to speak of them in our language. We may then argue that these phenomena which we already know to be different from the physical have the further differentiating feature of intentionality, but this cannot be the way we come to know of the distinction in the first place.

There are thus difficulties in Brentano's theory, but it does emphasize one distinguishing and important characteristic of thinking. The concept of intentionality is of outstanding interest in itself;[1] here we merely note it as one feature of thinking. In thinking I am free to direct my thought on objects which do not exist, the issue of existence or non-existence does not arise. Thought is free-ranging contemplation; it is not tied ontologically. There are other characteristics of thinking which now need to be considered, but this characteristic is as important as any, and Brentano's account of it, together with the subsequent development and discussion of his views, are significant contributions to the theory of thinking.

41. Where then are we to look for further characteristics of thinking? We may consider what philosophers and psychologists take thinking to be in their discussions of its nature and its origins. What, for instance, do psychologists look for when searching for the beginnings of thinking in animal life? Admittedly some would condemn the attempt to pin-point the genesis of thinking, others would go further and state categorically that animals cannot think. Still, the evidence brought forward by psychologists to show that animals do think and where this thinking begins is worth considering at this stage, for it will at least show up the assumptions made by psychologists about the characteristics which belong to thinking.

Hull's well-known experiments on defence reactions in animals may be cited. A slight electric shock is administered

---

[1] Involved in its discussion are questions of deep contemporary relevance, such as existence and non-existence, logical intension, the nature of concepts, of universals, of nominal clauses, and of indirect reference. In *Perceiving* (ch. 11) and again in an article 'Intentionality' in the *Encyclopaedia of Philosophy*, 1967, Chisholm sets out working criteria by which to distinguish sentences used intentionally. Cf. four papers in *Proc. Arist. Soc.*, Supp. 1968, by William Kneale, A. N. Prior, J. O. Urmson, and Jonathan Cohen respectively; also G. E. M. Anscombe 'The Intentionality of Sensation', *Analytical Philosophy*, 2nd series, ed. R. J. Butler, 1965.

to a rat in a cage and its reactions are observed; at the same time a buzzer is sounded. This process is repeated on several occasions. On the final occasion the buzzer is sounded but the shock is not administered; none the less the rat shows the same defence reactions. Here, as Hull puts it, is a reaction 'to the not-here and the not-now'; something not present in the immediate stimulation conditions the reactions. Have we then an instance in this occurrence of elementary thinking, and can the buzzing be said to be in any sense a *sign* of the shock and pain to come? We are warned not to read too much into the phenomenon or to speak of the rat's experience as if it were our own. But a minimum at least seems to be true, that such behaviour is not explicable wholly in terms of present stimulation and response.

That an animal can remember and can make use of what it remembers are suggested too by many other experiments. For instance, animals are allowed to watch while food is being put away behind one of a number of doors, each coloured differently. They are then kept away from the doors for several hours. On being allowed to return they make for the correct door. Or again, an animal is set to watch another carrying out a task which the watching animal has never performed. It is then set the task itself, either straightaway or after the lapse of some time, and it is found to carry out the task more speedily than is normally the case with animals of this species. The suggestion is that such experiments illustrate the beginnings of remembering, imagining, and thinking.

Quite young children, too, of eighteen months or so, are held to be capable of delayed imitation. Child psychologists, particularly Piaget, have observed their first crude drawings of objects which they have seen in the past but which are not now present. Already at this age they appear to be able to recall, in, no doubt, a very primitive way, what is no longer before them and to hold it long enough to make the drawing. They imitate too in their games, pretending to be someone not now present. This it is held is more than just memory and recalling, it is dwelling upon what is absent and imitating it, the beginning of reflective intelligence. The child reveals the power to turn away from what is immediately present and to reflect.

And here it would seem clear is one feature which psychologists assume to be essential for thinking, namely, partial detachment and disengagement from the present immediate experience. In the phenomenon of delayed imitation, for instance, the animal or the child is being stimulated in various ways and is responding to certain of the stimulations. But it is also imitating, and the imitating is not of what is present but of what is absent. Again in Hull's experiment the rat hears the buzzer and proceeds to defend itself against the shock. It would be wrong, perhaps, to say that it anticipates the shock or that it is thinking about it, but we can say that what it reacts to is (in part) not a present stimulation, it is the not-here and the not-now. In all cases where animal behaviour seems to show intelligence this feature of detachment and disengagement is present. It will be remembered, for instance, how Köhler's chimpanzee, having made several unsuccessful efforts to reach bananas outside its cage, turns away from the bananas, in Köhler's words 'half turns its back' on them, sits quietly for a time, and then jumps up, puts the bamboo sticks together, and draws in the fruit. Half turning one's back on what is immediately present (if not literally, certainly metaphorically) does seem to be a minimum requirement for thinking.

To think one must not be too occupied with the present. An interesting suggestion has recently been put forward that one of the functions of the frontal cortex of the brain is to hold off part of the pressure of the present upon the organism, to check the stimuli affecting it, and so inhibit some of the responses. When, through frontal leucotomy a certain part of the cortex ceases to function, patients tend to be tied to the present stimuli, the memory of even the immediate past tends to be blotted out and the distractions of the present moment make thinking almost impossible. Perhaps this is a reason why animals, lacking a developed cortex, find thinking so difficult; there is nothing to inhibit sensory stimulation. Whether this particular physiological hypothesis be proved true or false, the deeper truth can hardly be denied, namely, that we cannot think if 'the world is too much with us'; the thinker needs freedom from the distractions of hunger, worry, pain, and particularly from bondage to the immediately present as it presses itself upon him in sense-perception. The claim that one essential characteristic of thinking is disengagement, a withdrawal from the here and the now, seems justified, and it is a characteristic obviously complementary to that other of contemplating objects without asking whether they exist or do not exist.

42. Another characteristic of thinking we are told is inventiveness. Thus in the Köhler experiment referred to the inventiveness of the chimpanzee (helped by the detachment from the present) was taken to be good evidence of its ability to think. Something in the situation creates a problem and the animal by thinking discovers the solution and so the equilibrium that was disturbed is restored. Such problems occur too in human life. Interpolation to fill the gaps in sense-perception is an instance of inventiveness. Seeing the fire an hour ago and returning now to the dying embers I think out the intervening stages. Seeing the top surface only of the table I provide an under-surface and legs. These procedures illustrate the rudimentary thinking present in sensory experience. The thinking is less rudimentary when, for instance, I seek to solve the more difficult problems of recognition. What can the black object on the photograph be? How would it look if the camera had been nearer? Would it be smooth if I were there to touch it? By asking myself such questions and seeking answers to them, using imagination and my experience of such objects in the past, I attempt to recognize the object. The identification may of course be erroneous, for the gaps may be wrongly filled, but this is a risk we have to run if we are to solve any of our problems.

Nor is invention confined to interpolation, for there is also the attempt to extrapolate. For instance, given certain items which we recognize as the beginning of a series we carry this series forward in thought and, if possible, complete it. In such extrapolation is the germ of system-building; we think in terms of a system of items of a certain sort. Here too are the beginnings of conscious grouping into classes and the ascribing of qualities which we suppose to belong to a class as a whole to a given member of that class. As thinking develops, inventiveness of this kind increases; we invent hypotheses and fit them into complicated theoretical systems which we have also invented. Whether we are guided in our invention by experience and in what sense these creations of ours can be said to be true or false remains to be considered, but the presence of an inventive element in thought is obvious.

43. A fourth characteristic of thinking is the tendency to generalize, with a consequent use of signs. In the rat's reaction to the buzzer the present differs in certain respects from the previous buzzing and the present reaction is not the same in all its details as past reactions. Yet the new buzzing is like enough to previous buzzings for the rat to react in roughly the same way. The assumption seems to be that for the rat it is the 'same' buzzing and this is to assume that in some rudimentary way the rat is generalizing. Some psychologists, though not all, speak of the animal 'anticipating the pain'. In this case too the pain anticipated would be pain-in-general, at least to this extent that it would not be the pain felt on the last or any previous occasion, but something like all these without being any one of them. But whether the rat anticipates the pain or not it certainly recognizes the buzzing sound; it not merely hears, it recognizes 'the same again'. How it is that animals (or men) come to recognize 'the same' is a difficult question; there is no suggestion that at this primitive level common features are consciously selected from sensory experience,[1] though at a later point a conscious selection of this kind may come to reinforce groupings already made. None the less the recognition of the same again comes early, and this recognition, together

[1] Cf. the discussion of this point in G. Humphrey, *Thinking* (1951), pp. 292 ff.

with the concern with what is general rather than particular is taken to be evidence for the presence of incipient thinking.

Together with generalization goes the use of signs and the interpretation of them. The rat took the buzzing to be a sign of the electric shock, at least it did so in this sense that it reacted defensively as if the shock was to come. Is this an instance of primitive sign-interpretation? Perhaps 'interpretation' is not the right word to use in this context. 'Learning from signs' possibly would be better, though this too might be too strong (particularly in view of the suggestion that the reaction is explicable wholly in physiological terms). But it is obvious in this case that the organism is reacting not to the buzz alone, but to the buzz plus the shock situation. If a farmer looks at the dark cloud and prepares for rain, he does not merely see and recognize the dark cloud, he recognizes it as a sign of rain. A dark cloud is a dark cloud, but to one familiar with changes in the weather it is something else as well, namely, a sign of rain.

It is interesting to note the assumption here about the sort of existence which the sign has. It is a sign for a thinker or interpreter, though not necessarily only for the thinker who is now interpreting it; it may be a sign that many poeple can interpret and be accordingly public. What exists, however, is the dark cloud and this is all that exists; there is not alongside it another existence, the sign. This remains true even though the sign is public. The word 'sign', has admittedly a secondary sense; thus if I say 'Remove that sign' then the sign I refer to is a perceived physical object. But in studying thinking our concern is with signs in the foundation sense, in which they have more to do with conception than with perception. We have sensory experience of rain, but we also have a concept of rain; around the experience have gathered many accretions in thought, amongst them being this link between rain and dark cloud. So the dark cloud becomes a sign of rain (and in this case it happens to have become a sign without our consciously setting out to make it a sign). The rat, it is supposed, is already thinking in a primitive way, because for it the buzz is not just a buzz but also a sign of the shock to come. The dark cloud is not merely a dark cloud for the farmer but a sign of rain; and in so far as this is so the farmer is said to be thinking, since something is being taken not as it is in itself but as a sign for something else.[1] Such is the account of the early use of signs which seems implicit here and on the whole it seems a sensible one and one well worth bearing in mind in what follows.

We can accept the general conclusion that certain things in nature become, for beings capable of interpreting them, signs and that the process of recognizing and interpreting the sign is an instance of thinking. Furthermore, as the powers of interpretation develop, a distinction can be made between natural and conventional signs. A dark cloud is a natural sign of rain; on the other hand the red traffic light is a conventional sign prohibiting crossing. In the former case the one becomes a sign of the other on grounds of natural association; in the latter the one has to be learnt to be the sign of the other, for there is no natural basis for the relationship. Again, we do not merely interpret signs, we also use them. Chronologically the interpreting comes first, for instance, predicting rain on seeing the black cloud. But at some stage in his long story man learnt to *use* signs and to create them for his use. Having acquired the knack of recognizing in one thing a sign of another naturally associated with it, he extended his skill and set up relationships of sign and signified where there was no natural association. The child leaves a mark on the rock to show the direction he has taken. The signalman on the railway line keeps his red

[1] Professor H. H. Price in his helpful study of signs in *Thinking and Experience* distinguishes between primary recognition, for instance, recognizing the black patch as black, and secondary recognition, recognizing the black patch as a raven. He says that 'secondary recognition is recognition by means of signs' (p. 46). 'Primary recognition is not recognition by means of signs. It is by primary recognition that we recognise the sign-characteristics themselves—the dull grey colour which is a sign to us of lead, the blackness and the visual *gestalt*-quality which are signs to us of a raven' (p. 47). Price's acceptance of a dualist doctrine of sensum and physical object makes it possible for him to distinguish between the black patch and the raven and to think of them as two entities such that the first can be used as a sign of the second. But if one rejects this dualism then the black patch, say, cannot be taken to be the sign of the raven, but rather *is* the raven. And the dark patch in the sky which is a sign of rain is not also a sign of the cloud, for it is the cloud. A sign can only be a sign for something else and never a sign for itself.

signal up to warn the engine-driver of danger. It is a purely conventional sign used by the signalman to give information to the driver who, he knows, will be able to interpret it.

It would seem true too that animals and birds not merely react to primitive signs—in view of the evidence, it would appear foolish to deny this—but go further and use signs, communicating with one another by means of them. The familiar alarm cries of birds when danger threatens their young, or again the paradings of male birds before their females, suggests that they so communicate, and the evidence from the insect world is pretty conclusive. Fire-ants lay trails of glandular secretions to mark the path from the nest to food and these are then used by other ants; bees convey to other bees in the hive, by means of movements of their bodies, both the direction in which food is to be found and its distance from the hive. No one who has seen the film of these researches can fail to marvel at the ability of the bee to carry out what appears to be a very complicated piece of symbolization, and at the ability of the others to interpret it properly. In reflecting on such occurrences as these it seems foolish to deny that insects at least, whatever one says of animals, do use signs to communicate information to other members of their species and that these signs are understood.

44. In concluding, what preliminary account can be given of thinking in the light of the points discussed in this chapter? First we say that thinking is a mental activity directed upon an object, but the term 'object' is not to be interpreted here as signifying an object in the sense in which this table or this person is an object. The thinker is not dominated by his experience and knowledge of the real world. There is a disengagement in order to think. What he needs most is to give his inventive powers the opportunity to function freely. Thinking is inventiveness. To invent with greater ease he generalizes and thereby enables himself to interpret signs and even to create signs of his own and use them.

Knowing and thinking are clearly different from one another, the former is marked by constraint the latter by spontaneity. Thinking demands freedom to manœuvre, to invent and build systems of thought. It is an activity that the thinker finds pleasing in itself. But though these two activities are distinguishable the one from the other, they none the less interrelate. Indeed when we speak of 'serious' thinking we usually mean thinking whose express purpose is to gain further knowledge, and the interrelation then is so close that the strands are not easily disentangled. Possibly it is when the function of reason is studied that the relation between them is best understood.

VI

THE USE OF LANGUAGE

45. Human thinking is for the most part verbal. So much is this so that one sometimes tends to suppose that all thinking is verbal and that no other thinking occurs; but this is mistaken. As we have seen it is difficult to deny that animals think, yet they certainly make no use of words. And even in the case of human beings, people, who, through accident or disease, have lost the power of speech and who cannot string a simple sentence together, may none the less carry out complicated pieces of non-verbal thinking. Nor should we forget imaginative or 'pictorial' thinking. Most often this is accompanied by language; one talks to oneself if not to others. But this is not essential. Thus a person who is quite capable of using language may not in fact use any when, for instance, he thinks out the next move in a game. Or again, in dwelling on past experiences, and in thinking how they might have happened differently, the imagining need not be accompanied by language. Some people, particularly the book-bound, find it difficult to think imaginatively without language, but children and many adults find it easy. It is argued too that as a consequence of the invention of photography, film, and television, such thinking will become easier in future. Certainly, we now *see* much that in the past we could only read or hear about. Moreover, by technical arrangement and emphasis, film and television producers help to deepen and concentrate the visual experience and so make any later imagining of it livelier. Few of the millions who saw the sludge burying the village school in Wales will forget it. When in their case the event is recalled and reflected upon it is likely to be recalled and reflected upon pictorially. In the days of the silent film one knew the villain by his behaviour, his look, and his stance, and children who would not know the meaning of the word 'villain' could pick

him out and knew what to expect from him. Recognition need not always be verbal recognition, and thinking too can be pictorial and not verbal. Yet whilst all this must be admitted, it still remains true that human thinking is for the most part verbal, even though some of the verbal thinking is imaginative as well.

But this conclusion might easily lead to a false account of language. Since so much thinking is verbal, the assumption is easily made that language exists to help us to think. And this is an assumption which philosophers, conscious of the prominent part that language plays in their thinking, are particularly prone to make. Language, they assume, is an instrument which thinkers have forged to enable them to think better.[1]

Locke's discussion of language in Book III of the *Essay* is fresh and lively. In the course of it he considers the suggestion that a linguistic dictator could dictate what words should be proper to use in particular contexts. Locke rejects this suggestion, and certainly there is little to be said in its favour; but the argument which he brings forward against it is unexpected. 'Every man has so inviolable a liberty to make words stand for what ideas he pleases, that no one hath the power to make others have the same ideas in their minds that he has, when they use the same words that he does.'[2] Language, that is to say, is the arbitrary choice of the thinking individual. Locke admittedly modifies this theory in the same section. 'Common use, by a tacit consent' brings it about that all who speak the same language use words in more or less the same way. But in principle each thinker has the right of 'arbitrary imposition'.

Now this view of language is not entirely unfamiliar in our own day; the so-called Sign Theory, in its various forms, is closely related to it. On this theory words are signs, just as the natural signs we considered in the previous chapter are signs. Words are unlike natural signs, however, in that whereas,

[1] Cf. J. S. Mill's comment on Bentham: 'Words, he thought, were perverted from their proper office when they were employed in uttering anything but precise logical truth.'

[2] *Essay*, III. ii. 8.

for instance, rain is naturally associated with black clouds, courage let us say is not naturally but only conventionally related to the word 'courage'. We must not forget onomatopoeic words and certain other exceptions, but generally speaking words do not signify on the basis of a natural association. They are signs, phonemic signs, that are conventionally chosen (though they are not the only conventional signs). On this theory, human beings arbitrarily choose certain sounds to be signs, for instance, the sound 'courage' for courage. This sound became the agreed sign for courage amongst the members of the English linguistic community, and so the word 'courage' became part of the English language, a sign that could be used and understood. And the English language is the totality of these signs. The whole doctrine is summed up in the sentence: 'Words are a species of conventional signs and a language is a plurality of signs.'

Philosophers and linguists are critical of this theory, that speech is first the conscious, arbitrary choice of phonemic signs to serve as words, and that then language becomes possible as a plurality or collection of words. For, they hold, the reverse is the truth. First comes speech or language (any distinction made between these two terms is irrelevant at this stage), and then by abstraction we become aware of words in speech. And on reflection this second view of the situation certainly seems nearer the mark. For how could two men, lacking language, ever come to agree amongst themselves that such and such a sound was to be used as such and such a sign? How could the first man make clear to the second that he was arbitrarily using this sound in this way, and that he wished him to understand that he was so using it and to agree to use it so himself? Could he do this by 'defining ostensively'. He could point to a dog in the presence of the other person and utter the sound 'dog'. Perhaps, after a time, the listener would grasp that the speaker wished to relate the two. Perhaps the listener would himself imitate the speaker to the extent of pointing at a dog and uttering the sound 'dog'. Even so, this would not be equivalent to understanding that the speaker was proposing to adopt the sound 'dog' as the sign for the dog to which he was pointing. To complicate the issue the speaker, we may suppose, was not in fact wanting 'dog' to be accepted as the sign for this dog but for any dog. How could he, without being able to communicate verbally with the listener, be able to get this point across? Supposing further he wanted to choose a sign for courage, or for something still more abstract? How could he proceed? How could he, for instance, explain that he had arbitrarily chosen the sign 'and' as a sign of conjunction to a person who could not speak with him? Throughout too we are to suppose that he himself has no language at this stage and no consciousness of what a language is, but that he has hit upon the idea of picking out a sound which he can utter and making it a sign for something or other.

46. It is thus difficult to see how language, interpreted in terms of the 'plurality of signs' theory, could ever have originated. But in fairness one should consider the objection that the theory was not in fact attempting to give an account of the origin of language, but rather a philosophical analysis of language as it now exists. Even so, the analysis seems to be inadequate and misleading. It is not true that the most helpful way of speaking and thinking of a language is as a plurality of signs each of which is a word. One suspects that these theorists were more interested in words than they were in language, and in words not as used in the living language but as abstracted from the flow and considered in themselves. What motivated them was the thinker's interest in precise and fixed terms. The contrast between words used in actual speech and dictionary words is a real one, and this is part of the distinction between speech and language. A word in the former sense is momentary and it is what it is in its context only; but in the latter sense the word is an abstraction which is fixed and is thereafter 'immutable and incorruptible'. The dictionary defines it once and for all. Thinkers know where they are with dictionary words; the aim of the lexicographer, even though it is not always realized, is to establish the word as a fixed sign having a precise meaning.

But linguists who concern themselves with the living languages, English, French, Chinese, Urdu, Swahili, etc., as they have developed and are developing, present us with a very different picture of language. They agree that one of the uses of language is illustrated in logical thought and discourse; none the less to think logically is not the primary purpose of the use of language. The development of the languages of mankind has not been dominated by the ideal of producing an instrument for precise, consistent thought. It has been dominated rather by the need for communication with others; the chief end of language is communication. It is not the only end; we *think* verbally and we express our emotions verbally. Furthermore, the various ends of language are interwoven. For instance, communicating with one another is likely to involve some thinking, an absolute distinction cannot be made between the different uses of language. But in so far as distinction is possible language is first an instrument of social intercourse. We use language to explain our needs to others, to ask questions, to inform, to command, to coax, to persuade—or just to talk and be together.

No evidence is available on how man first came to speak and little is to be gained by speculating. In the case of children's beginning to speak there seem to be at least two purposes, first, to communicate with others but also, secondly, to imitate others. As well as needing to communicate the child obviously finds pleasure in imitating the sounds others make. When, for instance, the child first uses the word 'milk', it has heard the sound frequently when there is milk around, it imitates the sound and is reinforced in the utterance of it by finding that if it says 'milk' the milk it needs is produced. There is certainly nothing to suggest that the child at this stage consciously uses the word 'milk' as a sign. Professor Skinner, the Harvard psychologist, prefers to speak of it as a 'tact', a contact in communicating.

The adult too uses language to communicate, and, generally speaking, this is for him its main use. His language is not something that he himself has brought into being. He has learnt it from others within his own language community, and they in turn have learnt it from other members of that community. Each of these languages goes its own way, not merely in matters of vocabulary but also in syntax. This means that a universal grammar is unattainable. In view of the likenesses between human experiences, and the fact that men everywhere have ultimately to face much the same situations, it might have been expected that any account of their experiences in speech, in whatever language, would have features in common with other accounts of them in other languages. Philosophers, as well as linguists, have hoped to be able to set out a universal syntax common to all languages without exception. But when one looks at languages as they are one finds that, in spite of common elements in the human experience talked about, it is difficult to discern the outlines of a syntax which could confidently be asserted to be universal to all human languages. Each language has its own practices.[1]

47. Nevertheless, though a universal grammar of languages is not, on the general view, possible, languages clearly do have features in common and some general statements can be made about them. One may begin by pointing out that all languages are phonetic. This, it is true, may be a matter of definition, since we refuse to acknowledge that other means of communication sometimes spoken of as 'languages', for instance the 'language of flowers', are genuine instances of language. All languages are spoken. Some of them are written, and literate people tend to think of language in terms of written language and, as a consequence, concentrate on words as the units. But languages are first spoken; very many of the languages of mankind are still unwritten. It is therefore mistaken to concentrate

---

[1] This is the generally accepted view today amongst linguists and anthropologists, but for a contrasting opinion, cf. Noam Chomsky, *Syntactic Structures* (1957) and *Aspects of the Theory of Syntax* (1965), especially ch. 2 of the latter. It is here argued that criticisms by modern linguists of the universalists apply only in the case of surface structures of languages. Since these linguists have not made the study of deep structures their concern, their rejection of the possibility of a universal grammar is to be discounted (cf. particularly *Aspects*, pp. 117–18). See further, p. 115 below.

on the written language; much that is essential may thereby be overlooked.

If we begin with spoken language it is then more sensible to take the speech utterance, the continuum of sound bounded by pauses, as the significant unit rather than the word. This utterance may be a one word phrase, as when I just say 'Tired' when you ask me how I feel: but most often it is a phrase containing within it many words. In either case the phrase is one continuum of sound. It is true, however, that we can, if we listen, differentiate within the one flow. Thus in listening to the spoken sentence 'Tom sits' we can pick out the initial 't' sound. Something like it turns up again towards the end of the flow. As usually spoken these two sounds are not precisely the same, and it is possible to discern some difference between them, but they are near enough for us to group them together, and to think of them as belonging to the same family. They are, for instance, nearer to each other than either is to any other of the sounds we hear when 'Tom sits' is uttered. We speak of them accordingly as the 'same' sound, namely, the sound written 't'. Here then is a unit of sound which is abstract as opposed to the concrete unit, that is to say, the unbroken flow of sound. Other units, 'm', 's', 'o', and 'i' can be differentiated within the same flow of sound. These abstracted units of sound are usually termed phonemes.[1] Now the number of phonemes between which the human ear can differentiate is limited, but no language uses up all the possibilities. Languages are content with anything between thirty and fifty phonemes. Nevertheless, in spite of the comparative paucity of phonemes, human beings manage to talk together successfully over a wide range of subjects, and they succeed in doing so because of their skill in placing and in combining the phonemes in so many different ways in the sound flow. Children pick up this skill from their elders and, considering its complexity, do so very rapidly. It is not surprising that they sometimes mistake the order of the phonemes.

[1] Defined by Bloomfield (*Language*, 1935, p. 79) as 'a minimum unit of distinctive sound-feature'.

Phonemes are abstracted from the flow of sound but they are not abstractions in the sense of subjective creations. They are concrete enough as sound, though, as has been seen, a certain generalizing is necessary to enable us to speak of a phoneme, say the phoneme 't', since the particular sounds for which 't' stands vary. But granted the right to speak of 'a family of sounds' as a phoneme, it is possible then to isolate the various phonemes in any speech utterance. Now, in addition to phonemes, words can be isolated within the one flow of sound. That we are capable of isolating words is obvious by the time we begin to write. We hear the one flow 'thepanisontheshelf' but we write 'the pan is on the shelf', where the spacing marks the limits of the different words, though the sound is one continuum. Further, in addition to phonemes and words, linguists speak of morphemes—for morphemes are not to be identified with words. They find it convenient to think of language as consisting of words, but also as articulated into phonemes and morphemes. We must now consider these divisions.

To speak of words first, a useful approach to their study is one in terms of Leonard Bloomfield's theory of 'the free form'.[1] He contrasts free with bound forms. 'A linguistic form which is never spoken alone is a *bound* form: all others (as, for instance, *John ran* or *John* or *run* or *running*) are *free* forms.' As an instance of a bound form he gives *-ing*, which is never spoken alone. Now a word, for instance 'running', is a free form. It can be spoken alone. 'What is John doing?' 'Running.' A word is not the only free form, the linguistic form 'John ran' can also be spoken alone. The word, however, can be regarded as the minimum free form. This is a promising approach to the problem of what words are, but there are difficulties. Does the theory fit those words which are prepositions, conjunctions, and articles? Consider the indefinite article 'a', which is a word. Is it ever spoken alone? Not, apparently, in any normal sense. In a secondary sense it may be spoken alone. 'What is the indefinite article in English?' Answer: 'A'. But then in this sense we should have to say that '-ing' stands alone. 'What is

[1] *Language*, p. 160.

Bloomfield's example of a linguistic form which is never spoken alone?' Answer: 'ing'.[1]

Still, in spite of this difficulty, the suggestion that a word is a 'minimum free form' is a useful one. It would go some way towards explaining why, when men came to write down the spoken utterance, they thought it best to divide it into words and separate them by inserting spaces between them. But if it goes some of the way towards explaining the separation into words, it does not go all the way. To say that the word can be spoken alone and that it is able to stand on its own feet is to imply that it carries with it, as it were, all the meaning necessary for it to do so. Semantic considerations enter. Yet words are not regarded as the smallest units of meaning. These are morphemes. Just as the spoken utterance can be divided into phonemes, so too, it is held, it can be divided into morphemes. André Martinet in his Waynflete Lectures[2] prefers the word 'moneme' to 'morpheme' because of the different and confusing uses of the latter term. He thinks of language as 'doubly articulated', namely into phonemes and into monemes. (The monemes he defines as 'the smallest segments of speech that have some meaning attached to them'.[3]) It is in terms of this double articulation that he puts forward his definition of language. 'A language', he says,[4] 'is a medium of communication according to which human experience is analysed, differently in each community, into units (monemes) with a semantic content and a phonic shape. This phonic shape, in its turn, is articulated in distinctive and successive units (phonemes), whose number in a given language is fixed and whose nature and mutual relations also vary from language to language.' When it is asked what is common to all human language the answer cannot be found in a common grammar or common syntactical structure; it can only be found in this core of double articulation into phonemes and monemes. 'Apart from

---

[1] Stephen Ullmann in *Semantics* (Blackwell, 1962), p. 47 suggests that prepositions, conjunctions, articles, and the like, should be regarded as 'pseudowords'. Cf. further his *Principles of Semantics* (Blackwell, 1960), p. 59.

[2] *A Functional View of Language* (O.U.P., 1962), p. 22.

[3] Ibid., p. 22.   [4] Ibid., p. 26.

this common core, nothing can be said to be linguistic which cannot differ from one language to another.'[1]

Now it will be seen why we cannot identify the moneme (or morpheme) with the word. 'The smallest segment of speech that has meaning attached to it' could be part only of a word. For instance, 'headache' can be divided into two monemes. So can 'cats', namely 'cat' and '-s'. None the less, most words in the appropriate context *are* monemes. It is consequently easy to think of words as separate units, just because they are likely to be monemes, and because too they are minimum free forms. Yet a word is not invariably a moneme, nor is every word a minimum free form. There still remains something puzzling in the division into words, and linguists have not yet altogether explained this feature of language.

48. But there is another puzzle in this theory of 'double articulation'. It is possible, as we have seen, to divide the flow of sound in speech into units of sound (though each unit is more correctly thought of as 'a family of sounds'). The linguist picks out the phonemes used in the language which he is studying, and he is able to divide any utterance in that language phonemically. But on this theory we have to think of linguistic utterances as divisible not only into phonemes but also into morphemes. Just as there are smallest units of sound, so, it is supposed, there are smallest units of meaning; hence the possibility of a double articulation of linguistic utterance. But underlying the double articulation theory is an assumption which ought perhaps to be questioned. Meanings are taken to be analogous to sounds. We can justifiably speak of a division of an utterance into the smallest units of sound. But are we justified in speaking of dividing an utterance into the smallest units of meaning? Consider the sentence 'Tom likes Bill.' As uttered it is one flow of sound, but we can pick out the minimum units of sound. The one continuum is a complex of phonemes. But now is the meaning of 'Tom likes Bill' a complex of the smallest units of meaning (or of morphemes)? What are the

---

[1] Ibid., p. 26.

'meanings' present in 'Tom likes Bill'? The proper answer surely (if it makes sense to speak in this way at all) is that only one meaning is present, namely, that Tom likes Bill. The 'smallest unit of semantic content' in this instance is the whole sentence. But, it will be said, 'likes' has a meaning in itself (or possibly two meanings 'like' and '-s'). It is certainly the case that it has a definition in a dictionary. But, in the above context, the meaning that it has is nothing apart from the sentence. We cannot think of the sentence as divided into three (or four) 'minimum units of meaning', as we *can* think of it as being phonemically divided into so many phonemes. The utterance is made up of phonemic units. But is the meaning of the sentence made up of a combination of so many indivisible, atomic units of meaning?

49. It would appear that the analysis into morphemes is not as well attested as that into phonemes. Many linguists admit that the concept of morpheme is not crystal clear.[1] Bloomfield asserts: 'A morpheme can be described phonetically, since it consists of one or more phonemes, but its meaning cannot be analysed within the scope of our science.'[2] It is a unit of meaning, but what meaning is is not evident. As Bloomfield says, 'the statement of meanings is the weak point in language study',[3] and Martinet questions whether 'meaning is to be mentioned in linguistics at all'.[4]

One thing is obvious, that every language has its phonemic and its semantic aspects. Now the acknowledged difficulties about the morpheme may in part explain the new movement towards viewing a further aspect, namely the syntactical, as the key to the linguistic situation. Both the phonemic and the semantic components of a sentence, it is suggested, should be

---

[1] Critics point to the following difficulty. The phrase 'animal doctor' would be said to consist of two morphemes but 'vet.' presumably is one morpheme, and yet these two phrases have the same meaning. Consider further 'hair-dresser' and 'barber'.

[2] *Language*, p. 161.

[3] Ibid., p. 140. He himself offers a behaviourist theory of meaning. Cf. ibid., p. 139.

[4] *Functional View of Language*, p. 95.

considered in relation to the syntactical component. A grammar is to be thought of as generative. It contains syntactic, semantic, and phonological components. 'The latter two', says Noam Chomsky, the leading advocate of this view, 'are purely interpretative; they play no part in the recursive generation of sentence structures. The syntactic component consists of a base and a transformational component. The base, in turn, consists of a categorial subcomponent and a lexicon. The base generates deep structures. A deep structure enters the semantic component and receives a semantic interpretation; it is mapped by the transformational rules into a surface structure, which is then given a phonetic interpretation by the rules of the phonological component. Thus the grammar assigns semantic interpretations to signals, this association being mediated by the recursive rules of the syntactic component.'[1] What is attractive in this doctrine is the promise of a new unity in language theory and a new account of the relationship between the syntactical and the semantic. By reflecting on basic syntactical features of a given language, which go some way to revealing the deep, innate, creative, linguistic principles of the human mind, 'universal properties of language' may be discovered.[2] But the strong rationalist implications of this theory are likely to offend many. In particular, the question remains whether by examining the basic syntactical structure of any given language it is in truth possible to arrive at principles that *must* be basic to all languages.

50. If there is obscurity in the account given by linguists of the morpheme, there is none in what they have to say about the flexibility of language. A language is the creation not of one individual, but of millions of individuals who have used it in the past or are using it now. It is not brought into being by any single act of creation, but develops constantly, being changed and modified with the passage of time. It is the linguistic

---

[1] *Aspects of the Theory of Syntax*, p. 141.
[2] p. 35, and cf. pp. 117–18. Cf. also *Listener*, 30 May 1968, pp. 687–91, for the valuable broadcast discussion between Chomsky and Stuart Hampshire on language.

community, for instance the people who have spoken English over the centuries, which has determined the phonetic structure of the language and it is it too which has determined the phonemic and syntactical changes appropriate to changing contexts. The living language is never static but is constantly changing and developing. It is possible today with the help of computers to collect reliable statistical evidence of these changes. Such evidence as has been obtained, we are told, appears to show two things; first, the strength of traditional ways of speaking and, secondly, the manner in which traditional ways, in spite of their strength, are being constantly eroded. One erosive factor is the desire to make communication easier —though it would be foolhardy to claim on present evidence that economy is the dominant factor in the growth and evolution of languages, since so many of the changes which do occur are obviously not economies.

The flexibility of language does not signify the absence of rules, but the rules themselves can change with the passage of time. Apparently none of them is immutable, though it is also true that rules are the slowest to change. Very sudden changes, particularly of the rules, will endanger successful communication. It is surprising how wide the changes in a language can be without causing failure of communication. The fact is that when we speak of 'the same language' we can accommodate within the 'same' language large differences in the way in which it is spoken. There are dialects and there are idiosyncrasies of individual speakers. There are malapropisms, but we are not unduly disturbed. We know what Mrs. Malaprop wants to say and understand her. Yet all this is within limits, there comes a point when the listener does not understand and communication by speech breaks down.

It will now be clear that the influence of any one individual upon the language of his community cannot but be slight. And this fact makes unreal much of the discussion of sign theorists. It is misleading to speak of language as if it were an invention of an individual. In one sense, language is an invention and it has conventional elements within it. But it is not the invention of the person now using the language. The linguists have made this point very plain, and it is one that philosophers of language should heed.

51. The first thing to be said about our use of language, it must be agreed, is that language is man's principal instrument of communication. In this book we are more interested in another use, namely, its use in the process of thinking; but the approach to this secondary use of language is through the consideration of its use in communication. The difference in effectiveness between speech and any other means of communication, say gestures, movements of the body, or again alarm cries, is immense. By this device of varying the phonemes and of varying their order, men have made the stream of sounds which proceed from their mouths a highly efficient instrument of communication. So greatly has language eased social intercourse, so effectively has it helped the sharing of information about the world and about ourselves, that its invention must be reckoned as momentous in the history of the human race.

But when this is said, it is also necessary to add that language is not a perfect instrument; nor do we rely solely upon it, but supplement it with other means of communication. In some contexts, though not many, language may fail us altogether; we sometimes cannot find the words to express what we want to express. The question asked by the poet Bridges remains: 'Who shall ever find joy's language?' Yet this situation is rare, usually we do succeed in communicating our experiences. Or at least we partially succeed, for it has to be acknowledged that the communication may be flawed and marred by the verbal medium itself. Consider the limitations of language. First, there is the historic limitation consequent upon the proliferation of languages. One can only communicate with someone who speaks a language one understands. And even when two people speak the same language there may be big variations within it. Usually even then one gets the gist of what is said, but not without losing much. It is not only that the speaker introduces words strange to the hearer, but that he uses familiar words in ways unfamiliar to the hearer. This latter point becomes particularly important in considering the attempted transmission of precise thought.

Or consider again the limitation set upon a language by the fewness of the phonemes that are used. The number of distinct sounds that could be used by the normal human being in speech is far greater than the number that he does use. But the use is not determined solely by what is physiologically possible. It is argued that the greater the number of the phonemes used the more complicated the language tends to become and the more difficult it is to communicate in it. So though more phonemes could in fact be used, economy and ease of speech demand that as few as possible be used. But this economy, it is then argued, is secured at a price; for fewer phonemes signify an increase in multiple meaning. The combinations of phonemes being fewer have to be worked harder. No one would attribute the occurrence of multiple meaning wholly to the fewness of phonemes, but it is part of the explanation.

It is certainly the case that there is such a phenomenon as multiple meaning and that it may be a source of confusion both in communication and in thought. It may take one of two forms and these are known as polysemy and homonymy respectively. In polysemy the same word or phrase has two or more senses. One need only open a good dictionary to see instances of polysemy on every page. Thus opening the *Shorter Oxford Dictionary* at the word 'find' we are given twelve different senses of the word. These senses are related, and the speaker is usually aware of the relation. But the net result of polysemy in this instance is that one word does the work of twelve. Needless to say polysemy makes for vagueness and for occasional failure in communication. The other type of multiple meaning is homonymy, where the same phonemes used in an identical order provide entirely different words e.g. 'ball' meaning (1) a globular object (2) a dance. Opening a random page of the *S.E.D.* again one finds the set of phonemes 'flush' used for 9 different words and 'fly' for 5 different words. Some of these appear to be related in meaning and it is difficult in the border cases to distinguish between polysemy and homonymy, but in the case of 'ball' the word signifying a globular object and the other signifying a dance are wholly different.[1] In some languages homonymy is a rare occurrence, but it is a frequent occurrence in English, so much so that Robert Bridges once described English as 'a foolishly imperfect and clumsy instrument'.[2] Certainly the presence of a comparatively large number of homonyms in English suggests that the use of a few more phonemes would have benefited the language.

In contrast, the linguistic feature known as synonymy, when it occurs, must be regarded as a waste of phonemes, for here two different words have exactly the same meaning. It is argued by linguists that pure synonymy is rare. In abstract thought and in scientific terminology there may be total synonymy, and we must later consider this possibility; but ordinarily when we use different words we expect them to mean something different, though the difference may occasionally be very slight.

But to proceed with the catalogue of limitations, the very conventionality of language can itself be a hindrance to communication. It cannot be denied that language is conventional, though there are also in it non-conventional features. We do sometimes use a word or a phrase not because this is the conventional way of speaking about such and such an experience in English, but for other reasons. For instance, what we say

---

[1] Incidentally, the set of identical phonemes may be *written* differently e.g. 'mean' and 'mien', but the spoken sounds are the same, and so 'mean' and 'mien' are homonyms though not homographs. To add to the confusion homographs are not necessarily homophones, compare 'convíct' and 'cónvict'. Accent, tone, length, etc., the suprasegmental or prosodic features of languages, are involved.

[2] S. Ullmann, *Semantics*, p. 181, quotes from a lecture by Robert Bridges, who calculated that English had 1,600 to 2,000 homonyms. 'Now it is variously estimated that 3,000 to 5,000 words is about the limit of an average educated man's talking vocabulary, and since the 1,600 are, the most of them, words which such a speaker will use . . . it follows that he has a foolishly imperfect and clumsy instrument.' Ullmann thinks this estimate of the average speaker's talking vocabulary is on the low side, but if it be greatly increased the proportion of homonyms would still be substantial.

may be an imitation of what we hear, e.g. 'the babbling brook' and 'the gurgling sound'. There is considerable onomatopoeia in our speech, more than we sometimes suppose. These phrases, it is true, become in time a convention, but they are naturally based. Onomatopoeia, however, is not the sole type of non-conventional motivation. For instance, given the convention that we refer to coffee as 'coffee' and to a cup as 'cup' our use of the word 'coffee-cup' is not then a convention. So too in saying 'Tom hit Bill', 'Tom' and 'Bill' are names decided upon conventionally and the word 'hit' is conventional. It is a syntactical convention too that we say 'Tom hit Bill' rather than, for instance, 'Tom Bill hit'. But that we say 'Tom hit Bill' rather than 'Bill hit Tom' is not entirely a matter of convention. Hence it is incorrect to say that language is conventional without qualification. Words, such as 'cuckoo', are usually termed 'transparent' by linguists, as contrasted with the 'opaqueness' of other words. On the other hand, the word 'book' is opaque, for there is no reason other than the convention why we speak of a book as 'book'. And in this sense words and phrases are usually opaque rather than transparent.[1] Language, that is to say, is conventional, and essentially so. Yet its opaqueness can be a serious hindrance in communication. The hearer does not understand the statement because he does not fully understand the convention or because the speaker does not fully understand it, and so there is a failure to communicate.

These are serious limitations in the efficiency of verbal communication, but perhaps the most serious limitation lies in what is sometimes termed the analyticity of language. This limitation is not so obvious in short categorical statements,

---

[1] Logicians are in the habit of using these terms 'transparent' and 'opaque', following Whitehead and Russell, in a somewhat different sense and the above linguistic distinction does not help in the discussion of the particular problem they have in mind. A true singular statement, say, may in one context be transparent and in another opaque in the following sense. It is transparent if another singular term which designates the same object can be substituted for the original singular term and the sentence remain true. If a is a name of x and b is also a name of it, then 'a is f' = 'b is f'. In this position of substitutivity the statement is transparent. But if one says 'He believes that a is f' it does not follow that he also believes that b is f and the substitutivity is lost.

such as 'He left the house', or in commands such as 'Open the window'. But consider a description of a scene or an event. We speak of it piece by piece, presenting each feature serially. A momentary occurrence, that is a totality taking place all at one time, has in its description to be set out seriatim, one statement following another in time. This is inevitable. Is it distortion? Certainly not complete distortion, for, on the one hand, what is talked about has features which permit of analysis and, on the other, language has its own way of presenting this analysed content as a totality. It synthesizes as well as analyses. Linguistic description, however, is laborious and many details in what is being described are likely to be omitted. It requires exceptional gifts to make the description of a scene, as we say, real. None the less, verbal description is frequently all that is possible. After all most of what we have learnt about the world in which we live comes from listening to others describe it or from reading what others have written. It is true that we observe what goes on around us, and that what others say would not be intelligible to us if we had not seen, heard, and sensed certain things for ourselves. Yet for the most part we depend on verbal communication for our knowledge of the world. Indeed custom has so established speech and writing as the media of learning that today we have to be reminded of the value of 'visual aids' and of non-verbal means of communication in learning. In particular, the invention of the photograph, and with it the film and television, has made it possible for us to observe for ourselves so much that before we could only hear of from others, or read about. No doubt these inventions will be used widely in future and their use will provide a valuable supplementation to verbal communication. But our main source of information will continue to be what we read and what we are told, and the analyticity of these descriptions in writing and in speech is a source of inadequate understanding and possible error. It is said truly that the historian, for instance, is limited because he cannot possibly give all the facts. He has to select. But it is also necessary to remember that he is limited in another way; he has to present verbally what he does select and this means presenting analytically. Speaking generally, to describe a happening in words is to be involved in a difficult piece of analysis which may easily go wrong.

No more need be said of analyticity at this point but it will clearly be necessary to revert to it later in discussing verbal thinking. Here we may merely conclude that its analyticity and its conventionality, together with the possibility of multiple meanings, that is, of homonymy and polysemy, and various other features, combine to make language less than perfect as an instrument of communication. The words of Robert Bridges that the language of the average, educated Englishman is 'a foolishly imperfect and clumsy instrument' may perhaps be too strong. But human language is certainly not flawless; its inherent limitations must be acknowledged and kept in mind. Yet while these need to be acknowledged, they should not be exaggerated. Many of the defects of language are corrigible. And even if there are some which cannot be corrected, it is still obvious that the advantages of verbal communication greatly outweigh the disadvantages. The fact that cannot be gainsaid is that language has proved itself to be a superb tool for communication.

VII

SPEECH AND THOUGHT

52. When discussing this topic of speech and thought people sometimes write as if the two were distinct phenomena and the problem was one of relating them. But it should be made clear at the outset that this is over-simplification. Admittedly, speaking is not the same thing as thinking. We talk of people 'speaking without thinking' and there is the cynic's remark that women knit 'in order to have something to think about when talking'. Certainly, we can utter sentences parrot-wise. But speaking significantly involves, we suppose, along with the uttering of sounds, a certain measure of thinking. There is no significant speech without thought. There is, we agree, pre-verbal thought, but speech and thought are linked together from the beginning of speech. Consequently, when in this chapter we speak of the influence of speech on thought we shall be considering how speech when it develops, a development involving thinking, influences further thinking. The speaker is also the thinker, and we shall be asking whether the manner in which he has come to communicate more effectively with his fellows has in any way influenced his own private thinking. As we have seen thinking proceeds, for the most part, in the absence of that which is thought about, and on such occasions we think at first imaginatively. But once we have learnt to speak, we use language to describe what is absent. Or we may employ imagination and description together in our thinking, and this in fact is what usually occurs. Thus the technique of speech, meant primarily for communication, becomes useful in one's private thinking as well. How does it affect that thinking?

I should explain at the outset in considering the influence of speech on thought that I do not wish to examine here the way in which specific differences in specific languages influence the thought of those who speak them. It is held by linguists, such as Sapir, Lee Whorf, and others, that different peoples using very different languages, say English and Hopi, or even English and Chinese, are determined by the structure of these languages to think of the world differently, that syntactical differences affecting, for instance, the subject–predicate expression, the tense, the number, the gender and so on, affect thought. These are matters to be discussed by linguists and anthropologists, possessing an intimate knowledge of the language, the history, and the culture of these peoples. There seems to be a strong case for the general thesis they put forward, however much they disagree amongst themselves when they come to work out in detail the extent of the influence. But I am not concerned with this thesis at present but with the wider question, how the use of language, meant primarily for another purpose, has influenced thought in general. And I want to ask this question bearing in mind in particular three features of speech which, it seems to me, have influenced verbal thinking deeply, namely its conventionality, its analyticity, and, thirdly, its ability to handle the general as well as the singular. Now there may have been in the course of human history very primitive languages which lacked one or more of these features. Certainly a child beginning to speak lacks the power of describing and the power of analysis necessary for description; it is further unable to distinguish verbally between singular and plural. But it does not remain long at this level; very little sophistication is needed for the beginning of conscious pluralization[1] and very soon it will attempt faltering descriptions revealing primitive analysis. It would appear that these three features are present in all but the most primitive use of language and I propose to consider how it is that they affect thinking.

Before we turn to this task, however, a word must be said about certain difficulties consequent upon the use of language in thinking. Language, as we have seen, cannot be described

---

[1] Though this does not mean conscious classification. Piaget's experiments on the behaviour of normal children of 5 or 6 reveal that they frequently lack the power of classification.

as a flawless instrument of communication, neither is it a perfect instrument of thought. Indeed the needs of the individual as speaker are in some respects fundamentally different from those of the individual as thinker, so that we should not expect an instrument forged to meet the requirements of the former to prove ideal for the latter. Thus, for instance, the speaker's need is to communicate with another, and if this other person understands him he is not bothered by an element of vagueness in his speech. The vagueness may even make what he says more easily understood by others, for if he is very precise and very specific it may be more difficult to follow what he says. Precision too demands a greater effort on his own and the listener's part, so that it is not surprising that the language of day-to-day communication tends to be vague. But vagueness is inimical to serious thinking in a way in which it is not necessarily inimical to successful communication.

Consider again the phenomenon of polysemy discussed in the previous chapter. It is obviously a source of ambiguity in communication and in thought. The fact that a word or a phrase has several different senses may not lead to ambiguity if each of the meanings is kept distinct by both speaker and listener, and the same holds for the thinker; but these different senses are related, sometimes closely related, and it is difficult to keep them distinct. Hence the tendency to ambiguity. This may not hinder communication; but it makes precise thinking almost impossible. A fundamental rule of thought is that a symbol must not change its meaning in the course, say, of a piece of deductive reasoning, but polysemic words are only too likely to change their meaning, and even though the change be slight it may still be large enough to vitiate the argument. The presence of polysemy in spoken languages is one of the factors driving the thinker to give up using words and to use, for instance, letters instead as his symbols. If he does use words he seeks to define them precisely. (It is ironical, however, that in this quest for precision he may even increase polysemy, for the word as now defined by him may well carry with it a slightly different sense from all its other senses.) As to homonymy, this feature of language, needless to say, is a source of confusion to speaker and thinker alike, although it is more likely to bother the speaker than the thinker.

But if multiple meaning, particularly in the form of polysemy, is a source of trouble to the thinker, it might be thought that synonymy is a feature of language very much to his advantage. In verbal thinking it is most useful to be able to paraphrase, to restate what is said in other words without changing any of its meaning. In definition too we seek to substitute for a word another word (or words) which has precisely the same meaning. In these efforts at verbal substitution synonymy obviously should help. Now we find an abundance of loosely synonymous material in speech which admirably serves the purpose of the ordinary speaker when he wishes to paraphrase. If, for instance, a phrase he is about to utter is socially awkward, or likely to create bad feeling for any reason, he knows how to substitute for it another phrase which is unobjectionable and which more or less says the same thing. But in precise thinking it is necessary that any substitution should be exact, and this signifies that the synonymy must in this case be perfect. Unfortunately perfect synonymy is a rare phenomenon. The truth is that a living language cannot stomach perfect synonyms; one expects that what differs in sound differs to some extent in sense. Ullmann remarks: 'Very few words are completely synonymous in the sense of being interchangeable in any context without the slightest alteration in objective meaning, feeling-tone or evocative value.'[1] Consequently the thinker finds in, say, English much loose synonymy, but very little that is absolute or perfect.

53. But to return to those features of spoken languages which are likely to be particularly influential in verbal thinking, namely their conventionality, their analyticity, and their generalizing techniques. The question is how they influence subsequent thinking and, particularly, that reflective or higher thinking in contrast to the thinking which seeks the solution of the simpler, practical problems of daily life. First, how has

[1] Ullmann, *Semantics*, p. 142.

the conventionality of language aided thought? To say that a language is conventional is to say at least this much, that, on the one hand, there is no natural explanation of why the syntax of the language is as it is, and, on the other, no natural explanation of why the vocabulary is what it is. We speak here of verbal utterance or phonemic symbolism and of the writing of it. And what has just been said does not rule out a natural explanation of some syntactical features and again of the use of certain words. Yet the syntax and the use of the phonemic and of the written symbols are even in these cases still conventional, as we realize if we recall the German 'kuckuck' with its difference (both in speech and in writing) from the English word 'cuckoo'. Different languages, as we have seen, proceed in their own way and have their own conventions, and it is not possible to give a wholly natural explanation of syntax or lexicon. There is no natural explanation of why we call a spade a 'spade'. The use of the series of phomemes that make up the sound 'spade' is a convention.

Since this is a convention, then in principle any other series of phonemes *could* have been used. This is so, but important principles of symbolization must be kept in mind if we are to speak sensibly. A change of symbol is not made in a vacuum but within a living language; it cannot be made significantly except within the context of some language or other. Supposing someone decided to speak of a spade as, say, a 'bute'. When using the word he would not at first be understood by others, but would have to explain that it was his substitute for the word 'spade'. It is unlikely that others would accept the word in sufficient number to oust the word 'spade', but if they did there would be no question of their ceasing to speak English. The originator of the change knew how to use 'spade' in English, and now he substitutes 'bute' for it, but is still speaking English. He explains to others in English what he is trying to do, and his listener must understand English. That is to say, the conventionalism of language enables us to substitute one symbol for another only within the limits of a particular linguistic framework.

Supposing a group of scientists bring into being, over a period of time, and for the sake of greater precision, a new technical language. The man in the street does not understand it, that is to say, he has not come across these technical terms and he does not know what the scientists are talking about. But if he is sufficiently interested to listen to what they say, he will at once grasp that they are speaking, let us say, in English; the syntax is English, many of the words, the articles, the prepositions, conjunctions, etc. are English. The 'new language' is not strictly speaking a new language, for it is still English, though it is not the English of the market-place. It is, we might perhaps say, an extension of English. Or consider another example. Did Frege bring a new language into being in his *Begriffsschrift*? In one sense he did; yet it was no creation *ex nihilo*. The language of the *Begriffsschrift* is German, and Frege is thinking in German throughout, as is clear when he explains the different elements in his system. Any symbol that Frege uses is a symbol in the German language, and any symbol that an English thinker uses, even if it be identical with one which Frege uses, is a symbol in the English language. If the Englishman, who advocated substituting 'bute' for the English word 'spade', went a step further and succeeded in getting every one of whatever language to substitute 'bute' for whatever word he used in his language corresponding to 'spade' in English, 'bute' would still be an English word for the Englishman and a German word for the German.

The language of logic and the language of mathematics are part of the spoken and written languages of mankind, albeit a very specialized part. They are the product of a sophisticated use of these languages and involve considerable abstraction, together with severe concentration on certain features with the neglect of others. Being sophisticated, they tend to stress the written language more than the spoken. But they are none the less English or German or whatever language the thinker uses; they are an extension of these languages, an extension in accord with the nature of the language. In particular they are possible because the phonemic languages are conventional. Languages permit free choice of symbols with use and substitution according to rule.

This conventionalist element inherent in language is a great boon to the thinker. It familiarizes him with the concept of a conventionalist procedure first in respect of symbols used, but also in the wider context of rules and laws pertaining to a thought system. The point that particularly concerns us here is the aid the conventionalism of language gives to the thinker, who thinks in his own language, but is able to use new symbols and make substitutions which can help him to formulate his own thinking more precisely and exactly, and which can be used too by others, who speak a different language, in this way making communication between him and them easier.

54. The symbolic procedures of advanced thought, for instance of mathematics and logic, are in no way alien to the genius of the natural languages but are rather extensions of them, owing their very possibility to the conventionalism of the natural languages. I want now to suggest that we might look to the second feature of language in communication to provide part explanation of another phenomenon, namely, the thinker's readiness to resort to analysis. Anyone who has learnt the technique of communicating with his fellows linguistically is already an expert in analysis and synthesis. To illustrate this we can consider some instances of communicating, beginning with a very rudimentary instance. I saw Tom yesterday and noticed that he was lame; today I meet Bill who knows Tom but does not know that he is lame. I want to convey this bit of information to Bill. So in Bill's presence I utter an unbroken series of sounds, which is one unit from beginning to end, from a silence to a silence. This utterance is written 'Tom is lame'. I know that Bill understands English and I hope to convey to him through this utterance that Tom is lame. He has to understand what I say. If he does so he and I have both gone through a process of analysis and synthesis. I saw Tom limp. I cannot point to him limping now (which would be one way of getting the information across) but have to pass it on verbally. So I

have had to analyse the situation. Here is Tom, he looks healthy, cheerful and so on, but I ignore these factors in the situation and fasten on his lameness. I say 'Tom is lame'. Since Bill understands the English language he will understand the analysis in which I was involved. He will understand that I am referring to Tom and he will understand that I am saying of him that he is lame. He did not know this before, so now, having followed me in my analysis of the situation, he makes a new synthesis. Tom, whom he knew as healthy, cheerful, etc., is also lame.

Thus this simple utterance, where it is a successful act of communication, involves analysis and synthesis on the part of both speaker and listener. As the reader will know, the further explication of this type of statement, the traditional subject–predicate statement, has kept logician and philosopher of language busy for a very long time. What is reference? What is a subject? What is ascription of qualities? Is it too a reference? What is a predicate? The problems of simple subject–predicate statement are so many that they have absorbed most of the attention of philosophers, and left little time for the consideration of other types of simple utterance, for instance, the relational statement. Yet it is clear that if one remains at this level of simple utterance one does not see the full extent of the analysis and synthesis in speech-communication. A description of any ordinary occurrence is likely to involve far more complicated analysis. Reference was made to this point in the last chapter and we may now consider it again more carefully. A person is describing a scene which he recalls in memory. He saw it as a totality, but it was complex, too complex for him to describe it now in a single statement. He breaks it up into parts, selects one of them and describes it, proceeds to the next and describes it in another statement or statements, and so covers all the parts. Note that he is compelled to this method by the physiological and physical factors in speech. The statements are, and must be, spoken seriatim; they cannot be spoken together. Thus in addition to the analysis involved in the significant utterance of any simple statement such as a subject–

predicate statement, there is the more complicated analysis where the whole occurrence which cannot be described in one statement is described in many. There is then a double analysis, first the analysis involved in the simple utterance and secondly the analysis in the total description. Further, with analysis goes synthesis; each single statement involves synthesis, but then the individual statements have also to be linked up in such a way that together they make up one description. It should be remarked too that along with all this the speaker is constructing sentences, that is to say, he is selecting the correct phonemes in the correct order and setting them together in complete sentences.

Thus in the act of speaking with one another we are necessarily involved in complicated processes of analysis and synthesis. The exigencies of speech, and especially of description, demand almost constant analysis and synthesis. Consequently, the thinker when he comes to the study of his own problems is already well experienced in the use of this method, so much so that it is very natural for him to adopt the analytic–synthetic procedure. The analytic–synthetic procedure in the speech act is of course itself a thinking, but what is being said is that when one passes from communication with others to private (largely verbal) thinking it is not surprising that one continues to make use of a familiar method developed to meet the needs of communication through speech.

That the method of analysis and synthesis is present in, and central to, all serious human thinking is obvious. Whatever the problem, a common method of attack is to divide it into its parts. Descartes gives classical expression to this doctrine when he sums up his reflections on the conduct of rational thought. Having first determined not to accept anything for true which he did not clearly know to be such, he sets down, as the core of his method, the following procedure: to divide whatever is examined into as many parts as possible and then, by beginning with the simplest, to ascend to the knowledge of the more complex. One first divides and then synthesizes. This is the essence of the analytic method wherever it appears. Logical analysis is the analysis of an argument into its constituent statements, and an analysis of each statement into its parts; it reveals too the relationship between statements, and the relationships within a statement. When today we speak of 'philosophical analysis' we usually have in mind a special instance of analysis, that is, the analysis of a doctrine set forward by a philosopher, in order to find out, if we can, exactly what the doctrine is. We analyse it statement by statement, examining each in turn and relating statements the one to the other within the doctrine as a whole.

This analytic–synthetic procedure pervades our intellectual thinking. It is not necessary to argue that this is due to the fact that the procedure is already central to speech and, particularly, to description in speech. Thinking might have proceeded analytically even though men had never learnt to speak. It is difficult to conjecture what intellectual thinking would have been like if it were other than verbal, but we are certainly not in a position to deny that it could still have been analytical in its procedure. It might be argued that this procedure is the human mind's 'natural' procedure, that it is innate and essential to it. This, however, remains to be proved. We cannot say that the presence of analysis and synthesis in thought is the direct consequence of the analysis and synthesis in speech. What we can say, however, is that human speech involves analysis and synthesis, and that the use of language in advanced thinking is an additional incentive to the adoption of the analytic–synthetic method of procedure in that thinking. And when it is said that the analyticity of speech influences human thought the doctrine is true at least in this sense.

The most advanced human thinking is pure logical thinking and in it the analytic–synthetic procedure is seen at its best. This is apparent, for instance, in strict logical deduction. The analysis of the argument consists in setting out the propositions which are the premisses of the argument. Each premiss must be set out explicitly and none is to be hidden. No proposition is to be introduced which is not essential to the argument. Every necessary item is to be included and every superfluous item excluded. The complete analysis presents all that is necessary and sufficient for the deduction of the conclusion. With the drawing of the conclusion, the act of synthesis that brings the whole argument together is complete.

A word should be added at the end of this section about the 'analytic proposition' or 'analytic judgement' of the textbooks, for it might be thought that this is the outstanding case, the instance *par excellence*, of analyticity in thought. But this is not so. 'Analytic proposition' or 'analytic judgement' is a technical term used, for instance, by Kant for any proposition which is said to be true in virtue of the meaning of its terms. What is signified by the subject term is, on analysis, shown to contain what is signified by the predicate term. As Kant puts it 'the predicate *b* belongs to the subject *a* as something which is (covertly) contained in this concept *a*'. The analysis is of the subject. We have, Kant says, to 'break it up into those constituent concepts that have all along been thought in it'.[1] That such a proposition is said to be true 'analytically' is understandable, but the name 'analytic proposition' may none the less emphasize a secondary feature. For the important feature here is not the analysis but the identity, the identity of the *b* ascribed in the predication with the *b* covertly contained in *a*.

Since this is so there must be no question about the genuineness of this identity. It happens, however, that in many so-called 'analytic judgements' the identity is loosely assumed. Even the statement 'No bachelor is married' is necessarily true only in so far as 'bachelor' is completely synonymous with 'unmarried male', and one can point to frequent uses of these terms in ordinary speech in which they are not synonymous. We have seen that perfectly synonymous locutions are rarely found in speech. Thus it would be erroneous to suppose that the identity required is invariably present when someone says 'No bachelor is married'. What of logically true statements of the 'No un-*x* is *x*' form? 'No unmarried man is married' is necessarily true, given the constancy of the logical element 'no' 'un' '~' (in whatever way we symbolize it) and assuming

[1] *Critique of Pure Reason*, A 6–7, B 10–11.

that 'unmarried' signified solely the denial of the 'married' of the predicate term. But in this case too the more important feature is identity rather than analysis. We shall have more to say of 'analytic statements' later and of their alleged *a priori* character. The point to be made now is that the discussion of analysis in thought is far wider than that of the so-called 'analytic judgement' and is not to be confused with it.

55. We may turn to consider the influence of a third factor in speech. One of the skills which the speaker has to acquire is that of speaking of many individuals, as well as of one individual. The evidence shows that a child knows how to group things together manipulatively before it learns to speak, and well before it understands the use of general words. Grouping (*pace* some nominalists) is chronologically prior to speaking. But when the child does begin to speak then in due course it has to learn how to use general words, and it is clear that children take some time to learn this art; the basic distinction between singular and general is not made easily by them. It takes time to become aware of the fact that something is singular and that it is to be contrasted on that account with what is general. In our adult life we understand the grammarian's distinction between proper name and common noun and the logician's between a singular term and a general, but distinguishing between these is not an easy task for the very young child. Even for adults some nouns remain difficult to classify. For instance, what do we make of the word 'water'? Is it a singular or a general term? It is difficult to say.

There is an interesting discussion of such words as 'water' in a paragraph of J. N. Keynes's *Formal Logic* (1884) in which he is examining Bain's position, and a part of this paragraph may be quoted. Is the word 'water' a general word? It is obviously not a proper name. Keynes comments as follows:[1] ' "Water" is general. Professor Bain takes a different view here; he says, "Names of material—earth, stone, salt, mercury, water, flame are singular. They each denote the entire collection of one

[1] pp. 9–10.

species of material." But when we predicate anything of these terms it is generally of *any portion* (or of some particular portion) of the material in question and not of the entire collection of it *considered as an aggregate.* . . . We can distinguish *this* water from *that* water and we can say, "*Some* water is not fit to drink"; but the word "some" cannot, as we have seen above, be attached to a really singular name.'

Bain, that is to say, held that 'water' was a singular word because it referred to one stuff throughout the world; Keynes that it was general because one can speak of 'some water'. Which view is correct? To ask this question is to suppose that there is one and only one answer, but this may not be the case, and on reflection it is obviously not the case. Clearly, there are uses of the word which do not admit of articles and pluralization but we speak too of 'taking the waters', 'the water in the cup', 'some water', 'Derwent water', and so on. It is manifest that on the one hand we can speak of water in the bulk or, on the other, of discrete portions of water. Hence we might solve the puzzle by saying that in one use of the word 'water' is singular, in another general. Yet it is questionable whether this is a satisfactory solution. For is 'water' in the first of these two senses properly described as a singular term? Linguists as well as logicians have felt that there was something distinctive about words of this kind, and it was the linguist Jespersen who coined the term 'mass words' by which they are now known. 'Water', 'wool', 'beef', 'iron', and so on, in the first use, do not admit of articles and cannot be pluralized, so they are not general words; but they are not singular words either. It is best to think of them as mass words.

Now the suggestion is that when children use nouns they use very many of them as mass words. Quine suggests[1] that at first they even use the word 'Mama' as a mass word but that later it becomes a singular word. Whatever of this, it seems true that children must often begin neither with the singular clearly apprehended to be such nor with the general, but with something which may be said to contain both in germ. And if

[1] *Word and Object*, p. 92.

this is so it follows that the order of knowledge suggested by empiricists, first of singulars, and then of the general as a consequence of abstraction from singulars, is not always the true order. To judge by the earliest utterances of children, and by their first vocabularies, their words seem very frequently to be mass words and this would signify that the general is at least as primitive in speech as is the singular. What we begin with is as general as it is singular, though at the time we are hardly conscious of the distinction.

It is to be emphasized that the distinction between singular and general is not in the first instance syntactical. The words of languages are not divided into two classes, singular and general, as they are divided syntactically into nouns, verbs, adjectives, etc. The syntactic division that corresponds most closely to the singular–general division is that between the proper name and the common noun, but in living languages the function of the former is not solely to designate the singular or particular, it can carry with it a general connotation, it can pluralize ('some of the Tudors'), and in some respects it can function as a general word. No doubt the proper name is more of a designating word than of a characterizing word, but the difference between it and the general word in this respect is one of degree. In the second place, it would be obviously wrong to identify general words exclusively with common nouns. Adjectives, verbs, adverbs are certainly general words. In addition there are many syntactical classes of words, such as prepositions, conjunctions, and the like, which are not usually thought of as either general or singular. The grammarian in classifying words is not dominated by the distinction between general and singular, and this because the languages of the world have arisen in situations in which the speaker himself was not dominated by it, but merely aware of it. He was aware of things, individuals, possibly of himself and other persons, as unique beings, but this awareness was not such that it became the very basis of syntactical form. The singular–general distinction remained vaguely in the background.

Is it wrong to suggest that something of the grammarian's

indeterminateness—or should we perhaps say flexibility?—on this issue seeps through into logical thought? If so this would provide an interesting example of how our daily linguistic attitudes influence advanced thinking. In traditional logic canons of reasoning (i.e. syllogistic reasoning) were set down almost without reference to the singular statement. The latter had then to be fitted into the scheme. Should the affirmative singular proposition be an A proposition or an I proposition? For most it was an A proposition, but Ramus for one took it to be an I proposition. As is well known there are difficulties too in fitting the singular proposition into the canon of modern logic. Quine argues[1] that singular statements, whether indefinite or definite, need to be paraphrased with the help of the 'such that' clause, so that they fit the requirements of modern logic. Even those singular statements that have proper names as their subject terms, are to be treated in this way. 'Socrates is wise' can be paraphrased 'There is an x such that x is Socrates and x is wise'. The phrase '. . . is Socrates' is now treated as a verb '. . . being Socrates', and is predicative. It is a general predicative term—though in this instance it would be true of just one object. The criticism made of this move is that in the paraphrasing we lose Socrates and have merely 'something socratizing'. In some senses, Aristotle may be said to 'socratize' as well as Socrates. This criticism has some force. Portia was 'a Daniel come to judgement'; we may say that she danielized. But of course she wasn't Daniel. Why should the x that socratizes be Socrates? Yet possibly this over-simplifies the position. If our concern is with the existence of this unique person, the historical Socrates, the criticism is relevant, but if we concentrate on the wisdom, the honesty, and the truthfulness of Socrates, then what is general in the singular statement is foremost in our minds, and the paraphrase does then bring out its essential meaning and at the same time fits it into the logical scheme.

Perhaps the best instance of the way in which singular merges into general is found in that fountain-head of so many

[1] *Word and Object*, pp. 178–9.

modern theories, namely Locke's *Essay* together with Leibniz's subsequent reflections upon it in the *Nouveaux Essais*. Locke feels that the propositions that we use in reasoning are ultimately about particular things and he questions the principle that no syllogistic reasoning can be conclusive unless it contains at least one universal proposition. He thinks we argue from particulars. Leibniz in reply takes a singular proposition whose subject term is a proper name, namely 'St. Peter denied his Master', and argues that it is also general or universal. 'For', he says,[1] 'although it is true that there is only a single St. Peter the Apostle, we may nevertheless say that whoever was St. Peter the Apostle denied his Master' [Car quoiqu'il soit vrai qu'il n'y a qu'un seul St Pierre l'Apôstre, on peut pourtant dire que quiconque a été St Pierre l'Apôstre a renié son Maitre]. Leibniz, that is to say, analyses the given singular statement as follows: (1) There was one St. Peter; (2) There was only one (or not more than one) St. Peter; (3) Whoever was St. Peter denied his Master. By the third step he brings out the general feature hidden in a statement that is about a singular or particular and so shows that it is also a universal statement; at one and the same time it is both singular and general. The link between this analysis and the modern theory of descriptions is obvious.[2]

56. It is clear from the foregoing section that whilst man's ability to use general words in speech deeply influenced the character of his subsequent thinking, it did not do so by presenting a clear-cut distinction between singular and general, nor did it present a neat division of words into singular words and general words. Yet the ability to use general words successfully did contribute to the development of thought and, more, was essential if thought was to develop in the way it did. We may now consider how this was so.

Fundamentally the technique of the use of general words is

[1] *Nouveaux Essais*, iv. xvii. 8.
[2] During the years in which Russell worked out his theory of descriptions he was also studying Leibniz. Did he find in such passages as the one quoted above the first suggestions of his theory?

the predicating technique. It is the technique of using a characterizing expression where the same expression can be used as predicate term for more than one subject term. It enables us to use one and the same expression, without multiple meaning, to describe different things. In addition, with the help of such pointers as 'this', 'here', 'now', and of the articles, we may use these expressions to refer to single objects. We use them too to speak of groups, as when we speak of 'the rich'. Further the technique enables us to pluralize. In contrast the proper name, in the strict logical sense, does not admit of pluralization (though as we have seen proper names are used loosely and we talk of 'three Johns being in the room' or again of 'the Tudors', 'the Forsytes', and so on). But the use of the general word and of general expressions makes pluralization possible, and it makes possible the use of 'some', 'all', 'each', 'any', 'every', that is to say it enables us to quantify. More important still, it makes possible sentences that are eternal, in the sense of not being tied to the here and now, as when we say that the atomic weight of oxygen is 16.

Now a characteristic of human thinking, as we have seen, is its endeavour to free itself from too great a concern with the present and from the pressure of the present, and clearly the use of general words helps in the effort to attain this end. With this help man's thinking takes in a wider field and it does so by having less to do with immediate experience and by becoming more and more conceptual in character. The question then arises as to the nature of conceptual thinking and in what sense it is implied that this sort of thinking is only possible if one knows how to use general words. What are concepts, and what are the relations between concepts and general words that make facility in the use of the latter essential if we are to think conceptually? These are difficult questions.

The difficulty is heightened when one discovers that frequently when people speak of concepts, particularly what they call empirical concepts or empirical schemata, they have in mind images (usually memory images) along with words. Such schemata perhaps should not be called concepts. But if they are, the theory that there is no non-verbal conceptual thinking is endangered, and so is the theory that conceiving presupposes the use of general words. For empirical schemata may be wholly the product of imagination and may not presuppose any verbal ability. Consider the case of a deaf mute who has never been taught to communicate verbally and so has no language in the strict sense, though he can communicate through gesture. Could he have a concept of a particular shade of colour, say ultramarine? Could he see an object coloured ultramarine and could he recall the colour and recognize it when next he sees it? He could not name it. Has he a concept of ultramarine? He has more than a percept and more than a bare memory image. But he cannot apply a name in recognition. Perhaps this can be reduced to a matter of definition. If we define conceptual thinking as thinking that is necessarily verbal, though it may also have its imaginative elements, then the deaf mute has no concept. Only a person who can speak, and understand when he is spoken to, can think conceptually. This may appear a high-handed procedure, but we may at least agree to think only of verbal conception in what follows.

57. When we do use words in conceiving what is the relation between the word and the concept? The temptation is to say that the word is the name of the concept, but this temptation is one to be avoided. The English word 'freedom' is not the name of the concept of freedom. This today is generally accepted amongst philosophers. The function of the general word is not to designate, though general words can be used with words such as 'this', 'that', or the articles to make up singular expressions referring to unique individuals. The general word is essentially a characterizing word. In the second place, to say that the general word is the name of a concept is to presuppose that the concept is the sort of thing that can be named, an entity of some kind, not to be found, it is true, amongst the existing entities of the physical world, such as tables and chairs, but existing in the mind, or perhaps we should prefer to say existing intentionally. As has been seen, however, this is not

a position to be taken up without due consideration of the risks involved. It is dangerous to speak of a concept as an entity of any kind, and particularly dangerous to speak of it as an entity which is neither physical nor psychical but intentional.

For both of the above reasons, therefore, the theory that the relation between general words and concept is one between a name and the entity named is not acceptable. But if this is not the relation then what is it? To attempt an answer we may look again at the conceiving of empirical concepts where language is involved. I have a concept of a house; imaginative and verbal factors are both present. I recall houses seen, and may now be remembering a particular house, but it is more likely that I have a vaguer image. Further I know how to use the word 'house' in speaking English. In this context what is it to have the concept? It is having an image, more or less generic, and being able to use the word 'house'. But it is certainly more than this. It is having too the abilities and capacities, having the dispositions, having the body of knowledge about houses, which have gathered around the image. That I then have the concept is made manifest in many ways, for instance, when I recognize this to be a house, or when I say that it is not a house but a factory or a hall, or when I expect it to contain a living-room, a bedroom, a kitchen, and so on. Or we may take another, less complicated, example. People speak of having a concept of a specific shade of colour, for instance, ultramarine. Having the concept in this case normally involves having seen the colour, usually on many occasions, and having either consciously abstracted it or having become very familiar with it. It involves too having learnt how to use the word 'ultramarine' in speaking English, and this involves in turn having learnt the scheme of colour words and the place of the word 'ultramarine' in the scheme, and further having learnt to associate the word 'ultramarine' with the specific shade. Having the concept of ultramarine is then, for instance, being disposed to reject the statement 'This is royal blue' when it is spoken of an ultramarine object, or to accept the statement 'This is ultramarine'. Now the core of the concept in such a case is that which is retained in imagination, that is to say, the retained colour image. But it would be wrong to say that the concept *is* the image; but rather that around this core has gathered all the capacities and dispositions which must be there if one can rightly be said to have the concept of ultramarine.

What now of the conceiving which is less empirical and more intellectual, where the language factor has become more important and the imaginative less so, though some imaginative factors are still likely to be present? The core in this case is clearly not an image; it would seem rather to be the general word (or general phrase). But if we say this we do not mean that the concept *is* a general word, any more than that the general word is the name for the concept. We may consider an example. It will be agreed that a person has the concept of, say, reciprocity if he uses the word correctly in conversation or if, when questioned, he explains satisfactorily how he uses it; if he says, for instance, that it is a state between two parties in which there is mutual action in giving and taking. If we are satisfied, possibly by further conversation with him, that he is not repeating these words parrot wise, we say that he undoubtedly 'has the concept'. Our test, first and foremost, is the presence of a verbal skill, namely, being able to use this word 'reciprocity' successfully. But having the concept does not consist merely in having the verbal skill. For presupposed in the successful use of the word 'reciprocity' may well be our experience of our own co-operation with others, or of our attempts to co-operate when they were unsuccessful, or the recalling of how others have reciprocated with one another, or of how groups of people, societies, and nations have co-operated and of the benefits that have accrued from such co-operation, and so on. These are the associations, the memories of social behaviour, and the linguistic capacities, which have accumulated around the general word, but the core, it would seem, is the general word 'reciprocity' itself. The concept, *reciprocity*, that is to say, is not (1) an intellectual entity of which the word 'reciprocity' is the name, nor (2) the general word 'reciprocity', but neither (3) is it any capacity or disposition, or any set of capacities or dispositions. It is the general word, *plus* the associations stored up in images and in words, the word *plus* the acquired skills and dispositions.

Now if this approaches to being a true account of the concept, the deeper sense in which thinking presupposes the acquirement of linguistic skill becomes clear. The more intellectual thinking is anchored, not in the memories of the past and not in imagery, but in words, and again not in proper names (used as proper names) nor in operational words, but in general words—fundamentally, in characterizing words, be they adjectives, verbs, or nouns—or general phrases. It is in this special sense that ability to use general words is a necessary condition of the higher, conceptual thinking of mankind. This is not to say that the ability is of itself a *sufficient* condition of conceptual thinking; for experience of the world, of men, and of oneself, together with many non-verbal abilities, skills, and dispositions, are also requisite. But it is to say that it is only because man learnt the technique of using general words that he was able to develop that thinking which we call conceptual. And though we may still have to concede that there are pre-verbal empirical concepts, our final justification for speaking of conceptual thinking as essentially verbal is now made plain.

58. To sum up the argument of this chapter, human thinking is not wholly verbal or conceptual; some parts of it may be described as pre-verbal. Further, verbal thinking itself is not to be explained wholly in linguistic terms; empirical elements are likely to be present as well. But if this is granted, it remains true that the form which man's higher thinking has taken has been determined very largely by his success in acquiring certain speech skills. There are ways of thought which come easily to a person who has mastered certain linguistic techniques, and other ways which do not. I have selected three features of speech to illustrate the point. First, its conventionalism; a phonemic articulation with its own syntax tacitly agreed upon by those who speak the language is used in order to

communicate with others. The thinker later grasps explicitly what is here in implicit form only, and consciously uses symbols and arbitrary principles to further his thought. Secondly, its analyticity; communicating involves describing, and the speaker in order to describe is forced to analyse and then to synthesize. This analytic–synthetic procedure is essential for communication, if only for physiological reasons, and is at hand for thinking. Finally, the describing involved in communicating itself involves statement, in particular that form of statement in which something, a, is said to be characterized by a character, f, and this characterizing involves the use of the general word. And certainly, if we single out the speech skill which has the greatest relevance to human thinking, we find it to be this skill of using general words, for without it conceptual thinking would not be possible.

Living language is a species of human behaviour in a situation in which man desperately needs to communicate with his fellows. When alarm cries, gestures, and the like proved inadequate speech was evolved—not all at once by one individual but over many centuries by countless millions. And once a cultural group had learnt to speak, its way of speaking undoubtedly influenced its thinking about the world, not merely in the sense mentioned at the opening of this chapter, that peoples using very different languages such as, say, English and Hopi, were determined by the structure of these languages to view the world differently, but in the deeper sense that procedures evolved by the speaker later become procedures used by the thinker. It is difficult to imagine how human thinking would have developed if man had never learnt to speak, but had solved the problem of more effective communication with his fellows in some other way. Some of the factors in the situation would have remained the same. The man himself, who uses his abilities to solve his problems, would remain, and so would the fundamental problems he had to solve. In any case it is no part of our argument that linguistic procedure is the sole determinant of thought procedure, but only that it deeply affects it.

We seem justified in saying that were there no speech using general words there would be no conceptual thinking. There would also be no statement. What would have come in its stead, in the absence of speech, it is impossible to speculate. It is agreed that some of man's thinking is pre-verbal and pre-statement. For instance, a kind of pre-verbal induction may occur, an expectation resting on imaginative thinking but using no language. Yet inductive reasoning is greatly assisted when it can consciously set out its hypotheses in statements. And if we consider deduction it is evident that there can be no pre-verbal deduction, since deduction is from premisses, that is to say, from statements. To put it simply, the ability to reason deductively presupposes the ability to speak one of the world's languages—and this goes for deductive reasoning in mathematics and in logic too, since mathematical and logical 'languages' are but extensions of one or other of the languages of mankind.

The invention of language, spoken and written, went far to solve the problem of human communication. But it did more. It made possible a vast expansion of human thinking. From the thinker's point of view the verbalization of thought was not all gain; certain features of language, as we have seen, invite confused thinking unless steps are taken to prevent this happening. Yet this verbalization was none the less vastly gainful, for it provided those procedures of symbol-using, analysing, abstracting, and generalizing, which had been worked out to meet the needs of communication through speech, but which now became the instruments whereby countless new outlets were found for the free development of human thought.

One point more needs to be added. In concluding the chapter it would be well to return to that with which it began. In speaking of speech and thought there is a tendency to think of these as two separate forces interacting the one upon the other. This can be taken in too extreme a way. It might quite fairly be said that speech is still the finest achievement of human *thinking*, and this makes any suggestion that first speech came and then thinking appear absurd. To put it concretely, we are dealing with men. It is man's creativity that revealed itself in the emergence of speech and it is the same creativity that is again apparent in what we call the higher, the more intellectual thinking. At the end of this chapter it is good to recall this elementary truth in order to avoid being misled by too great abstraction.

VIII

THE SPONTANEITY OF THOUGHT

59. We singled out constraint as the most prominent feature of knowing; in contrast the most prominent feature of thinking is undoubtedly its spontaneity, and it is the spontaneity of thought which is to be considered and illustrated in this chapter. In particular, since this is an epistemological study, it is spontaneity in the attempt to extend knowledge which primarily concerns us. It is unnecessary to discuss, say, the spontaneity of creative, artistic thinking. More to the point is the spontaneity claimed for acts of decision or of determination, whether in practical or in theoretical matters. Kant argues that even though I have no knowledge of myself as I am, but merely as I appear to myself, I am none the less conscious of the spontaneity of my acts of determination, and 'it is owing to this spontaneity that I entitle myself an *intelligence*'.[1]

The spontaneity which entitles us to think of ourselves as intelligences is equally apparent in our efforts to extend our knowledge. We may think of these efforts as operating at two levels, that of our daily life and that of more precise thought, and it is the latter which most concerns us, since here the spontaneity is the more evident. Beginning with the analogical element in thinking and the use of models, we may then consider inductive inference in general. This will lead to a consideration of deduction and, finally, of system-construction. In this chapter we are not concerned with the question whether through these efforts we do gain greater knowledge of our world—indeed in, for instance, system-construction the question may seem irrelevant—we merely wish to familiarize ourselves with the element of spontaneity in thought.

It will be well before we proceed further to explain how the word 'spontaneity' is used here. There are two related senses

[1] *Critique of Pure Reason*, B 158 note.

to the word. On the one hand we speak of spontaneous development, meaning by this development from within in the absence of any external stimulus, that is spontaneous movement or change—for instance we speak of the 'spontaneous combustion' of a haystack. On the other hand, spontaneity may characterize a person's thinking in being not merely from within in the above sense, but also free, unrestrained, and original. It carries with it a sense of innovating. And when we speak here of the spontaneity of thought it is in the second of these senses more particularly that we use the term.

A further point needs to be made clear. We tend to assume that however bound a person may be in his actions he is completely free in thought: a slave, we suppose, can think as he chooses although it is not always wise for him to say what he thinks. Yet it is necessary to qualify the assertion that nothing ever can or ever does impede the thinker's freedom. A person may be conditioned (though not wholly determined) in his thinking by various factors, for instance his upbringing and his education, but he himself may not be conscious of the extent to which he is conditioned. His thinking may be limited too by the narrowness of his experience and by his comparative ignorance of the world around him, both the world of things and the social world of human relationships. On the other hand, as we have seen, he may be hindered by too much concern for the world; the clamour of the world around him may be so great as to inhibit fresh thought. Further, since he thinks imaginatively or verbally or both, anything which hinders the development of his imaginative or linguistic powers, for instance defective sense organs, may limit his thinking.

These are impediments to the spontaneous development of thought, and it would be foolish to deny that they exist. There is always too the further restraint upon the spontaneity of thought—though this can hardly be termed an impediment— namely, the restraint imposed by the knowledge already gained by the thinker. We shall later pay considerable attention to this aspect of the matter. Nevertheless, the existence of such impediments and restraints does not prevent us from speaking of the spontaneity of human thought, and we may now proceed to consider the form it takes in different kinds of thinking.

60. In this chapter pre-verbal thinking is not discussed, but this should not be taken to mean that the characteristic of spontaneity is absent from it. Here again the invention of speech is itself ample testimony to the spontaneity of pre-verbal thinking. But the present discussion is concerned with thinking after the technique of communication through speech has been acquired, though some of the thinking discussed may still be non-verbal, that is to say, imaginative with no use of words.

I have spoken of different levels of verbal thinking; roughly, the thinking of daily life on the one hand, and the more precise thinking of philosopher, logician, and scientist on the other. Our main concern here is with the second level. The former is less spontaneous and more ruled by custom and habit, though it too reveals spontaneity. Spontaneity is present, as has been seen, in that elementary interpolation and extrapolation which helps to fill in gaps in the information provided us. Frequently these gaps are filled in dispositionally without the necessity of fresh thought, but sometimes thinking becomes necessary. However well established the habit, and however expert one becomes, genuinely puzzling situations arise. Sometimes the thinking has to be done quickly and a decision arrived at rapidly, but more often we have time to ponder over the difficulties which face us and think out our solutions; we have time too to bring what is relevant in our past knowledge to bear on the present problem. Thus in the face of these difficulties we may look around for, or recall, situations which are alike to the one now being considered, in order to see whether what we know about these situations applies at all here. For instance, we want to know whether something, a, has such and such a quality, f, and we have no means of knowing this directly. We recall that b is in many respects analogous to a, it shares many qualities in common with a, and b we know is f. This gives us some ground, we think, for supposing that a too is f. In this case our thinking may be imaginative and non-verbal, though most usually it is verbal. In contrast to it, is a second procedure which is strictly verbal. To find a solution to our puzzle we do not seek analogies but consider what is known and established. We set this out in statements about which we have a certain measure of assurance. Given these statements does anything follow? Can anything be inferred from these which will help us in our search?

Here are elementary instances of two forms of thinking, namely, analogical thinking and deduction, and they clearly differ from one another. Much attention has been given to deduction, but comparatively little to analogical thinking. If analogical thinking has been considered at all it has usually been considered as an item in inductive reasoning. Yet whilst the latter does involve the use of the analogical method, it is wrong to assume that the only analogical thinking which occurs is that which is part of inductive reasoning. This is not the place to consider fully the important issue which arises here. But it is clear that the assumption that there are two sorts of reasoning, the inductive and the deductive, and two sorts only, needs to be questioned. There is no justification for confining the use of analogy to inductive argument, for reasoning on the basis of analogy occurs which has nothing to do with induction. As we shall see, the concept of induction lacks clarity and consequently the difference between induction and deduction is not clearly defined. In this situation it may well turn out to be the case that the contrast between deduction and analogical reasoning is a more profitable study than that between deduction and induction. In this present chapter, however, the three kinds of reasoning will be recognized and I shall seek to illustrate the spontaneity of thinking in analogical thinking, in induction, and in deduction. In the case of the first, analogical thinking, I shall confine myself to two instances, first in the use of models and, secondly, in the establishment of generalizations.

61. The thinker has a set of phenomena before him which he does not wholly understand, and in seeking to understand it he turns to another set which is analogous to the first and which

he does understand. He asks whether the second can serve as a model of the first. When we wish to understand S_1 we may look at S_2 which resembles it and then use our understanding of S_2 to enlighten ourselves about S_1. S_2 may then be said to be a model, and the thinking is analogical because it rests on the observation of the likeness or likenesses between S_1 and S_2. There are many types of models and the uses made of models in thinking differ greatly from one another. We may now consider some of these uses.

Models are used widely at the everyday, pre-scientific level. The soldier tries to explain to his family the disposition of the battle forces with the help of plate, cup and saucer, knife, and spoon. Uncle Toby and his servant Trim did the job more professionally with their well-kept model of the battlefield in the garden. Our speech shows that we have models for action and behaviour. 'He swears like a trooper', 'He reads like a parson', and so on. A model may lurk behind any metaphor we use (although a metaphor is not to be identified with a model).[1] Consider a more conscious use of a model. A problem worries us which is difficult to tackle because of the physical size of what we are considering, so we look around for a like set of phenomena on a smaller scale. In a physics laboratory an experimenter is working on the problem of wind-movement in large tunnels, but for his convenience and to save expense, he experiments with a small model. The first experiments on hovercraft, we are told, were made on models operating in tanks of water. The model in such cases is a concrete individual object, possibly of the same material as is the original, and the experimenter knows the precise extent of the differences in size, weight, etc. and allows for these in his calculations. In so far as the structure of the original and the model is of the same form, they are said to be isomorphous.

Many of the models of the natural sciences are straightforward, concrete replicas of this kind, being useful because of likenesses both in form or structure and in material. But there

[1] On the relation between model and metaphor cf. Max Black, *Models and Metaphors* (Cornell Univ. Press, 1962).

are other models which are analogous in form only and which are used in ways somewhat different from the above. Thus Rutherford suggested that the theory of the atom in his day could best be developed if the structure of the atom was thought of in terms of a planetary system. In this case material likenesses, if any, were not the basis of the analogy but only likenesses of form. If the form or structure of the atom was taken to be analogous to that of a planetary system, could the theory of the atom be then more easily developed? The analogy was fruitful and a new hypothetical theory of the atom was set up for testing. Many models in biology, physiology, and other sciences (including the social sciences) were used in much the same way. Sometimes models have been used to help in presenting part only of a new theory, it being understood that the models in this case cannot possibly be representative of the whole; the experimenter wishes to concentrate on some part of the theory and finds it useful to think in terms of a model in doing so. Sometimes again a theorist may use two models to help him set forward his theory. An excellent and familiar example is the use of particle and wave models in quantum mechanics. H. J. Groenewold comments on this use in these words: 'Compared with classical mechanics the theoretical formalism [of quantum mechanics] is more abstract and its relation to observation is less direct. In classical theory one has particles and waves and these two concepts mutually exclude each other. In quantum theory the same entities, e.g. electrons or photons, show particle aspects and wave aspects in the peculiar sense of complementarity—they exclude each other and complete each other. . . . In treating a special problem it is often useful to transform from one particular representation to another one at appropriate moments. Now the particle picture and the wave picture are inadequate approximations to the formalism. . . . In speaking in terms of them during the treatment of a special problem it is often necessary to jump from one picture to another one at appropriate moments.'[1]

[1] 'The Model in Physics', in *The Concept and the Role of the Model*, ed. H. Freudenthal (Reidel, Holland, 1961), p. 102.

This is to say, two models are used that are inadequate as models apart, but adequate in so far as they complement each other.

It will be noticed that the models here are still concrete ones, namely, the wave and the particle; although, as Groencwold says, the formalism is more abstract. But analogical thinking is not confined to the concrete, nor are all models concrete. For example, to take the most obvious instance which happens to be a highly important one, an analogy is observed between (*a*) a complicated set of phenomena, having qualitative as well as quantitative features, and (*b*) an abstract mathematical model. A study of the latter helps to give insight into the nature of the former. It enables us to express the set of phenomena mathematically, and in expressing it mathematically new insights about its structure are gained. This type of analogy becomes highly formal when the model is a pure deductive system. The system has its own axioms and from these follow its theorems.[1] Now we find a set of phenomena which seems to us analogous to a system of this kind and the system becomes itself a model by which our understanding of the structure of the set of phenomena before us is deepened. Knowing one system (that is, being acquainted with its calculus) we find in the other set of phenomena something which may be thought of in the same terms, and it is this analogy we seek to develop. In the case of the model we are able to move from the axioms downwards, but in the case of the theory we begin with phenomena which suggest the presence of a system explicable in terms of these axioms. In *Scientific Explanation* Braithwaite puts the point in this way. Of the two deductive systems the first, the model, is such that 'the logically prior premisses determine the meaning of the terms occurring in the representation in the calculus of the conclusions; in the theory the logically posterior consequences determine the meaning of the theoretical terms occurring in the representation in the calculus of the premisses'.[2]

[1] The system itself can be interpreted in many interpretations, and each such interpretation is spoken of as a *logical* model. The various interpretations are then alike and structurally identical.

[2] R. B. Braithwaite, *Scientific Explanation* (Cambridge, 1953), p. 90.

At this stage analogical reasoning is a potent factor in the development of human thought. The thinker comes to sets of phenomena with established deductive systems in mind and seeks to find analogies. The ever-present risk in this situation is that the thinker, having established certain analogies, then assumes that the analogy extends further than it does. Braithwaite warns against the danger 'of transferring the logical necessity of some of the features of the chosen model on to the theory, and thus of supposing, wrongly, that the theory, or parts of the theory, have a logical necessity which is in fact fictitious'.[1] Speaking more generally, he remarks: 'Thinking of scientific theories by means of models is always *as if* thinking; hydrogen atoms behave (in certain respects) as if they were solar systems each with an electronic planet revolving round a protonic sun. But hydrogen atoms are not solar systems; it is only useful to think of them as if they were such systems if one remembers all the time that they are not. The price of the employment of models is eternal vigilance.'[2]

This is sound advice. The satisfaction of finding theory match model over a wider and wider field tempts the thinker to claim a greater isomorphy than is in fact present. Clearly the thinker's use of models is a procedure which may easily lead to error. Still, any inventive thinking may mislead; the fearful are right when they say that thinking is dangerous.

62. We may now consider the part which the observation of analogies plays in the making of generalizations. We shall again confine the discussion to verbal generalization, without denying that there is generalization already in the child's grouping before it learns to speak, possibly even in the dog's anticipation of a walk when it sees its master put on his coat and pick up his stick. That these generalizations rest on the observation of likenesses would be admitted. What of verbal generalizations? We assume that such statements, too, normally presuppose the observation of likenesses. Consider the general statement: 'All the books on the shelf are red.' I may now be

---

[1] R. B. Braithwaite, op. cit., p. 94.   [2] Ibid., p. 93.

looking at the books on the shelf before me and seeing that they are alike in colour. They may differ somewhat in their shades of red, but their colours are well within the limits recognized by me as red. Or I may be out of the room and relying on my memory of what I observed when I was in the room. It is, of course, also possible that I may never have been in the room and may never have seen the books on the shelf but have been told that there are books on the shelf and that they are all red. It is assumed throughout that I know how to use the English language, and know that 'red' is the correct word to use in this context.

The word 'red' is not the only general word in the statement; there are too the words 'books' and 'shelf'. As has been seen, the successful use of such words as 'books', 'shelf', and 'red' involves the retention, either consciously or dispositionally, of a complicated network of previously gained information, and much of this information is about likenesses between things which have either identical or resembling qualities. The predicating expressions are '. . . is a book', '. . . is on the shelf', and '. . . is red', and it is stated that all the objects which are books and which are on the shelf are also red. Thus what is immediately presupposed in the general statement is that I see or have seen (or my informant has seen) a likeness in colour between the books such that they may be described as red, but presupposed too are all the observations of likenesses necessary for the significant use of '. . . is a book' and '. . . is on the shelf'.

Such are the observations of likenesses. What now of analogical *reasoning*, that is to say, of the argument that arises out of the observations? If in looking at the shelf I observe the likeness in the colour of all the books, no argument is then necessary to enable me to say: 'All the books on the shelf are red.' The enumeration is complete, covering all cases, and no analogical argument is required. The argument becomes necessary when not all the cases are covered but only some of them. Consider the general statement 'All swans are white'. I have observed the likenesses between swans, and all the swans

I have seen have been white. I now argue that all swans are white. I realize that such an analogical argument from some cases (that is, all the cases I have seen or have read or heard about) to all cases is logically weak. The fault does not lie in the observation of the analogies but in the passage from some cases of x being f to the conclusion that all cases of x are f. This is the crucial step present in ampliative induction (to use Peirce's term) but not present in summative induction or complete enumeration. The argument on which the ampliation rests is the argument from analogy and it is not always reliable —as I come to realize when I first see a black swan.

Analogical reasoning may lead to error, but it does not always do so. We help ourselves to avoid error by, for instance, defining as precisely as possible the extent of the positive analogy. Moreover, a factor other than analogy enters into inductive reasoning, namely that of the number of analogous instances, for this may corroborate the results gained by analogical reasoning. We shall consider this further factor in the next section. But analogy in itself is a basis of argument. The fact that entities are alike or analogous, and that we can observe these analogies, means that we are presented with a world of related particulars rather than of isolated particulars. We concentrate on the relations, find likenesses of quality and of structure, and this discovery enables us, on the one hand, to use models to further our thinking. On the other, our experience of likenesses suggests the possibility of more likenesses. The fact that entities are analogous in some respects suggests that they may be analogous in other respects. This may possibly lead to new knowledge, and in any case it provides the thinker with clues that open up new lines of thought, which he may follow, and with new hypotheses to test. As Mill says, speaking of the value of analogy: 'Any suspicion, however slight, that sets an ingenious person at work to contrive an experiment, or affords a reason for trying one experiment rather than another, may be of the greatest benefit.'[1] It is of benefit to the thinker even though he fails to establish new knowledge on the

[1] *System of Logic*, III. xx. 3.

basis of the clue provided him. Here, in the use that he makes of analogies, is a pointer to the liveliness and effectiveness of his thinking.

63. John Stuart Mill defines induction as 'the operation of discovering and proving general propositions',[1] and the discovery begins with the observation of particular instances. Now the number of like instances matters as well as the likenesses between them. Thus in complete enumeration or summative induction all the possible instances are known, all the x's on this shelf which are books are known to be red. The certainty of the generalization 'All the books on the shelf are red' rests on the completeness of the enumeration. On the other hand, in simple or incomplete enumeration many cases remain unexamined and this gives rise to doubt about the universality of the general statement, though the analogy in the cases examined is strong. But if consideration of the number of observed cases in relation to all possible cases may cause doubt in our minds, it is argued that the discovery of more and more cases in which the analogy holds, with no case in which it does not hold, gives a certain degree of assurance. The basis of this assurance may well be psychological rather than logical; we are disposed to expect what has always been turning up in past experience; we have a propensity, possibly a compelling propensity, to assume that the resultant generalization is universally true. The continuing analogy and the increasing number of corroborative cases strengthen the growing confidence. We feel that our expectations are reasonable —in Mill's phrase, 'what we should reasonably expect to find' —in view of the evidence we can put forward.

None the less ampliation, involving a passage from 'Some x's are f' to 'All x's are f', is not logically justifiable. There is no valid way of deducing the second statement from the first. Consequently, ampliative induction must be regarded as a species of non-demonstrative inference. Inferences occur which make no pretence to demonstrative certainty but give probable

[1] Ibid. III. i. 2.

knowledge only. They tell us what a reasonable man can be expected to believe. This might vary from one man to another, but the assumption is that the beliefs of one reasonable man would not vary widely from that of another. Being reasonable they would set down rules, rules not for gaining certainty admittedly but for gaining probability, and in so far as these rules were generally accepted a certain objectivity would be introduced into their procedure. Hume sets down a specific set of such rules[1] and adds a cryptic remark: 'Here is all the *logic* I think proper to employ in my reasoning; and perhaps even this was not very necessary, but might have been supplied by the natural principles of our understanding.' Mill took over Hume's rules with suitable modifications, and adumbrated his celebrated Inductive Methods or Methods of Experimental Inquiry.[2] As every beginner knows, however, these were not flawless, and Mill did not succeed, in the opinion of his successors, in providing the requisite logic of inductive reasoning.

Nor has twentieth century speculation provided a satisfactory logic of induction. It has been confused by uncertainty about the relation between the logic of induction and the logic of probability. The latter has become increasingly adequate on lines that become more and more mathematical, but it does not solve the problem of induction, namely, ultimately, the problem of justifying ampliation. Thus Reichenbach, following von Mises, sought to establish limits to relative frequencies of events occurring in long sequences or 'collectives', such as a series of tosses of pennies or throws of dice. These would then provide him with exact and wholly objective probabilities, for instance, the probability of a double six occurring with this pair of dice over a sufficiently long series of throws. If it were then possible to reduce all items of induction into probability inferences of this order a truly objective logic of induction could be provided. But logicians are not at all convinced that the probability that von Mises and Reichenbach talk about is the

---

[1] *Treatise*, I. iii. 15, a section showing the influence of Bacon of Verulam.
[2] *System of Logic*, III. viii.

probability of ampliation and they do not find a safe basis for inductive logic in the relative frequency theory of probability. Efforts have been made to analyse more fully the process of inductive reasoning. William Kneale in *Probability and Induction* makes a significant distinction between primary and secondary induction. Primary induction is the passage from the observation of likenesses and from the consideration of the number of cases to the generalization, be it hypothesis, law, or probability rule (if these are distinguished). Secondary induction then consists in the further process of finding a wider and possibly transcendent hypothesis, a theory explanatory of this and other generalizations. Kneale has doubts about speaking of this second process as induction. He concludes: 'The best convention is perhaps to extend the use of the word "induction" to cover the hypothetical method but at the same time to distinguish this new application of the term by adding the adjective "secondary".'[1] On this view then the inductive process would not end with the acquiring of the generalization or law but would also include the attempt to fit it into a wider theory, so that its consilience with other generalizations or laws could also be tested. This phase too should be regarded as part of the inductive process, but it should be distinguished from primary induction.

Now it is generally agreed that an account of inductive reasoning in terms of the passage from the observation of particulars to the general cannot be adequate, a second phase is necessary and it is emphasized that the method of this second phase is different from that of the first. The first is a passage from some to all; the second is the hypothetical deductive method wholly devoid of ampliation. The doubts about speaking of the latter as induction, even secondary induction, can well be understood, yet for a full account of inductive reasoning both phases would have to be recognized. In this situation it is not difficult to understand the impact of Karl

---

[1] Kneale: *Probability and Induction* (Oxford, 1949), p. 104; and cf. further, §§ 43–7, pp. 226 ff.

Popper's 'denial of induction' in the *Logic of Scientific Discovery*. When Popper speaks of induction he means what Kneale means by primary induction. He argues that 'there is no such thing as induction' if by induction be meant 'inference to theories from singular statements which are "verified by experience" (whatever that may mean)'.[1] How we acquire a hypothesis, whether of a simple rule or law or of a complicated theory, is not a matter susceptible of logical analysis. 'The initial stage, the act of conceiving or inventing a theory, seems to me neither to call for logical analysis nor to be susceptible of it . . . there is no such thing as a logical method of having new ideas or a logical construction of this process.'[2] Once the new hypothesis is acquired, however, it can be tested by deductive methods, which seek in particular, Popper thinks, to prove it false. But there seems no reason for calling this procedure an inductive procedure.

Now here certainly is one way of solving the problem of ampliation and so of inductive logic. Popper does not deny the tendency to pass from some to all, but he does deny that this is a logical process. There is no such thing as rational induction and so no logic of induction, though there does exist a logic of science; but the latter has to do with testing and comparing theories and is deductive. Now Popper's is a drastic solution of the problem and not every one accepts it. Carnap, for instance, views induction as a process involving more than simply the acceptance of a hypothesis, there is also in the accepting a rational estimation of its probability. Consequently induction can be, and needs to be, studied logically.

It will be noted that, in spite of their differences, all these accounts agree that we do pass from the observation of particular cases to generalizations, though there is disagreement whether the passage is susceptible of logical analysis. Here is a form of extrapolation that enables us to extend the boundaries of our thinking (though not necessarily of our knowing), and in view of its usefulness in thinking it may be regarded as the

[1] Popper, *The Logic of Scientific Discovery* (London, 1959), p. 40.
[2] Ibid., pp. 31–2

most important instance of extrapolation. Clearly, not every acceptance of a generalization is the outcome of a conscious movement from particulars to general. Indeed some new hypotheses appear to come to us out of the blue. Yet usually they come after considerable preparation of one sort or another. It would be absurd to argue, for instance, that the fact that Darwin had so wide an experience of the world of animals and plants had nothing to do with his making his famous hypothesis. Relevant in this context are certain remarks by Einstein quoted by Popper.[1] Speaking of 'the highly universal laws' of science Einstein says: 'They can only be reached by intuition, based upon something like an intellectual love (or sympathetic understanding, *Einfühlung*) of the objects of experience.' The intuition—to be distinguished from a Cartesian infallible, intellectual intuition—is a leap of the mind, but not a leap which anyone could make, irrespective of his experience. And this point seems equally applicable to our ampliations at a lower level. They may not be completely justified logically, yet when Einstein stresses the need for sympathetic understanding of the objects of experience he is only reasserting in other terms the empiricist insistence, from Bacon onwards, on the need for wide observation and complete familiarity with the subject-matter of one's study.

The importance of such ampliations or extrapolations as these in thinking requires to be stressed. The thinker needs them for both practical and theoretical reasons. If he is to survive he must learn how to predict the future, and inductive ampliation is the primitive procedural response to this practical need. Admittedly it is not the only procedure possible; one may, for instance, consult an oracle or resort to crystal-gazing. But human beings prefer to trust inductive ampliation, that is to say, prediction of the shape of things to come in the light of one's experience of the present and the past. On the theoretical side, the thinker uses the generalizations derived from his observations of the world as material wherewith to build his systems. Since the generalization is linked with particular

[1] Ibid., p. 32.

observations the thinking is to that extent linked with the world; but the link is not one that logic guarantees, and the generalizations cannot be assumed to be true. Nor is it easy to verify or falsify them: certainly not by appeal to positive particular instances; and there is some doubt whether bringing forward negative instances always does falsify.[1] Hence the thinker cannot be sure that, in relating these generalizations the one to the other and fitting them into his system, he is in so far increasing his knowledge of the natura lworld. None the less, these ampliations do provide him with hypotheses, general statements in an eternal present, wherewith to build his systems. Consequently, the value of inductive generalizations for the thinker does not depend wholly on their being applicable to the world; they provide material for the free speculation of active thought.

64. Finally, we turn to deductive reasoning. Is spontaneity of thinking conspicuous in such reasoning? Here the answer clearly varies with the differing accounts given of deduction. For instance, if we take the extreme syntactical view and suppose that the rules of deduction are identical with linguistic transformation rules, then to know the language in question is to be able to deduce. Now it is agreed that there is spontaneity enough in acquiring language, but, on this theory, once we have acquired it, there is then no more fresh thinking in passing from premiss p to conclusion q than there is, for instance, in putting the verb in the middle of the sentence, if one is speaking English. Neither of these acts could be said to reveal spontaneity of thinking. Nor is spontaneity conspicuous in those less syntactic accounts of deduction which present it as passive, almost automatic, and in no way active thinking. One may recall Russell's dictum: 'The mind is as purely receptive in inference as common sense supposes it to be in perception

---

[1] Cf. R. G. Swinburne, 'Falsifiability of Scientific Theories', *Mind*, July 1964, and D. W. Peetz, 'Falsification in Science', *Proc. Arist. Soc.*, 1968–9, 17 ff. Cf., further, P. B. Medawar: *Induction and Intuition in Scientific Thought*, 1969, pp. 53–4 n. 44.

of sensible objects.' Aristotle's account of syllogistic inference in the *Prior Analytics* could be interpreted as saying much the same thing; the mind is receptive of the inevitable conclusion. Syllogism, he says, is an argument 'in which certain things being stated, something other than what is stated follows of necessity from their being so. I mean by the last clause that they *produce the consequence* and by this that no further term is required from without in order to make the consequence necessary.'[1] On the other hand, this passage could be interpreted in terms of a potential becoming actualized; the inference is potentially there given that 'certain things' are stated. This line of thought in turn, treated more subjectively than Aristotle would have treated it, may suggest a theory that inference is the self-development of ideal content. F. H. Bradley's phrase may be recalled: 'Every inference is the ideal self-development of a given object taken as real.'[2] The 'object' develops of itself and in its own way, and it develops just in this way and in no other. On the other hand, the development is ideal and is in that sense subjective. If we are to speak in this context of spontaneity at all it can only be in terms of the spontaneous self-development of ideal objective content, analogous in its spontaneity to, for instance, spontaneous combustion, but different from the spontaneity that is being considered in this chapter.

We may contrast these views of inference with the view that to infer is, in part, to intuit. On the above-mentioned theories, with the possible exception of Aristotle's on certain interpretations, no intuitive element is necessary, but on the theory to be now considered inferring does involve the intuition of a relation. The theory has been advocated by more than one writer, but since the celebrated phrase with which Bradley sums up his doctrine about inference in the second edition of his *Principles of Logic* has been quoted, namely, that inference is the ideal self-development of an object, the reader's attention should be drawn to the very different account of inference in

[1] *Prior Analytics*, 24^{b}19–22 (my italics).
[2] *Principles of Logic*, 2nd edn. (1922), p. 598.

the first edition, written some forty years earlier.[1] In the first edition Bradley speaks of inference as 'an ideal experiment' and remarks 'Every inference combines two elements; it is in the first place a process, and in the second place a result. The process is an operation of synthesis; it takes its data and by ideal construction combines them into a whole. The result is the perception of a new relation within that unity. . . . . What is given to us is terms conjoined; we operate on these conjunctions and put them together into a whole; and the conclusion is the perception of two terms in relation, which were not related before the operation. Thus the process is a construction and the result an intuition, while the union of both is logical demonstration.'[2]

In this account of inference Bradley speaks of its 'result' as an 'intuition'. The thinker 'sees' or 'perceives' a relation within the whole which has been constructed by him; and is sure that the relation holds. This element of perceiving is contrasted with that of constructing. The latter is said to be 'an operation of synthesis', involving a search for relevant material, accepting this item and rejecting that, trying out one combination and then another. Inference is conceived here not as a self-development of an objective content but as a constructing and an intuiting, and if we now ask where spontaneity of mind most clearly shows itself in inference as thus analysed, the answer must be in the constructing, that is to say, in the, possibly, difficult and prolonged quest for premisses through ingenious experiments that aim at setting out the data in such an order that the thinker can perceive the new relation.

It may be argued against Bradley that inference cannot be divided in this way into 'two elements'. Setting out the premisses in such an order as to make the relation perceivable already involves seeing the relation. This is so, but one may entertain propositions without having such and such a conclusion in mind and come to realize that, say, two of these

---

[1] Very different, but the reader should note the qualifications in the second edition's account; cf., for example, 'Terminal Essay on Inference', 1 (c), pp. 598–9.

[2] *Principles of Logic*, II. iii. i, p. 256.

propositions do imply this conclusion. Or again one may begin with a conclusion which is entertained, but not yet proved, and seek for demonstrative proof. One will then search for the necessary premiss or premisses. This is the constructing that Bradley speaks about. On the other hand, the intuiting is seeing two terms in relation 'which were not related before the operation'. The question arises whether there is not another intuiting in inference, namely, intuiting that the premisses imply the conclusion.[1] But one might argue that seeing the two terms in relation in the conditions of inference is seeing the implication of the premisses, so that in fact there are not two intuitions in inference but only one. It might be further questioned, however, whether it is necessary to speak of intuition at all as an element in inference. Bradley himself, in the second edition, in line with his general emphasis on evolution and development, substitutes the notion of self-development of an ideal content for that of constructing and intuiting.

Our concern in this chapter is with spontaneity in thinking, and we may ask about the bearing of such discussions as these on this matter. Now, if it were satisfactorily established that intuition is an element in inference this would be an element of constraint rather than of spontaneity. If, on the other hand, it were held that inference is the self-development of an ideal content then such inference would reveal spontaneity, but spontaneity in the first of the senses mentioned above, namely the producing of something from within itself. In this situation the other element in Bradley's teaching would need emphasis. For whether there is or is not intuition in deductive inference there certainly is what Bradley referred to as a constructing; there certainly is a preparing and laying out of material, and this in the most convenient notation. Now spontaneity, in the sense of free innovation or extemporizing, is the characteristic mark of such constructing. In all theories of inference, and not merely Bradley's, this is the direction in which we should expect

---

[1] The question of the logical form of the implication, whether for instance, it be entailment or material implication, is irrelevant here. Of any such form it can be asked whether the implication is intuited or not intuited.

to find spontaneity in this second sense. The thinker, in order to further his deductive arguments and build his systems of thought, freely arranges his materials and freely tries out and chooses likely premisses. Let no one say that spontaneous constructiveness of this order is of no importance in reasoning.

65. In the construction of such intellectual systems human thinking reaches its maturity. The main characteristics of thinking are all prominent; the subtle inventiveness and the search for new procedures; the determination of the most precise notation which is at the same time the most economical; the withdrawal and the abstraction which give freedom to manœuvre; and the generality and tenselessness of the system's statements.

Now the system-building may have applicability to the real world. This is a matter to be considered later. But the thinker does not necessarily have the system's applicability in mind when he builds it. On the contrary he may well wish, as he builds, to be free from having to secure a correspondence between system and that which is. System-building is never haphazard in method, it is governed by rule, yet applicability to the real or correspondence with the real is not the rule. In this sense the system may remain throughout uninterpreted. The thinker chooses the rules which will guide him in building the system and, even if some of the rules are derived from experience of the world, it is not for that reason that they are chosen. He wishes as a thinker to be free from external constraints and rests his system finally on its internal consistency. If at any time the empirical phenomena can be interpreted in terms of the laws of the system well and good, but the system is not built for this purpose.

The thinker is guided by the ideal of a pure, formal, uninterpreted system which makes the following demands upon him. He must state precisely the principles upon which his system rests; these principles must be basic and not themselves derived; they must be sufficient for the system (that is to say no other principles are needed for building this system) and necessary (that is each and every principle is needed by the system); furthermore, since they are basic they must be independent of one another, for if a principle could be derived from another it would not be basic to the system. As is well known the quest for axiomatized, pure, deductive systems of this order, promoted by the mathematicians, led to alternative systems, for instance, of geometry, each system being consistent in itself and no system being such that it could be described as *the* one true system of geometry. The question of factual truth does not arise in such system-building. But the truths of each system are true within that system, that is to say, they are true as following necessarily from the axioms and deductions of the system.

Nor are such systems confined of necessity to geometry or to mathematics. The case could be, and has been, made out for alternative logics. Different axioms will give different logics and a principle deemed necessary in one logical system, for instance, the principle of excluded middle, may, if the thinker finds it more convenient, be excluded from another, so that a deductive system is constructed which makes no use of it.[1] In principle it would seem to follow that entirely consistent logical systems could be set out having no basic principles in common. Carnap in his *Logical Syntax of Language* gave forceful expression to the conventionalism of this general standpoint. The thinker is an experimenter in systems and he is justified in constantly seeking the new conventions which will help him to develop new systems. Carnap advocates the Principle of Toleration. There are no right and wrong conventions. 'It is not our business to set up prohibitions, but to arrive at conventions.'[2] The thinker chooses, and what he chooses is correct for that system; he is not to be 'hampered by the striving after correctness'. 'In logic there are no morals. Everyone is at liberty to build up his own logic, i.e. his own form of language, as he wishes.'[3]

There has been considerable criticism of extreme conventionalism, and Carnap himself has modified his position. One

[1] Cf. Waismann, 'Are There Alternative Logics?' *Proc. Arist. Soc.*, 1945–6, 76–104.
[2] Carnap, *Logical Syntax of Language* (1937), p. 51.
[3] Ibid., p. 52.

criticism is not open to us at the present stage of the argument, namely that such conventional systems may not be applicable to the real world. This is a problem to be faced later when we consider how, through thinking, knowledge of the real world can be extended. Here we are considering thinking as spontaneous, speculative activity, and its applicability to the real world does not arise. None the less, even within the framework of the present chapter, extreme conventionalism has its difficulties.

The thinking we are now considering is verbal thinking and the systems are linguistically expressed. Hence, says the conventionalist, building a new system is in effect constructing a new form of language and the thinker is free to construct his own forms of language as he chooses. Yet if we talk in these terms have we not already limited the thinker's freedom? Our reflections on language and thought have led us to conclude that no thinker is free to create a language *ex nihilo*; the most he can do is to extend what is to hand, what already exists. He can choose features of it, concentrate on them, and develop them. The symbols used are, it is admitted, basically conventional, but they have an agreed use if communication is to be possible. The rules of syntax too are conventional and vary from language to language (making a universal grammar, it would appear, a utopian dream), but the person who wishes to use a language has to accept the syntax of that language. No individual person can create a completely new language; in this sense he is not free, he is only free to extend.

Supposing, however, we cease to talk in mere linguistic terms of the thinker's speculation, and cease to speak of logical rules as linguistic rules, it might then still be argued that the speculating is conventionalist since it is axiomatic. The thinker first sets down the rules of procedure governing his system. They are not necessarily his own creation but he chooses these rules rather than any other, and his system-building is conventionalist in that sense. His aim is to build up a logical system, consistent within itself, but a system that is one only of many other logical systems that he himself or other thinkers might freely bring into being. In theory these systems can differ *in toto* since they are free creations, and they need have no principle in common. But there too is a fundamental difficulty. For it might well be replied in the fashion of Leibniz: no common principles are necessary in these self-consistent systems *except consistency itself.* Surely consistency is a requisite for all system-building. Only to the extent, the conventionalist might argue, that the thinker himself chooses to make it a principle for each system. But this argument is not acceptable, and it is not acceptable because the thinker in fact has no choice about *this* principle. To build a system he must be consistent. He is free to give up the attempt to construct a system if he so chooses, but if he wishes to build a system he must observe the demands of consistency. This means that if we speak of alternative logics, and if we mean that two alternative logics may in theory differ wholly, so that they have no principles whatsoever in common, then we are speaking of what is impossible, since the principle of consistency is common to all possible logical systems. We may continue to speak of alternative geometries since the demand for consistency is not regarded as a geometrical axiom but as a logical principle presupposed in all geometrical system-building. But we are not free to speak of alternative logics if we mean that in theory two logical systems may exist having no basic principle in common.

To be consistent is not to contradict oneself and in this sense the principle of consistency is identical with that of non-contradiction. There have been speculations recently[1] about the possibility of a 'negationless mathematics', a system of arithmetic, for instance, in which there would be no negative numbers. But this could not possibly signify that a general system of thought is possible containing no negation. There is no thinking without determining or setting down limits and, as Spinoza held, determination is negation. In this wider sense, therefore, there cannot be a negationless system of thought.

[1] One such attempt is mentioned by A. Heyting, *Intuitionism* (1956), viii. 8. 2, p. 120; he refers to G. F. C. Griss's papers in *Proc. Akad. Amsterdam*, 1946–51 on 'Negationless Mathematics'.

Given *p* then not-*p* can always be thought. Now when a person contradicts himself he is at one and the same time affirming both *p* and not-*p*. We assume that he does this without fully understanding the position and that he will correct himself when he does understand it. He may of course consciously put forward apparent contradictions and paradoxes to stimulate thought, but this is something different. We shall consider in the chapters which follow why one must not contradict oneself in thinking, why consistency is an essential principle. Here we note the fact that the thinker's systems must be consistent and coherent.

66. The thought systems we have just been discussing are the highest and most sophisticated products of thinking. Their constructing has its counterpart in the less sophisticated activities mentioned earlier, the elementary interpolations and extrapolations of our daily life, the use of metaphor and of model, analogical thinking, hypothesis-making, and inductive reasoning. All of these, along with system-building through deduction, illustrate that spontaneity which Kant picked out as the mark of intelligence. Here is active intelligence. The ancients, when they spoke of *intellectus agens*, had frequently in mind intellectual intuition, but it is possible to speak of active intellect in another sense, namely as the activity of the thinker, innovating, planning, extemporizing, speculating, making hypotheses, classifying, and system-building. If it is true that he is in part passive to influences in his environment which mould him, he is not wholly passive. By theorizing and experimentation he seeks to fill the gaps in his knowledge so as the better to understand and master his world. But this is not all, for he also finds delight in speculation for its own sake, and the system-building becomes an end in itself.

Our attitudes to free, spontaneous thinking are ambivalent. We acknowledge the skill, the concentration, and the vigour; we admire the order and beauty of the system produced; and we acclaim the originality and sheer adventure of the thought. At the same time we harbour suspicion. Is speculation for speculation's sake really worth while? Does it lead anywhere? Does it lead to the extension of true knowledge? Our attitudes show, on the one hand, a deep respect for speculative thinking and, on the other, a doubt and even a fear of it. Unless the thinker finds a corrective, he may, we feel, be led astray by this very spontaneity and freedom.

PART THREE
THE FUNCTION OF REASON

IX

THE FUNCTION OF REASON

67. What is the function of reason in human life? Let us approach this question from a new angle, that of the contrast between human knowledge and human thought. The function of reason is to bring the constraint of knowledge to bear upon the spontaneity of thought.

Without hardening distinctions and reifying abstractions it is possible to distinguish between three features in the cognitive situation. I do not speak of faculties, such as the Sensibility, the Understanding, and the Reason, which are sometimes spoken of as if they had a life of their own in the mind, and as if capable on the one hand of co-operating with each other but also of warring against one another and of creating unhappy tensions. To speak in this way obviously *is* to reify abstractions. What is necessary is to distinguish between knowing and thinking (whilst yet not making them distinct faculties) and to recognize a third feature in addition to knowing and thinking, namely reason, whose function it is to check and moderate the spontaneity of thought by bringing what is known to bear upon that spontaneity.

In using the term 'reason' in this way it is acknowledged that the word has been used in many other ways and that there is a certain arbitrariness in the present use. It is even true that the term 'reason' has been used both for the knowing and for the thinking from which we are now trying to distinguish it. In the course of philosophic reflection knowledge in the narrow sense, that is to say strict knowledge which is certain, has frequently been referred to as Reason (νοῦς, *intuitus*, or *ratio*). On such occasions the knowing is usually taken to be infallible, completely certain, and absolute. The term is used, too, when referring to thinking. We have a recent instance in Blanshard's *Reason and Analysis*, in which four characteristics of 'human reason' are enumerated: first, not being tied to perception; second, being able to abstract; third, being able to infer explicitly; and fourth, being self-conscious.[1] These characteristics, particularly the first two, approximate to the four characteristics of thinking we considered earlier,[2] and Blanshard speaks of 'the thought of a rational being' as reason. There is nothing abnormal in this identification; speculative thought in particular is traditionally identified with reason. Kant recognizes this, and is critical of 'the bare speculative use of reason'.[3] Reason (*Vernunft*) has its legitimate empirical employment in, for instance, scientific thinking, but it can also be employed to generate ideas which 'detach themselves completely from experience and make for themselves objects for which experience supplies no material'.[4] Kant condemns such speculative thinking; it seeks to apply principles, which are applicable to the empirical world, to a world which is possibly illusory. Such speculation is in Kant's view a misuse of reason.

Thus the term 'reason' has been used to refer to intuitive knowledge or infallible insight on the one hand and to thought, particularly the higher speculative thought, on the other, and these are legitimate uses. I think it more profitable, however, whilst recognizing the legitimacy of the two uses mentioned, and others which have not been mentioned, to use the term in a different way. Our concern here is with the factors present in human knowledge. I set down, as the central factor in the situation, being sure. Little is to be gained by calling this central factor 'reason'. It is easy to understand why the term νοῦς was considered appropriate by the Greeks for infallible, god-like, intellectual intuition. But for being sure, which is less exalted, some such term as 'primal knowledge' or 'assurance' may be preferred. Little is to be gained too by speaking of human thinking as 'reason' (to speak of it as adducing 'reasons' is something different). I find it most convenient to refer to these two features as knowing and thinking, and to

[1] Brand Blanshard, *Reason and Analysis* (Allen and Unwin, 1962), pp. 50–1.
[2] Chapter V.
[3] Cf. *Critique of Pure Reason*, A 631–42, B 659–70.
[4] Ibid., A 565, B 693.

reserve the word 'reason' for this third feature, namely the checking, judging, or testing of thought in the light of what is known. Thus, to speak concretely, the person who knows also thinks, speculates, and puts forward hypotheses about what he does not know, but he then tests his speculation by what he is sure of and by what he feels constrained to accept, and in doing this, I hold, he proceeds in a rational manner.

How does this differ from the traditional rationalist theory? The rationalist would agree that a man's thinking, which might be influenced, for instance, by prejudice, whim, or assumption, should be checked by knowledge. But he also views reason itself as a source of knowledge, a knowledge of basic principles that cannot be acquired in any other way. Such principles (1) may be known by acts of intellectual intuition, or (2) they may be known innately. In either case their source is pure reason and they hold universally and necessarily. Now, as we shall see, there are grave difficulties in the doctrine that it is reason that provides principles basic to thought and knowledge. The account of the function of reason put forward in this chapter does not include this provision as part of that function. In its view reason is not itself a knowing, nor is it a source (and the sole source) of principles known *a priori*; reason's task is to test thinking by what is known. It is not the function of human reason to lay down absolute standards of truth in accordance with which thinking must be tested, nor to pass infallible judgement on what is thought.

68. On the practical side it would be generally acknowledged that a man behaves rationally if he faces his present problems in the light of the knowledge he possesses. The peasant, who has learnt from life, acts as rationally in this sense of the word as does any philosopher. A hungry man behaves rationally if he eats the food he has found nourishing in the past. The gardener acts rationally in sowing seeds in spring and not in the autumn. Sometimes the practical man is uncertain how to proceed, and then it is rational for him consciously to recall his past experience, and to question others about theirs, and in the light of

this evidence to weigh the alternative actions one against the other. In his deliberations about the best action he thinks out possible situations, carries on primitive experiments, and finally tests all by what he knows. This is a rational procedure.

In this book I wish to apply this interpretation of rationality to the theoretical field. The role of reason is that of checking and guiding thinking in the light of the available knowledge both of what is certain and of what is probable. To think rationally is to think in accordance with what one knows about the natural world and about oneself and others. This seems true, to begin with, in the case of elementary inductive thinking. In our daily life we find ourselves anticipating certain occurrences and behaving with definite expectations. We are familiar with these occurrences and our expectations of them are so strong that we do not normally ask for justification of our anticipations. But if it becomes necessary to find justification we appeal to what we have experienced in the past, for things have always happened in this way. Our present thinking, that is to say, is guided by our past knowledge.

When the thinking becomes a little more sophisticated we realize that large assumptions are being made and we seek to make these explicit. For instance, we are assuming that the future will be like the past, that is to say, that nature is uniform. Is this assumption justified? For an answer we turn again to experience; sometimes what we expect does not turn up. It is not completely rational therefore to affirm that the future will always be like the past. Sometimes what we discover may suggest a special relationship between a and b such that if a occurs then b is likely to occur. If any such hypothesis is suggested we test it further by what is known, and if, as is frequently the case, what is now known is inadequate to verify or falsify the hypothesis, we await further knowledge which will be evidence for or against it, this being the rational thing to do in the circumstances. Any ampliation from 'some' to 'all', where our knowledge guarantees some cases but not all, cannot be justified rationally, any more than can the assumption that the future will be like the past. On the other hand, a genuine negative case could rationally falsify a hypothesis if such a case could be found. So the thinking, which may be suggested in the first place by what is known, is thus checked and, possibly justified, or again falsified, by further knowledge.

This same general procedure is rational too in the case of the analogical reasoning discussed in the last chapter. A situation now being examined is known to have features *a*, *b*, *c*, *d* in common with certain past situations which had also the feature *e*, and this suggests the possibility that *e* too may be a feature of the present situation. It is rational in these circumstances to search for this further feature and if we find it the discovery justifies the hypothesis.

The knowledge we make use of on such occasions as these may be habitual and the checking of the thought may involve little conscious effort. What is retained may be imaginative or conceptual or both. We retain imaginative schemata and verbal concepts, and it is these that are likely to provide the content of the thinking, the content then being information stored up in the mind. The thinker is not, however, tied to the retained schemata and associations but is free to experiment afresh and think out new possibilities. His procedure is adjudged rational to the extent to which it then accords with what is known. And though some habitual elements of the kind mentioned are no doubt always present, he is yet for the most part conscious of the items with which his thinking starts; he is conscious too that he is now thinking and that his thinking needs to be verified or falsified.

69. Two criticisms may be made of the account here given of the function of reason in human knowledge. It may be held in the first place that it is a mere rejection of the rationalist theory of reason and the substitution of an empiricist theory in its place; and, secondly, that it involves a denial of the very possibility of *a priori* knowledge. I hope it can be shown that these criticisms as they stand are defective; none the less they touch on deep issues and it is these that will need our attention in the remaining chapters of this book.

Both criticisms are defective in greatly over-simplifying the issues. The first seems to rest on the assumption that if one denies rationalism one is thereby affirming empiricism. There is a tendency, mentioned earlier, to think of rationalism and empiricism as alternative theories in epistemology, such that if any particular doctrine is not rationalist it must be empiricist and vice versa. But this tendency is to be resisted. Not only are there many forms of rationalism, so that one may give up one form and yet, by accepting another, remain a rationalist, but one may reject rationalism in all its forms and yet not accept an empiricist theory. A theory of knowledge is possible which is neither rationalist nor empiricist.

I am quite ready to believe that the account of the function of reason put forward in this chapter is not a rationalist theory. For, although there are different rationalist theories, it seems to be the case that they all demand a certain minimum, namely, that reason itself is a source of knowledge. If this is so then the account of reason given in this chapter is admittedly not a rationalist account, for in it reason is not thought of as a source of knowledge. But neither is it empiricist.

Presumably, the minimum required in the case of any empiricist theory is that knowledge is gained either directly in sense-experience or is derived from what is so gained. Knowledge, on the empiricist theory, begins with the acquiring of what is vaguely termed a 'sensory manifold' and out of it by a process of complexing and constructing, by generalizing, by making and testing hypotheses, further knowledge is gained. But if this be empiricism, the theory of knowledge put forward in this book is no more empiricist than it is rationalist; it cuts across both rationalism and empiricism. It begins with what remains of the traditional intuitionist theory. The latter was rationalist. Reason provided knowledge, for instance of basic principles, which was absolute and infallible. But what remains of it is the doctrine central to the Three Condition Theory, namely, that the first thing to be said about knowledge is that the knower is sure and that knowing, though not to be identified with being sure, is only to be understood in its light. Now a person can be sure of things which are adjudged empirical in the traditional sense, for instance, that the book is red, but he may also be sure of what is not empirical in that sense.

We may conclude that the account given of the function of reason in the present chapter is not a rationalist doctrine, but this does not mean that it must be empiricist. The account given rests on the earlier accounts of knowing and thinking, and the presentation of knowing and thinking has been neither rationalist nor empiricist in the usual senses of these terms. The same can be said of the account given here of the function of reason, that it is neither rationalist nor empiricist in the usual sense.

70. Does the present account of the function of reason involve a denial of the possibility of *a priori* knowledge? Again the charge over-simplifies the issues. What has been said does involve a denial that reason is the source of a special kind of knowledge. This knowledge is usually termed *a priori*, but not all *a priori* knowledge is of this kind. Consequently, the denial that reason is a source of *a priori* knowledge does not involve a denial of all *a priori* knowledge. There may be other kinds of *a priori* knowledge which are not being denied. I may take one instance. We know from the meaning of the terms that all bachelors are unmarried males. This has been described as *a priori* knowledge. But if it is so described, it is a piece of *a priori* knowledge which is not denied here, and is different from the *a priori* knowledge under consideration in this chapter. We are here concerned with the view that it is part of the function of reason to provide, for instance, knowledge of basic principles of being and existence, such principles as causality on the one hand and of non-contradiction on the other. They are not known by experience, but independently of it and prior to it. But now to deny the existence of such *a priori* knowledge as this is not necessarily to deny the analytic knowledge that a bachelor is an unmarried male.

Thus it is not true that the account given of the function of reason in this chapter necessarily involves a denial of all *a priori* knowledge. What is denied, in the effort to put forward a more acceptable theory of the function of reason and of its relation to knowledge and to thinking, is that reason is a source of *a priori* knowledge. Reason is certainly an arbiter, but not in terms of information which it itself provides *a priori*. This is to introduce mystery where there need be no mystery. The function of reason is to arbitrate in the light of what is known.

Yet is it possible to defend what has now been said? Have not the traditional intuitionists shown that we do intuit *a priori* certain principles and that without such intuitions no advance in knowledge is possible? Or, if doubts about intuition arise, can we really deny that there are conditions for the very possibility, not merely of advance in knowledge and in thought, but of experience itself, and that these conditions include the *a priori* knowledge of principles by reason? Experiencing involves understanding; this means, it is argued, that experience is conditioned by principles which the mind does not gain in experience but which it knows *a priori* and which it brings to experience. It is a condition of our sensory intuitions that we think in terms of space and time, and of our experience of the world that we understand it in terms of substance–attribute, causality, and the other categories. The categories, says Kant,[1] 'are nothing but the conditions of thought in a possible experience, just as space and time are the conditions of intuition for the same experience. They are fundamental concepts by which we think objects in general for appearances, and have therefore *a priori* objective validity.' They are known by reason. Kant, for instance speaks in this connection of 'unserer Vernunfterkenntniss *a priori*'.[2]

But this philosophy speaks of objects of experience as having to conform to our knowledge. The world is a world amenable to determination by the principles of reason. This doctrine could no doubt be defended if one adopted an idealist or Hegelian metaphysic. But the case for idealism must be made out independently. That the world is fashioned by Spirit is not a matter to be decided by our needs as epistemologists. Alternatively, it could be argued that the experienced world is

[1] *Critique of Pure Reason*, A 111.   [2] Ibid., B xx.

phenomenal only, and not noumenal, and because it is merely phenomenal it can be moulded by us. In that case we should not know whether or not the noumenal, as opposed to the phenomenal, obeyed our principles; but could only make the claim that the phenomenal was principled by us, that is to say, by our reason. Phenomenalism, however, as has been seen, involves so much inner self-contradiction as to be discredited, and it is hardly likely to provide the foundation required for the defence of this philosophy. It is thus not going to be easy to show that we are justified in demanding of the world obedience to principles which we ourselves have laid down.

But if we reject the traditional rationalism, it may be replied, then we deny the possibility of knowledge of the necessary, and this will mean that science is not possible. This obviously is a very serious objection. Yet what is the necessity we have to know? Are we speaking here of metaphysical necessity, of what must exist, or of logical necessity, of what must be thought? Presumably of the first—although it may be, and has been, argued that one cannot finally distinguish between the two. It may even be argued that this distinction is unreal, since necessity is a concept pertaining essentially to logic. In Wittgenstein's phrase: 'There is only *logical* necessity.' Certainly it is possible to appreciate the need for logical necessity. A logical system is ruled rigorously by principles which are accepted at the outset and adherence to these principles secures logical necessity and validity. That a logical system must be necessary is obvious; though there may be argument as to the source of the principles mentioned, whether they are known innately by reason, or whether they are intuited by reason in the course of the thinking, or whether, thirdly, they are accepted conventionally or dispositionally or in some other way. Yet whatever account is given of their origin there cannot be objection to the statement that a condition of thinking a necessary thought-system is the acceptance, explicit or implicit, by the thinker of principles holding rigorously throughout that system. The reflections of theorists over the past century on the manner in which systems are constructed in abstract thought have helped to make this point clear. The ideal is that the thinker should consciously choose his axioms. Once chosen they must determine the system and be necessary and sufficient to the system. Each system is then valid and consistent with itself, but it may happen that the necessary conclusions of one system contradict the equally necessary conclusions of another system.

The principles apply necessarily and universally; they must apply and they apply throughout. They are not found or discovered in the course of thinking out the system, they are accepted from the start. They are there from the beginning, i.e. *a priori*. This too is a legitimate use of the term and we may go on to speak of the acceptance of the principles as an *a priori* condition of the thinking. But this is not to justify the view with which we started, namely, that we are aware *a priori* of principles which condition *knowledge* of the world. The principles we are speaking of here are principles of thought-systems and they need have no applicability whatsoever to the existing world. One can think them without even attempting to interpret them in terms of what exists. On the other hand, one is not inhibited from suggesting that some such system, say Riemann's system of geometry, applies to the physical world or to some part of it, and then setting out to discover, if one can, whether it does apply. But in that case the a-priority does not apply to the knowing. When it is agreed that the acceptance of principles is an *a priori* condition of thinking the logical systems, it is not at the same time admitted that the accepting of principles (whatever their source may be) is an *a priori* condition of knowledge of the world. Unless care is taken this point may be neglected, with consequent confusion. Granted that thinking has *a priori* features in the sense described, it does not follow that knowing has *a priori* features. Nor is it the case that the occurrence of thinking itself presupposes a knowledge of *a priori* principles holding of the world. Universality and necessity in thought-systems are secured by adherence to principles laid down and accepted at the outset, but it is not necessary that these principles should apply to the existing world. Consequently, the applicability of these principles to the existing world, if they do apply at all, need not be established before they can be used by the thinker to think out his system. The argument, therefore, that an *a priori* knowledge of principles of the existing world is presupposed in the thinking of necessary thought-systems has not been established. This means that the further argument that principles known by reason *a priori* must be presupposed in the thinking of necessary thought-systems has also not been established. Admittedly this of itself does not dispose of the case for *a priori* knowledge by reason, but it weakens it.

71. These considerations, however, leave us with considerable difficulties. It is essential to recognize logical necessity; but this means admitting the acceptance of principles as a condition of logical thinking. In addition we ordinarily suppose and hope that our thinking may advance knowledge of what exists, though it need not always do so; it may be applicable to the existing world, and may enable us to gain new knowledge of that world. In that case, it would seem, the *a priori* principles hold of the world itself and do not merely determine the course of the logical thinking. It would follow that the world must obey these principles and is determined; some part of what happens in it, to say the least, happens out of necessity.

But if any of the thinker's principles determine the world it then seems incorrect to suppose that he himself chooses them and that it is he who lays them down as axioms. The individual thinker can legislate for the logical system which he brings into being, but this is no basis for the argument that he can legislate for the existing world or that he can lay down the principles operating in that world. How then is logical thinking ever applicable to the world? Supposing in answer to this it be argued that the principles operative in the world must be discovered by the knower. How are they discovered? Experience, we are told, cannot give them; we experience what happens but not what must happen. If the principles are known, therefore, they must be known *a priori*; and this not merely in the sense that they secure necessity and universality in the system, which is the sense in which the principles of a logical system are held to be *a priori*, but also in the sense that they are known *a priori* and not set down freely by the thinker. This, it is claimed, must be a special kind of knowing other than experience, deeper and profounder than it and epistemologically prior to it, which makes necessary and universal knowledge of the world possible. The special kind of knowledge is reason.

Now the strength of this theory lies in the undoubted a-priority of logical thinking determined by principles, and as long as no clear distinction is made between thinking and knowing it follows that in fundamentals the process of knowing the world is identical with the process of thinking, so that in knowing the world necessary and universal principles are known *a priori* to operate within it. But, once distinction is made between thinking and knowing, then it need not be assumed that the process of knowing is identical with the process of thinking in this particular, that the principles of the existing world must be known *a priori*, that is, definitively and once and for all, before detailed knowledge of that world is possible. The analogy of thinking must not be allowed to play too great a part in the account given of knowing.

What has been said of the function of reason in this chapter would of course be held to be erroneous by those who interpret knowledge of the existing world in the *a priori* manner, for it denies that it is part of the function of reason to provide knowledge of *a priori* principles. What other theory of knowledge then can be offered, it will be asked, if, granting that experience does not provide the necessary and the universal, a science of the world which is systematic, necessary, and universal is none the less claimed to be possible? I wish to suggest that if we question the view that reason exists as the provider of knowledge of *a priori* principles, so too we need to question the above notion of experience. Are there these two grades of knowledge, (i) reason, giving definitive principles, and (ii) experience, giving the stuff to be principled? Just as we query the conception of reason as provider of *a priori* principles, so we must query this conception of experience. This will be difficult, since theory of knowledge rests on the assumption that any account of human knowledge must be in terms of the contrast between reason and experience.

In the chapters which follow I want to consider certain problems which immediately arise. In the first place I shall return to the question what it is that we know. We know physical objects, ourselves, and other selves. Is all knowledge a knowledge of particulars? Is knowing to be identified with being acquainted with real, concrete individuals? If it be so identified, what account do we give of the natural sciences which deal with the general? Do we say that these sciences are not knowledge? Is the purpose of the natural sciences to make us familiar with certain abstractions and relations between abstractions, so as to be able in some strange way to handle and, up to a point, to control the existing world of individuals without knowing that world? Or is it ever possible to know, and not merely to think, the general?

In the second place, our knowledge of what is is not unprincipled. In that case we come back to the problem of how we have gained the principles used? We have argued that they are not known by reason *a priori*. What account then shall we give of them? And here it is not the special principles or laws of a specific science, say, the laws of physics or botany, we have in mind but the principles held to be basic to all sciences. I wish to examine in the last two chapters of this book five such principles; in the first the principles or categories of substance and of causality; in the second the principles of identity, non-contradiction, and excluded middle. I shall here face the none too easy task of seeking to explain the use of such principles within the terms of reference of this chapter, that is, without conceding to reason any function other than the one set out in the first paragraph.

X

KNOWLEDGE OF WHAT IS

72. In dealing with illustrative cases of being sure we made the claim that we know what exists. I am sure that I am sitting here, that my friend is sitting opposite me, and that there is a table between us; I am sure that I myself, my friend, and the table exist. It was admitted that being sure is primal knowledge, that one may be in error even though sure; but my recognition of my general fallibility makes no difference to my assurance in these specific cases. I claim to know that I myself, my friend, and the table exist. They are individual things, real things, and not copies or representations of things. They are particulars; each is a substance existing, at least temporally, in its own right and having qualities.

It is now time to look further into these claims. Do I, in fact, know the real (the noumenal) or a representation (the phenomenal)? Is what I know a particular entity and, if it is, what is the status of the general? These are matters to be discussed in this chapter. Related to the discussion are the further discussions of the concepts of substance, entity, and identity in the two chapters which follow.

When I claim to know the existence of something or of some person I then claim to have knowledge of it itself and not of a representation of it that permanently veils it. It is not the case that what I know is phenomenal only and that I never penetrate beyond this phenomenal to what is. I do know what is, though this does not mean that whenever I know that so and so exists I know all there is to know about it. I do not know all there is to know about my friend, but I do know that he exists. I could not say that an object x exists if I knew nothing at all about it, but the assertion of its existence does not presuppose that I have an exhaustive knowledge of its nature.

I am sure of the existence of a table, a particular physical object, having length, breadth, and depth, having a certain weight, and lasting through a certain amount of time. The traditional empiricist sees grounds for doubting the alleged knowledge. David Hume thought the arguments brought forward against claims to know the existence of physical objects were so strong that it was folly to suppose that rational justification of these claims would ever be possible. None the less he is not deeply distressed by this; outside his study his doubts disappear and he takes it for granted, as does the next man, that physical objects do exist. With tongue in cheek he recommends his readers to give up the attempt at rational justification. 'Carelessness and inattention alone can afford us any remedy. For this reason I rely entirely upon them.'[1]

I have tried to show earlier[2] that our plight is not as desperate as Hume makes it out to be in this passage. It is possible to give rational grounds for rejecting traditional empiricism. The fundamental error of such empiricism is to say, or to imply, that we 'began with sensa' and that consequently any knowledge we have of physical objects is indirect. It is just not the case that first the mind is a *tabula rasa*, that, through the senses, so many simple impressions are impressed upon it, for instance, a red colour, a sweet taste, a round shape and so on, and that we put these together to form a complex idea of an apple and have finally to determine, best we can, how the complex idea of apple thus acquired corresponds to the real apple. Less naïve empiricist theories have been put forward which hold that sense-perception consists in awareness of colours, sounds, tastes, etc. by a mind which is a relating, co-ordinating, and unifying agency, very different from a *tabula rasa*. Yet what is finally perceived in sense-perception is still phenomenal, so that the fundamental doubt about the empiricist theory remains. For whether we take the naïve or the more sophisticated view, neither of them bridges the gulf between the sensory phenomenon and the physical object. The dualism persists, and our assurance that non-phenomenal physical objects exist cannot find justification in either theory.

[1] *Treatise*, I. iv. 2, final paragraph.   [2] Chapter IV, above, §§ 34–7.

The truth that needs to be emphasized, as we have seen earlier, is that we do not 'begin with sensa'. From the start of our cognitive experiences we find ourselves in a world of physical objects acting upon us and to which we react. There never is a time when we are aware merely of sensa, after which we deduce the existence of physical objects from them. The question before us is not whether beginning with sensa we can ever prove that physical objects exist, nor whether we can remove the veil that hides the physical world from us, for there is no veil. The real question is the following: Being quite sure that there are physical objects, that we ourselves are physical, and that we affect, and are affected by, other physical objects, are there any philosophic arguments which can now, as we reflect, make us doubt what we are sure of? The arguments would be the ones we considered in Chapter IV, those arising from contradictory appearances, mistaken identification, delayed perception, illusion, hallucination, and the like. What we then found was that our assurance of the existence of physical bodies was not at all shaken by these arguments. And as long as this is true—and nothing has arisen in the development of the argument of this book since Chapter IV to suggest that it is not true—we go on affirming the existence of physical objects and reject scepticism. An additional question may then be asked, namely, how the evidence gained in sense-perception can be used to further our knowledge of the world of physical objects. But this cannot sensibly be asked as long as we remain sceptical about the very existence of these objects.

73. As well as claiming to be sure of the existence of the table, I also claimed to be sure of the existence of myself and of my friend. Does this further assurance survive reflection? It does in respect of one part of the assurance, namely that both myself and my friend exist as physical objects. What has been said about physical objects generally applies here. I am sure that my friend, whom I see and touch, exists as a physical body, and I am sure that I too exist as a physical body. Nothing has arisen to shake this assurance. But of course this is not all. My friend

and I are not mere physical bodies; something more needs to be stated. A minimum was argued for in Chapter IV. In addition to being a physical body I am a being who has experiences which can only be talked of significantly in psi-sentences, a term whose use was explained. So too my friend is a visible and tangible, public, physical object, who also has experiences which can only be talked of significantly in psi-sentences.

Now I cannot doubt my own existence, and it would be paradoxical to say that I can. *Dubito ergo sum.* Further, how could anyone else without contradicting himself claim to be putting before me for my approval arguments to show that I do not exist? Yet, I can be deceived as to what I am, and since this is so do I really know that *I* am, for the term 'I' may be used by me ambiguously even though I take it at the moment to be free from ambiguity? I claim that I exist as a perceptible body. Having subjected this claim to re-examination I continue to be sure that these hands and feet and the rest of my body exist, just as I am sure, in spite of the sceptics, that other bodies exist. But the existence I am sure of is not merely physical, I am sure that I exist as a willing, feeling, thinking being, that is to say, as a conscious being. I am both the physical and the conscious object. It is sometimes said, or assumed, that the conscious entity is the more 'real' I. This would be to assume that there are two I's, a mind–body dualism; one might even be assuming a dualism of physical substance and mental substance. But I do not claim that what I am sure of is a dualism of this kind. I am one; one body, but an animated body and (if this is more) a conscious, animated body.

Yet what is it to be a conscious, animated body? We have spoken of a minimum answer in terms of a physical body having experiences which can only be described in psi-sentences. Now, in view of our discussions of thinking it would seem clear that this minimum must be expanded at least to contain within it the notion of a unity through time. I am a being who continues to be through a period of time, for it is a condition of my present thinking and my present recognition of objects and situations that I remember my own past experience. Certainly I must continue to exist through the period in which I build up a thought-system, or through the period in which I retain a piece of knowledge to use it later to test my thought; I continue to exist through this period as retaining, recalling, and recognizing. I am now sure that this is so, that I existed in the past and that I had these experiences, and that I now remember myself having the experiences.

Kant speaks here of a 'unity of apperception' presupposed in all experience, and finds in 'pure apperception' the permanent and abiding I (*das stehende und bleibende Ich*).[1] For Kant, however, this is not an entity of which we are directly conscious; we are directly conscious of our empirical selves, we are conscious of our pains, our strivings, and our reflections, but we are not conscious of this abiding I which is the condition of consciousness. Yet it must exist; in thought we see it to be inevitable. This position, it seems to me, is a difficult one to sustain. I am conscious of my empirical self, but do not know my permanent self which I nevertheless affirm to exist. Indeed such a position can be sustained only in so far as one accepts Kant's strong representationalism, which enables him to regard the self one is conscious of as a representation, an appearance only, and consequently not the abiding self, the self as one is. He is thus enabled to make the puzzling remark: 'I have no *knowledge* of myself as I am, but merely as I appear to myself.'[2] There are for him three elements in the situation: first, the physical body in space; second, the introspectible self, a bundle of experiences; and third the 'I as I am', the real self, whose existence is *thought* but not known and whose nature remains a mystery.

This unknown I is the subject of considerable later philosophic speculation and proved useful as well to Romantic writers. Jean Paul in his *Titan* has a character who asks: 'Here sits a man and I am in him, but who is it?' Obviously no

---

[1] *Critique of Pure Reason*, A 123.
[2] *Critique of Pure Reason*, B 158. 'Ich habe also demnach keine *Erkenntniss* von mir wie ich bin, sondern bloss wie ich mir selbst erscheine.'

answer is expected, for the mystery is too deep. In Kant's philosophy there is the partial answer, that the real but hidden I must be there to account for experience and to provide the necessary unity of apperception. One may agree with Kant in acknowledging the need for a unity of apperception, but does this necessitate a hidden unknowable self, which turns out to be the real self? I extend the minimum theory of the self put forward in Chapter IV to cover unity of apperception; but no more is requisite for this purpose than the perception of my physical body in space together with the consciousness of myself as continuing through time and as experiencing experiences which are spoken of in psi-sentences. Any account of the existing self in terms of body alone is inadequate. It is admittedly possible to know a good deal about a person by observing his behaviour; it none the less remains true that I may be conscious of experiences which are never revealed to others in any bodily behaviour of mine, not even in speaking of them.

I am conscious of a self, which is physical, but also a unity that can be talked of adequately only if psi-sentences are used as well as sentences describing physical bodies, and I am conscious of it as continuing through time. I (and others) are aware of the continuance of my body through time, just as I (and others) are aware that this table was here yesterday and has been here for many years. But I am also aware of myself as an abiding consciousness. I remember enjoying a walk yesterday. My memory is of myself walking on the sea-front, it is a memory of my body and the physical environment at the time, but I also remember the pleasure which I had. What is important, however, for our present argument is that I remember all this as something that happened to me. It was I, who am here now (and not merely my body), who was there yesterday. One is conscious, that is to say, not solely of an immediately present self, but of a self continuing in time. My experiences it is true are a succession, but I am conscious not only of them as successive experiences but also of myself as the one who experienced them all. Since this is so it is not necessary to accept Kant's unknown self as the only self that can give unity of apperception. If it be said that there is no permanence in the passing, ephemeral experiences of the mind and so no possibility of finding the requisite unity of apperception there, it may be replied that what we are conscious of is not a series of experiences, but a self which is a physical body lasting through time, but which also has experiences of which it is conscious and conscious of as its own. It could even be said that the permanence of the body provides a basis for the unity of apperception, but not in any merely materialist sense for this is a body which has experiences, including the experience of being a self lasting through time.

Thus I may continue to be sure that I exist as a physical body having experiences that can be described only in psi-sentences. And we can now add that this means being sure that I exist not momentarily but as an abiding self. This is still a minimum. It is obvious that a good deal more needs to be said about this self. More needs to be said about the inner experiences. The world of inner experience is a private world which no one can enter but the person himself. Other persons understand my descriptions of my state and I theirs. In this sense the experience ceases to be wholly private and becomes something that can be talked about publicly; within limits, too, I can talk sensibly of what I have not myself experienced. But this does not mean that I can feel another's pain or another's joy. There remains the private world and this is a very real world. When I claim existence for myself I claim it not just for my body but for my self, the conscious being, to whom the world appears, who knows joy and sorrow, who strives to attain his ends, who believes, doubts, and judges, who is sure or not sure. It is he, both body and mind, who exists.

Finally, my friend also exists, I see him this moment and I have certainly as much reason for supposing that he exists as I have for supposing that the table exists. I have perceptual assurance of both. But in my friend's case I also know that he too has inner experiences as I have, that he is more than body. He has spoken to me of his experiences and I understand him. Further a certain sympathy on my part may deepen my awareness of his inner life. My feeling of the privacy of my own inner life, strong as it is, is not strong enough to lead me to suppose that I alone have such experiences and to make me a solipsist. I am sure, and have evidence that I find totally convincing, that my friend and the table exist not merely as experiences of mine, but independently of my experiencing them, and I am also sure that my friend has inner experiences and is no mere physical body. This does not mean that I know all there is to know about the nature of a physical body, of another person, and even of myself, but I have primal knowledge of this difference between being a mere physical body and being a body that at the same time has consciousness and inner experience. This is involved in saying that I have primal knowledge of the existence of the table, of my friend, and of myself.

74. The table is a particular object, so is my friend, and so am I. I am sure that these three particulars exist, three of a very large number of particulars existing in the world. What else exists? Does the general exist? Most of our thinking has to do with the general rather than with the particular. But is the general a part of the world that exists, and can it be known as part of that world? If the empiricist doctrine were true that only particulars exist, would it mean that our thinking about the general could never be a thinking about what exists, could never, as the phrase goes, have ontological relevance? A knowledge of some sort might be gained in thinking the general, but not knowledge of what is. Here is a source of scepticism about human thinking; thinking is general and abstract and so not applicable to the real world.

There have been philosophical schools—the schools of Bergson and of Croce come to mind—that tended to favour the view that abstract, general thinking, though of great use in the world, does not provide us with knowledge of what exists. We gain knowledge of existence in the intuition of the concrete particular, but thinking, and especially scientific thinking, is an activity intended not so much for knowing that which exists but rather for handling it. Science is a techique for living, whereas intuition is knowledge of the world as it is. This kind of doctrine, though it has its adherents, is not widely held today, and its method of dealing with the problem of the particular and the general is not one that can be accepted. If science provides the means to deal effectively with the world it does so because it illuminates the world and gives us understanding. Yet it cannot be denied that the concern of science is primarily with the general.

It seems necessary to probe more deeply into this distinction between particular and general. Where does the distinction originate? It is worth noting that no one has claimed that knowledge of this distinction is *a priori*. The distinction between one and many is connected with that between particular and general, and so is the distinction between substance and attribute, and these have been held to be known *a priori*. But the distinction between the particular and the general is not claimed to be so known. This may be due to its vagueness. Not all the principles which are claimed to be known *a priori* are entirely free from vagueness, but this distinction between the particular and the general is very vague, and not the sort of distinction we should expect to be known *a priori*, especially if *a priori* knowledge be interpreted here to be the infallible and clear knowlege of pure reason.

How then has the distinction originated in our minds? Of the two concepts it is the particular which seems to be the clearer and more positive, though this concept is not entirely clear nor entirely positive. As Aristotle remarked, there is something elusive in the particular existence, no totality of attributes that we can think of as applying to it can exhaust its nature. Hence the demand for a direct acquaintance or intuition of it, since no description of it will be adequate. In the case of physical objects the intuition in question may be basically a sensory intuition. Thus the cricket-ball that I grip in my hand is felt to be a solid entity, a particular. The Matterhorn seen from Zermatt stands out; it certainly exists. (It is of interest here that the word 'exists' is connected etymologically with *ex+sistere* and so with *stare*. What exists is what stands out.) In a secondary sense we are prepared to say too that a figure in a portrait exists, that Mona Lisa exists, and so does the mirror-image, for, though its outlines perhaps are not so well defined, it is there. Further I now remember particular objects that no longer exist, the house destroyed in the War, the old elm tree that was burnt, and my friend who died. They stand out in my memory. Experiences of this kind help to explain our consciousness of the existence of particular objects. Other experiences of the ways in which these entities affect and are affected by the world around them, and of how they react to the stimulation of other particular entities, strengthen our awareness. Nor should it be forgotten that each person is aware of himself as a particular entity, whatever be the final analysis of this awareness.

Now granted that the particular in these varied senses exists, what are we to say about the existence, or non-existence, of the general? Does it make sense to ask whether the general exists? If we ask the question are we involved in some category mistake that makes the question nonsensical? It may be suggested that we indeed are so involved and that we fall into error in taking it for granted that the same questions can be asked about the general as can be asked about the particular. There is no 'general' in the sense in which there is a particular. When we speak of what is general, it may be said, the existences we speak of are still particulars, but we now speak of them in a general way. This, however, is a theory which is not yet examined and it cannot be assumed to be true. Can the whole class of alleged general objects be so easily dismissed as a class of non-existents? And what is meant by speaking of a particular (or particulars) existing in a general way?

75. An example may be considered. We are sure that the particular mountain, the Matterhorn, exists. What of mountain in general? Does it exist in any sense? It has been suggested that it exists as a generic image. We have already admitted that a mirror-image may be said to exist. Can existence be ascribed

to the generic image, mountain in general? It would be an existence retained when one has seen many mountains and has, as it were, run them together and forgotten the detailed differences. The clear lines of the particular mountain are lost and what remains is shadowy and nebulous. In addition, what remains (if we are justified in speaking in this way) can only remain subjectively, that is to say, not independently of the mind, and is in this respect, we suppose, different from the particular existent, even from the mirror-image, which (so we suppose) is out there independently of the mind. In a word, we are assuming that there exist images 'in the mind', a thesis not yet proved, and that the generic image is one instance of such images.

Now it may be that when I think of mountain in general and speak of a mountain, without having any particular mountain in mind, I have an experience which may be described as having a generic image of mountain. If the image were less vague than it is, then possibly it would be worth asking whether the image itself is not a particular used in a general capacity. But it is so vague that such a suggestion could not profit the discussion. In any case, even though it may be necessary to admit that we do experience such generic images as these and may have one in mind when using the general word 'mountain', yet it is not the case that whenever we use this general word we then experience the generic image. Most often, in using the word in speech, no experience of a generic image accompanies it.

Another suggestion is that mountain in general *exists* as a concept. There may be some vague imaginative elements in one's consciousness of mountain in general, but essentially it is an experience of having a concept, that is to say, the concept of mountain. Mountain in general is one with the concept of mountain, and it exists as an object of conceiving, being internal to the mind. Concepts must exist, it is said, since conceiving must have objects. Mountain in general is no particular mountain but exists as an ideal object. There is, however, one immediate objection to this theory, namely that in introspection we are not conscious of any such objects. But, in spite of this, many arguments have been put forward in support of their existence, though it is highly doubtful whether the case for them is proved.[1] The classical empiricist theory of the concept inevitably finds difficulty in linking ideal concepts with particular objects. On this theory concepts are our own creation, though in creating we may follow the suggestion of nature. To a certain extent concepts can be representationalist, but we are free to create them as we choose. The material from which we frame them consists largely of abstractions out of what is experienced and this, it is claimed, to a limited degree, does link the conceptual with what is experienced, though the link is weak. In such a situation, however, it is particularly difficult to defend the view that conceiving the conceptual is a means of extending one's knowledge of what exists.

An alternative to the conceptualist account is the nominalist. In its extreme form, resting on the philosophy that particulars only exist, nominalism holds that the general exists as a word but in no other sense. There are real mountains, but the general word 'mountain' is not the name of anything; it is not the name of a real mountain in general, for there exists no such entity, nor is it the name of a concept. It is not designative. Particular objects exist but the general does not exist and this means that classes, qualities, and relations do not exist. General words are solely a linguistic convention enabling us to speak and think of our world.

I attempt here no complete analysis of conceptualism and nominalism, but merely wish to bring out the point that these doctrines certainly do not make it easier to understand how verbal thinking can be relevant to the real world. They have, in fact, bred scepticism—though they are not for that reason false. Yet it is natural for epistemologists to look for theories which do not end in scepticism as these tend to do. We may now consider briefly two such theories, which if true would give thinking, though it be general, a genuine ontological relevance.

---

[1] Some of these arguments have been listed and examined in my *Theory of Universals*, 2nd end., pp. 201 ff., and I need not repeat them here.

On the one hand it is argued that a better understanding of the phenomenon of language may modify the degree of scepticism. It cannot be denied that language is conventional, yet this does not necessarily mean that the principles on which it proceeds are chosen arbitrarily. These principles are in any case not chosen by the individual speaker, as we have seen, and are not subjective in that sense. They are chosen—if 'chosen' is the right word—by the people who use the language. Nor did the people choose the principles arbitrarily. Language emerged out of the interaction of the millions of people who brought it into being and out of their need for communication, but it arose too out of the interaction of these people with their world. If language is to be regarded as an instrument, it is one forged with a view to the requirements and needs of those who forged it in the world in which they found themselves. It ought to follow that to a certain extent a language shows what the people who use it experienced and learnt of their world. Further, one might expect some correlation between the language and the world, even possibly in the sense that the syntactical rules of the language regulating the use of general words would be correlated, to some degree, with the principles of the world. If this were the case then the successful use of language would involve *ipso facto* a measure of understanding of the world talked about, and the use of language would itself keep the user in touch with the principles of the world.

This is an interesting argument, that a speaker acquires in the very use of general words some knowledge of the fundamental nature of the real world, since the language itself stores up a sense of the structure of what exists. Yet if this argument were correct should we not expect to find much closer agreement between the syntactical principles of different languages than does obtain amongst them? Speaking generally, the conditions which have met the human race have not varied profoundly and, if this hypothesis of a correlation were true, the syntactical principles of the different languages (particularly those of peoples who have lived in close proximity) should correspond closely to one another, reflecting the experience of one and the same world. Yet linguists, as we have seen, would be unhappy with such a doctrine, for the syntactical principles of languages used by neighbouring peoples may vary considerably and do not show the uniformity that the argument would require. Accordingly it would be unwise to take it for granted that syntax can in some way provide clues to the nature of the real world; at most the syntactical principles of a language might possibly throw light on what the people who used that language assume the structure of the existing world to be. But there is no safe ground here for supposing that a successful use of language keeps us in touch with the real world, that is to say, that principles of syntax are closely correlated with principles of being.

The second of the two arguments has little to do with language, but arises from the belief that the representationalism of empiricism, and the abstract character of that which is thought, together necessitate a drastic modification of our views on knowledge. Mere thinking must be shown to be capable of establishing truth of itself. The mind knows *a priori* the final principles that determine the nature of what exists, and thinking which proceeds strictly in accordance with the principles so provided must lead to an extension of our knowledge of the real. If, for instance, we begin with the admittedly inadequate and sometimes contradictory experience of the world gained through sense-experience, and if we see to it that our thought upon the sensory phenomena is throughout dominated by the principles we know, then some part of the truth about what exists will always emerge. Since the *a priori* principles regulating rational thought are principles of being, then thinking, determined solely in its procedure by the demand for complete consistency with its own internal principles, must extend our knowledge of the existing world. Particular things are to be understood in the light of the general scheme; their particularity is relative only, for they finally fit into the scheme of the whole. In this way the human mind can by thinking alone establish what exists, that is to say, secure universal and necessary knowledge of what must be.

This is an exhilarating prospect, but there are many difficulties in the theory. I shall merely mention four of these to
explain why this line of argument is not followed further here.
First, is there adequate assurance that the particulars will lend
themselves to the scheme? Second, the thinking is abstract
throughout. How can we through such thinking come to know
what is not abstract? Thirdly, strict adherence to the principles
would enable us to set up a valid thought-system. But we have
seen that such valid thought-systems may well have no reference
whatsoever to what exists; they need not apply. It is not clear
what element in this theory makes possible the application of
thought to what exists, enabling us in this case to ignore the
distinction between thinking and knowing. Finally, the whole
argument rests on the supposition that we do have exact knowledge of the principles of being. Even if we did, it would be
doubtful whether further knowledge of being could be gained
by thinking alone. But can we accept the above supposition?
This is a matter that will concern us in the next two chapters.

76. The arguments just considered do not relieve us of the
anxiety that in thinking the general we lose touch with the
existing world. Our doubt is not allayed by the argument that
to think verbally is inevitably to be guided by syntactical
principles which are linked with the structure of things, or the
further argument that rational thinking can of itself reveal
what is real, since what is real is rational. The doubt does not
affect the recognition of the value of the logical thought-
system, nor of the value of the study of the latter's structure,
and this study is equally worth while even if no application of
the system to the existing world is possible. It is simply a doubt
about the relevance of abstract general thought to our knowledge
of the existing world. None the less, before we sink into complete scepticism, certain further points need to be considered
which may lessen the scepticism, even if some part of it
will still remain.

Nominalist accounts of the general, though they may
facilitate the task of the logical analyst, drive the epistemologist

to despair, and though classical conceptualism may appear to provide links between the concept and what exists these turn out to be weak. But nominalist and conceptualist doctrines are, in my opinion, suspect in themselves quite apart from their effect on epistemological problems. A modified realism, I believe, gives a more successful account of the use of general words, and at the same time provides the epistemologist with better foundations upon which to build. We may here examine this alternative theory.

First, we note it challenges the over-facile pairing of the particular with the concrete and the general with the abstract. It challenges too the assumption that the particular is substantival and that the general is either an attribute of a particular or a relation between particulars, and consequently that substance is always concrete and attribute and relation are always abstract. This presupposes that the distinction between concrete and abstract is clearly determined, is fixed, and is wholly free from ambiguity. But this in fact is not so. The distinction is ambiguous. For the purposes of the present argument I shall confine myself to two ways in which it is used, first, to mark the difference between a whole and something abstracted from a whole, and, secondly, to mark the difference between what exists and what is thought only but does not exist.

Thus we may in the first instance mean by the abstract some part of the whole which is abstracted or singled out, singled out by the mind for possibly closer study. The mind concentrates on this part of the whole. But what is so abstracted is still a part of an existent and is still concrete, since the part is as concrete as the whole. If a zoologist concentrates on a particular frog's leg rather than on the whole frog he is still studying what concretely exists, although he also abstracts. If we grant this we should grant the next point, namely, that if one concentrates on the colour of this rose one is still concerned with the concrete. Yet if this be granted then the thesis that the concrete is always the particular individual thing and that the quality is always abstract is shaken. Further, what applies to a quality applies to a relation. Consider an individual object A that has the quality q and is related in a certain way r to another object. I concentrate on q and q is, in this sense, abstracted; in the same sense r may be an abstraction. But this does not justify the view that A is concrete in contrast to q and r which are abstract. For though abstract in one sense q and r are concrete in another. The assumption, therefore, should not be made that q and r are abstract in a sense which does not permit them to be concrete whereas A is concrete in a sense that does not permit it to be abstract. Indeed I can concentrate on A amongst all these objects before me, and, if I do so, A is an abstraction too though it is still concrete. A, q, and r can be all abstract and at the same time all concrete.

But then, it will be argued, in the other sense of the contrast between concrete and abstract we cannot handle A, q, and r in this way. A is always concrete, q and r are always abstract. A is thought and it exists, q and r are thought only. Suppose we grant that the red of the rose is as concrete as the rose itself—incidentally, this is not to say that it is as particular as the rose—the quality red, which we ascribe to this rose, is none the less not concrete. The reason for this, it will be said, is that it is general or universal, this same quality belongs to this rose and to that rose. Therefore, it is argued, it cannot be concrete. When I say 'This rose is red' the subject-term 'this rose' refers to the rose, but '. . . is red' does not refer to anything; it is the predicating expression. As has been seen, the use of this expression can be interpreted in nominalist or in conceptual terms. We know how to use the phrase '. . . is red' in predication, or again we have the concept of being red and this enables us to ascribe redness to the rose, so that the listener (who also has the concept) will understand. In neither case do we recognize a concrete quality, but we either use a locution '. . . is red' which we know to be appropriate for communicating what we now wish to communicate, or we convey linguistically the appropriate concept-term by which to determine the subject.

The reader may find this somewhat mystifying, and taken on their face value these accounts of the general are mystifying. What precisely are we seeking to communicate about the rose, and why should it ever apply? Now the fact of the matter is that much is presupposed by nominalists and conceptualists, which if taken into account at this point makes their doctrines somewhat easier to understand. First, predication is possible within a system of thought which has no reference whatsoever to an existing world. Secondly, when on the other hand we consciously predicate a quality of something we know to exist, for instance of this rose, then to a certain extent we do depend upon past experience of the existing world; not that, on these theories, we find the general quality itself in experience, but we find resemblances there. We get used to these resemblances and qualify in terms of them. This shows, the conceptualist would say, that we already have concepts, though possibly rather rudimentary concepts; or, if we do not wish to speak of concepts, it shows, says the nominalist, that we have learnt how to link certain of the words of the language we use with these experiences of resemblances.

Resemblances observed then suggest certain lines of thinking and speaking, that is to say certain procedures, which are not entirely unrelated to the world we want to understand. This does give some ground for supposing that our thinking can be relevant to the existing world, and no doubt conceptualists in particular have found in this supposition a source of comfort, since apparently their conceiving is to some extent suggested by their experience of the world. Yet the comfort cannot be great when they reflect on the looseness of the resemblances on the observation of which their concepts partially rest, and on the freedom they possess to frame their concepts as they choose.

But now whilst much of our thinking is in one way or another the outcome of consciously observing resemblances or of becoming familiar with them over a long period, this is not the whole of the story. It has been argued above that the colour seen is as concrete as the thing which is coloured. The point has now to be made that this colour, thus concrete, recurs. Identically the same colour recurs, and we are conscious that it is identically the same. One and the same shade of colour is here *and* there. This means that we experience qualities which are concrete and yet general. The general ultramarine, a specific shade of blue, is the very colour which I now observe. In other words, the particular individual has no corner in concreteness; the general or universal quality may also be concrete in this sense that it is what exists, though as a quality only. This is realism. Where realism holds that all universals are of this order it errs. But in a limited sense it asserts a truth of considerable importance for the epistemologist. The thinker may think of the general and still be thinking concretely; his thought at this point may be decidedly relevant to what exists.

What holds for qualities holds also for relations. I am aware of these relations. For instance, I am sure that my friend, myself, and the table exist, but I am equally sure that my friend is on that side of the table and I am on this. I know this spatial relationship as well as the individual entities. This does not mean that the final questions about the nature of space are answered, any more than the final questions about my friend's existence, or my own, or again about the existence of a table as a physical object. But I do know that my friend is there on the other side of the table. What we are sure of is not isolated individual persons or things but individuals in relation with one another. Furthermore, just as the quality ultramarine can be here and there simultaneously so too can the same relation be in many places simultaneously. As is the case with qualities so with relations; they are concrete but they are at the same time general. Thus we may say of certain qualities and relations that they do not differ from things or individuals in being always abstract, whereas the things are concrete; they differ rather in that a thing is in one place at one time, whereas one and the same quality or one and the same relation can be in many places at the same time.

This seems to be a truer account of the situation than that given by nominalist, conceptualist, and traditional realist, and is to be accepted on this ground solely. But it is also a far healthier starting-point for the study of our knowledge of the existing world. Some starting-points are such as apparently to make thinking irrelevant at the outset in our attempts to know the world. But it is not so with this starting-point. Thinking is verbal but not merely verbal; nor is it a study of abstract concepts, only vaguely linked with what is. Rational thinking is bringing the knowledge we already possess, and which is retained in the mind, to bear on the present problem. This knowledge, which may be to a great part dispositional, prepares us beforehand for the new situation, as Hume explained; the experience of the past is conceptually available, frequently 'not really and in fact present to the mind, but only in power'. It may be questioned whether the full significance of Hume's teaching on the concept has been completely grasped by us. Emphasis has been mainly on the theory's propensity basis, but possibly the most significant feature in Hume's account is, not so much the role of dispositions in conceiving, but rather that of the mind's retentiveness. Having a concept is a species of mental retention which enables us to behave in certain ways; for instance, it enables us to use language. It is retaining in association a web of empirical and linguistic material, retaining it for the most part dispositionally, but always in such a way that something seen or heard can revive what is so retained; in particular, hearing a verbal expression or seeing a written word or phrase revives the relevant capacities.

Not everything in Hume's teaching on the concept is acceptable to us today and perhaps he over-emphasized the importance of the dispositional or propensity element, but the general outlines of his teaching are sound, particularly if we now acknowledge its stress on retention. Needless to say this is an element of considerable significance for epistemology and we emphasize it now in dealing with the problem of this chapter, namely, that of the applicability of thought to the world. The classical conceptualist theory, for which thinking was an activity concerned with concepts as internal objects, did not wholly remove the scepticism bred by nominalism in its various forms. But the position is different when conceiving is viewed as in part the reviving of what is retained of past experience, and when it is further understood that, though most of what is retained is general, this need not signify that thinking is out of touch with what exists. For we have now seen that the experience of qualities and relations can itself be an experience of the concrete. Hence the thinker when thinking is not inevitably cut off from the existing world; he does not then lack all points of contact with that world. On the contrary, he carries the points of contact with him, so that in this sense his thinking is throughout in touch with the world.

This is not to say that his thinking is wholly determined by what is retained of experience, ultimately by the nature of what is. The thinker's own spontaneous speculation must not be forgotten. We have stressed earlier his independence, his power of withdrawal, his ability to innovate and to experiment; and what is now said in no way contradicts what was said then. But it is also true that though there is withdrawal, the knowledge already gained is retained and remains a factor, frequently dispositional, in the thinker's guidance and control of his thought. The thinker speculates freely about possibilities and is free to consider even what is inconsistent with his experience and knowledge; but for the most part he tends to rest his speculation about the possible on what he has learnt of the actual. And this we think is rational procedure, the point at which man's rationality is well revealed.

What man has learnt is that the actual world is patterned—at least it is patterned in this sense that there are resemblances and, even more, that the same recurs. It is a world that lends itself to grouping and classifying, and not a world of bare particulars. It accordingly invites the use of general words in speaking and thinking of it. Because the thinking is in general terms it is not on that account irrelevant to the existing world. We may safely reject the extreme sceptical view that by thinking man can never help himself to extend his knowledge of what is.

XI

THE FRAMEWORK OF CONCEPTUAL THINKING: SUBSTANCE AND CAUSALITY

77. The fact that conceptual thinking is predominantly in general terms does not make extension of our knowledge of the existing world through such thinking impossible. Let us now consider a further question, namely, the nature of, and our knowledge of, the framework within which we think. This framework is to be conceived in terms of its linguistic, logical, and categorial elements. We have already examined the manner in which linguistic considerations affect thought. Since thinking is, for the most part, verbal and carried forward in a specific language, the syntax of that language must be regarded as part of the framework within which the thinking occurs. It is a comparatively permanent element within the framework, although, as we have seen, language is not static but changes syntactically and semantically over the years, for the meanings of expressions and locutions change as well as the syntax. Still, the language is permanent enough to enable those who use it to communicate with one another, and it is always the shared language which is used by the individual in his thinking, and this fact, needless to say, influences his thinking. In addition to these linguistic factors there are logical factors which, so we assume, are wholly permanent and do not change. The sentences or statements we use in thinking are affirmative or negative. They say something of all, of some, or of one. They may be predicating a property of a subject; they may state the relation between two or more subjects; they may place something in a class; they may place one class in another class; they may relate classes. Further, the development of our

thought, if it is exact, will proceed by way of logically permissible relationships between statements, namely, implication, alternation, disjunction, equivalence, independence, and conjunction (always assuming that 'p and q' is one statement and not two, for this assumption has been denied[1]). We think within this logical framework.

But other factors are at work in determining the framework of our thought in addition to the linguistic and the logical. What we take to be pervasive features of the world are just such factors. We take the empirical world to be a spatial world and a world in time. We assume too that anything whatsoever that can be thought about must possess features which are pervasive and universal, and must be thought in terms of these features if they are to be thought at all. Plato in the *Sophist*, discussing these features under the heading 'the greatest of the kinds' ($\mu\acute{\epsilon}\gamma\iota\sigma\tau\alpha\ \tau\hat{\omega}\nu\ \gamma\epsilon\nu\hat{\omega}\nu$),[2] names three 'kinds'. Whatever is thought about, he holds, is thought about as existing (or not existing), secondly, as in motion or at rest, thirdly, as different from something else and the same as itself. We may use this passage as a helpful clue. Thought has to do with existence or non-existence. Whatever exists is in motion or at rest. Whatever exists is different from anything else and the same as itself. For the purposes which follow I link the concept of existence or being with that of substance. Secondly, I link being in motion or at rest with change and with bringing about change, that is to say, with causation. Thirdly, there is difference and identity. I shall assume that these three are indeed fundamental categorial features without attempting to adjudicate on the question whether they are, or are not, the 'greatest of the kinds'. I shall deal with substance and cause in this chapter and with identity in the next.

78. To what extent is it true that the concepts of substance and cause form part of the framework within which the world

---

[1] For instance by J. S. Mill, *System of Logic*, I. iv. 3: '. . . we might as well call a street a complex house.'

[2] *Sophist*, 254 b–d.

is conceived by us? What is the source, or what are the sources, of our knowledge of substance and cause? These are the questions immediately before us.

To begin with substance. We think of the world as existing or being; but if no more is said this concept is empty. It is a concept of 'first being' in Aristotle's sense, we know that it is but not what it is. To say anything about it would be to attribute features to it, and this involves thinking of it as substance having attributes. To think significantly about the world on this view is to think of it in terms of substance and attribute. We may adopt a monist or a pluralist view of the world. If the former then the world itself is a substance; if the latter, the world consists of a number of individual things each of which is a substance. If we adopt the pluralist view we may still speak of substance in general, but the concept then is an abstraction and it is not necessary to suppose that the world is one substance. In the same way if we speak of the world as itself a substance it may still be possible to think, with Spinoza, of determinations within the one substance enabling us to speak of many individual substances, though such talk would be loose and lacking metaphysical precision.

It is clear that the conception of substance is part of the framework of our daily conceptual thinking about the real world. It is obvious too that the substances we think about at first are the finite things existing around us, and that we regard ourselves as substances. It is true that we early think of the whole world as one, as a universe; but we do not normally at this stage think of it as one substance or ask how a one-substance world is also a pluralistic world containing a vast number of substances. A substance we assume at this stage is a concrete individual thing, which has certain qualities. These qualities may change though the substance continues to exist, and in that sense the substance is not dependent on the qualities but is independent of them. They exist only as qualities of the substance and are dependent on the substances of which they are qualities. Substances are independent and have a certain permanence, in spite of the changes which may occur in their qualities and in their relations to other substances. They themselves, we assume, can bring about changes.

Such is the manner in which we tend to think of the world around us and this account of substance is roughly the account that Aristotle gives of it. Substance is 'that which is not asserted of a subject but of which everything else is asserted'. It is that which has qualities and relations; is independent; is a continuant in spite of changes within it and around it. Aristotle gets into difficulties when he tries to develop his doctrine, as when in Book Z of the *Metaphysics* he discusses the question what is the substance other than its qualities, that is to say, what is its matter, and thinks it then necessary to distinguish matter from form, looking to those properties which can be said to be essential to a substance to explain its form. But, speaking generally, Aristotle in his account of substance merely makes explicit what men normally take for granted.

How men acquire this fundamental concept of substance Aristotle does not consider. He takes it to be self-evident that they do so. Aristotle in other contexts talks of necessary knowledge; for instance, he thinks deductive inference is necessary, and he holds that prior to inference we know principles used in inference and know them as holding necessarily and universally. But he does not speak of our knowledge of substance or any of the other of his categories in this way. He simply finds himself, and finds others, thinking in terms of these categories. He certainly makes no claim to an *a priori* knowledge which dictates the form of experience.

The view that we have *a priori* knowledge of being, motion and rest, and difference (which, however, are not to be thought of as Aristotelian categories) could find greater support in Plato, particularly in the passages in the *Sophist* to which we have referred. In the discussion of the science of dialectic in that dialogue it is held that we possess knowledge of these kinds, now expressly declared to be Forms.[1] In the *Republic* Forms are said to be known by reason and our knowledge of them is said to be certain and infallible, in contrast to the

[1] *Sophist* 254 c.

fallibility of sense-perception. Here, undoubtedly is an archetype of the subsequent rationalist doctrine that such features of the real world as these are known by pure reason independently of empirical evidence, that is to say, of the evidence of the senses.

In modern times the champion of the rationalist view is Kant. He writes in reaction to the doctrine of the empiricists. Locke 'bantered' (to use Berkeley's word) the concept of substance and Hume that of cause. They argued that these concepts were not the clear and distinct ideas known by reason which the rationalist had supposed them to be. Kant acknowledges the *naïveté* of the 'dogmatic' rationalists, but none the less is dissatisfied with the empiricist account of knowledge. His main reason is plain, it is one that he shares with Leibniz. Though our knowledge begins with experience it does not follow that it all arises out of experience. He speaks of experience here in traditional empiricist terms, as the *anschauung* of the sensory manifold, that is to say of 'perceptions' or 'ideas' which pass before the mind. Such sensory intuition is needed in human knowledge, but because its information is wholly contingent it lacks the basis of order and regularity which makes prediction possible. Yet we find, even at pre-scientific levels, that men know what to expect and know how to predict. To some extent their world is a law-governed world. Consequently, though the order is not grasped as part of the sensory manifold, we must suppose that they are conscious of it; experience itself must be more than the mere reception of the sensory manifold. The manifold must be ordered by principles, by 'categories', meaning for Kant 'pure concepts of the understanding which apply *a priori* to objects of intuition in general'.[1] These give our knowledge such elements of necessity and universality as it contains, and these are features which, as we realize, cannot be found in the contingent sensory manifold but must have been introduced into it.

We may consider specifically Kant's treatment of substance. In the First Analogy[2] he puts forward a proof of 'the principle

[1] *Critique of Pure Reason*, A 79, B 105.   [2] A 182, B 224 ff.

of permanence of substance'. It will be seen that he fastens on one feature of the traditional doctrine of substance, namely permanence,[1] and attempts to show that human knowledge is impossible unless this principle is introduced. Here is one of three principles requisite to secure that necessary unity of apperception which 'lies *a priori* at the foundation of empirical consciousness'. He sets out the principle of permanence of substance in the second edition in these terms: 'In all change of appearances substance is permanent', to which he adds: 'Its quantum in nature is neither increased nor diminished.' We may concentrate on the first part of the principle. Its proof lies in pointing out that all appearances are in time, and changes in appearance are apprehended and thought in time. But time is not itself perceived, so there must be 'in the objects of perception' some permanent object 'which represents time in general'. So even to determine the temporal character of the sensory manifold appearing before us, to determine whether it is coexistent or successive, this concept of a permanent is essential. 'Our *apprehension* of the manifold of appearance is always successive, and is therefore always changing. Through it alone we can never determine whether this manifold, as object of experience, is coexistent or successive. For such determination we require an underlying ground which exists *at all times*, that is something *abiding* and *permanent*, of which all change and coexistence are only so many ways (modes of time) in which the permanent exists.'[2]

Kant's argument in this section moves from thinking of permanence to the thought of permanent matter and of a substrate in the traditional sense. The argument, however, is then complicated by the fact that he proceeds to speak of 'substances' rather than of the one permanent substance, as when he says that what is needed to determine change in time is 'to connect the coming to be with things which previously existed and which persist in existence up to the moment of this

[1] In A 182 the principle is spoken of as the 'Principle of Permanence' only, the words 'of Substance' being added in the second edition.
[2] A 182, B 225.

coming to be'.[1] Thus the argument is not after all one to establish an absolute permanent as an underlying ground necessary for the unity of apperception, since the relative permanence provided by different substances will do.

But the main difficulty with the argument of the First Analogy is that it does not prove what we expect Kant to prove, namely that substance is 'a pure concept of the understanding which applies *a priori* to objects of intuition'. The substrate which is permanent is found 'in the objects of perception', that is, in the appearances; we may grant that 'without the permanent there is no time relation',[2] but if the permanence we know belongs to substances in the phenomenal world it makes it easier at least to consider some alternative to the theory that the concept of substance is derived *a priori*. If we grant for the time being that the conception of permanent substance is necessary for the unity of experience, Kant still does not show in the argument of the First Analogy that it follows that this conception can only find its source in pure reason and is *a priori*. He may not have thought it necessary to prove this in the First Analogy, possibly assuming that he had established that point earlier, but this too, as we shall see, is doubtful.

In the meantime it should be reaffirmed that there are other features in the traditional concept of substance along with permanence. For instance, a substance is that which has its own independent existence. This is implicit no doubt in Kant's account of substance, but it is not made explicit. Yet it is central to other philosophies of substance—leading Spinoza, for instance, to conclude that one and one only substance can exist, namely 'God or Reality', or Leibniz to teach that each monad is a substance; whilst David Hume, preferring the psychological approach, finds true substance, that is to say truly independent existence, in what he terms 'a perception'.[3]

A more important characteristic of the traditional concept of substance is that it is something which can act and be acted

---

[1] A 188, B 231.   [2] A 183, B 226.

[3] Cf. the striking passage in *Treatise of Human Nature*, I. iv. 5, Everyman, p. 223, Fontana, pp. 283-4.

upon. Plato already stresses this point in the *Sophist*[1]—speaking, however, of 'a thing that has real being' rather than of substance. The mark of such real being is that it has power (δύναμις) to affect or be affected. Locke finds in the notion of active and passive powers 'a great part' of our idea of substance,[2] though he will not go so far as to say that substance *is* power. It is interesting to find Kant, too, in the course of the argument of the Second Analogy, when discussing action and force (*Kraft*), saying: 'Wherever there is action—and therefore activity and force—there also is substance.'[3] And it is particularly interesting to find him making no claim to a-priority of knowledge in this case, but accepting the knowledge as purely empirical. He speaks here of 'the empirical criterion of substance, in so far as substance appears to manifest itself not through permanence of appearance, but more adequately and easily through action'. Thus permanence is part of the *a priori* concept of substance, whereas having power to act is the empirical criterion of a substance.

79. Now there is a marked contrast between the teaching of the past on substance and that of today. This concept of substance without which, according to the rationalists, we are incapable of ordering our experience and so, in effect, of having any significant experience, is regarded by those who are engaged in the advancement of science as a mere superfluity. It is vague, and where attempts have been made to make it precise, for instance, in respect of the characteristic of permanence, it is not found useful. I may quote Russell's *Analysis of Matter*:[4] 'What appears as one substance with changing states should, I maintain, be conceived as a series of occurrences linked together in some important way.' A physical object is 'a group of events arranged about a centre. There *may* be a substance in the centre, but there can be no reason to think so, since the group of events will produce exactly the same percepts.'[5] Science deals with events rather than with substantival things.

[1] *Sophist* 247 e.   [2] Cf. *Essay*, II. xxiii. 7 ff.   [3] A 204, B 249–50.
[4] 1927, p. 152.   [5] Ibid., p. 244.

The only permanences it needs are the four-dimensional space–time continuum and, possibly, the conservation of energy. But in neither case must we suppose the permanence to be substantival. The most we can say, Russell concludes, is that persistent material substances are 'approximate, empirical generalisations', but they have ceased to be of value in scientific inquiry.[1]

In the forty years which have elapsed since Russell wrote the *Analysis of Matter* it would appear that neither physicist nor chemist has found it necessary to restore the traditional concept of substance as a permanent self-dependent entity; nor does the biologist speak in terms of a substantial core. Kant's insistence on substance as a pure concept of the understanding essential to scientific thinking clearly finds little support in our own day. It is always possible that future changes in scientific thought may make the traditional doctrine of substance more relevant, but it cannot now be said to be an essential part of the framework within which the scientist thinks. Having said this, however, it should be affirmed and emphasized that the concept of substance remains an important part of the framework within which we carry on our ordinary, everyday life and thought. We find ourselves thinking and speaking of the world as one made up of animate and inanimate individuals, each one of which is a substance, having attributes, persisting through a period of time though its attributes change, affecting other substances and being affected by them and yet having a certain independence of its own. It seems to be as true now as it was to Kant that such a concept is a necessary part of the framework of everyday experience, and may consequently be said to be a condition of the occurrence of our everyday experience.

But this should not be interpreted to mean that it is a necessary condition of any possible human experience and of any possible human knowledge. The concept of substance need not be a pure concept derived from pure reason and applying *a priori* to experience. Since this is so, what other account of the origin of this concept is possible? Could it itself arise from

[1] Cf. ibid., p. 355.

experience, that is to say, from our experience of the external world and our experience of ourselves? Consider again the experience of seeing the Matterhorn. It stands out; it is isolated and different from what is around it; it is real, solid, permanent. Now this perceptual experience may be in part illusory. The Matterhorn may not be as solid as it appears; very little reflection is necessary to make us reject the supposition that its permanence is more than relative. Yet seeing the Matterhorn is an experience which suggests the concept of a substance; it is a something that is able to stand on its own, is permanent through changes, and is a substrate of change; it is an existing individual thing which is concrete and a continuant. The observer presumably will have become acquainted with substances long before he sees the Matterhorn. It is obvious, too, that if he *speaks* of what is before him as 'a substance' he will have learnt the English language and knows how to use this phrase. But such an experience as seeing the Matterhorn could of itself set him on the way to conceiving the concept of substance, if he did not possess it already. It is admitted, further, that the having of the concept would normally involve dispositional factors. One look at the Matterhorn would not provide him with the concept of substance. But several experiences of it and of like objects would create within him a familiarity with objects having these characteristics, namely, apparent independence, permanence, and so on, and he would be disposed to expect objects having such characteristics. This disposition would have been acquired in the course of experience.

Kant knew of the dispositional theory and rejected it. In B 166–8 of the *Critique of Pure Reason* he argues that there are two choices before us. 'There are only two ways in which we can account for a *necessary* agreement of experience with the concepts of its objects: either experience makes these concepts possible or these concepts make experience possible.' Now the categorial concept he has concluded (for reasons already given above) is *a priori* and independent of experience, and so the former alternative is ruled out and the latter must be asserted, 'namely, that the categories contain, on the side of the under-standing, the grounds of the possibility of all experience in general'. But he also acknowledges here that a dispositional theory has been put forward as 'a middle course'. The theory he describes is Liebniz's theory of innate dispositions. He rejects it on two grounds, 'On such a hypothesis we can set no limit to the assumption of predetermined dispositions to future judgements', whereas correct theory demands that the number of categories should be stated and known. Secondly, there is 'the decisive objection', namely 'that the *necessity* of the categories, which belongs to their very conception, would then have to be sacrificed'. And no appeal to the fact that one was innately disposed to accept these concepts would help, for 'a man cannot dispute with anyone regarding that which depends merely on the mode in which he is himself organised.'

On these grounds Kant rejects the view that having the categorial concepts is having innate dispositions. On the first of the two arguments we could not, if we identified concepts with dispositions, put forward a list of categorial concepts and hold that these and these alone are all the possible categories. This must be admitted, but the question that arises is whether Kant is justified in supposing that the number of categorial concepts is in fact fixed and determined. As to the second point, one certainly cannot argue with a man who merely says that he is so and so disposed. But if he says his dispositions are acquired, and are the results of experiences of the world which others can share, argument might be possible. Kant might not have objected to this, but then he would have fallen back on his basic contention that experience itself cannot provide those concepts which make experience possible.

Kant rests his case for the need of an *a priori* rationalism on his conviction that wholly reliable knowledge is possible only if the phenomenal world is ordered by necessary principles and that these principles are necessary only if they are derived from pure reason. He instances the principle of the permanence of substance as one such principle. Now this principle is, admittedly, fully operative in everyday thinking, yet everyday thinking is loose and lacks necessity, so that the Kantian argument from necessity to an *a priori* origin does not hold in its case. On the other hand, where human thinking becomes more precise it apparently finds it expedient to dispense with the concept of substance, since this concept turns out to be a superfluity, if not a hindrance to accurate thought. It would seem to follow from this that in the case of substance Kant's argument for supposing it to be derived *a priori* is not strong and it is difficult to see what arguments could be used today to establish his thesis. The alternative view that having the concept of substance is having a disposition which has been acquired in the course of our experience of objects in the physical world remains however a promising theory.

One further point should be made in discussing our knowledge of substance. If we suppose that the notion is derived from experience, we should consider whether it is derived not merely from our experience of the external world but also from our experience of ourselves. For I experience myself as a continuant, persisting in my identity in spite of modifications and changes in the qualities that pertain to me; and I experience myself as an individual different from others though possibly influenced by them. It would certainly appear to be the case that my experience of myself must be reckoned as one of the sources of my concept of substance and attributes. More will be said about this source of empirical information when we come to consider it in its relation to the concept of causality.

80. If the concept of substance is part of the framework of our everyday thinking so certainly is that of cause, and we have to ask of cause, as we did of substance, how the concept is gained. Philosophers, particularly after Hume, have provided many theories of causation, but in studying these one has an uneasy feeling that not one of them answers the fundamental question that is being asked. For the truly basic question here is how we gain the concept of efficient cause, that is, of one thing bringing about a change in another. But the inquirer who wishes to learn about efficient cause finds himself fobbed

off instead with discussion and argument about regular sequence, law, statistical averages, limiting boundaries, systems of
determinism, and the like. All of these discussions may be
relevant, but none is immediately relevant. And this may be
the reason why the discussion of causality in European philosophy since the seventeenth century, even at its most brilliant,
seems somehow ineffective, as if it fails to get to grips with
what is of central importance to the problem.

It is not surprising to find today a reaction to what has now
become the established philosophical doctrine on cause and
effect. Writers, particularly those concerned with the analysis
of the notion of action, advise us to look less to theory and more
to the evidence. The prototype instances of causation need
to be examined again. The man stands on his feet, walks to
the door, and closes it. I see him close the door and I am
aware that this is a change which he has brought about. Or I
see the table-lamp fall over and smash the vase. In both instances, it is said, I am conscious of a causing. Persons, animals,
plants, and inanimate objects are causing changes around me
ceaselessly, and I have only to open my eyes to see that this
is so. This is what the theorists seem to ignore, and this is the
point at which a new beginning must be made.[1]

Now it is certainly the case that this is the fundamental
phenomenon one wishes to understand when dealing with
cause and effect. On that point these writers are wholly justified; the heart of the matter is efficient causation and somehow
philosophers have turned away from it and concentrated on
secondary issues. Yet how could this have happened if there
was in fact clear evidence on all sides of the occurrence of
efficient causes? Consider again the position of Cartesian and
empiricist thinkers at the beginning of the modern age. It is
clear that they were concerned from the first with the problem
of causation as a problem of efficient causation; the other
three Aristotelian causes (material, formal, and final) were of

---

[1] Of the many relevant writings I may instance Max Black's 'Making Something
Happen' in *Determinism and Freedom*, ed. Sidney Hook (1961), and A. R. Louch's
Explanation and Human Action (1966), ch. 3.

little interest to them. But an element in the theory of efficient causation itself became suspect. The grounds of dissatisfaction are set out at least as early as 1666, in Cordemoy's *Discernement du corps et de l'âme*, and they are such as to challenge the view that to find examples of a person, or an animal or plant, or again an inorganic thing, causing something one has only to look around and see. We say that *a* has caused *b* to move, and we assume that we see this, but 'if we examine carefully what we know with certainty here, all we see is that *a* moves, that it meets *b* which was at rest', and that *b* then moves.[1] We do not see *a* causing *b* to move. For all we know to the contrary, it may be the case that *a* is not the efficient cause of *b*'s movement. Thus it may be that God is the cause, that He takes the occurrence of *a*'s contiguity to be the occasion of the change in *b*. It may be that God is the one and only cause. But writers who did not accept such Occasionalism none the less admitted the force of Cordemoy's original criticism. Thus when we turn to the searching analysis of the causal relation in Hume, he in no way rejects the position that causal relations between things are never seen. He reaffirms it, and reaffirms it indeed in language that recalls that of Cordemoy: 'We find only that the one body approaches the other, and that the motion of it precedes that of the other.'[2] In Hume's language, we have no 'impression' of cause as efficient cause. As against modern theorists Hume would deny that we see causal activity. We do not see *a* causing *b* to move, or *a* making something to happen to *b*, or changing or affecting *b*—in whichever way we choose to describe it. We do not *see* the causing, though we do speak of it.

Hume explains our knowledge of the causal relation in terms of two impressions we receive in sense-experience, namely, that of the contiguity of *a* and *b* and that of the succession, first *a*'s movement then *b*'s movement. Further we are conscious of the constancy of the conjunction. Finally, it must be

---

[1] Discourse IV, Géraud de Cordemoy, *Discernement du corps et de l'âme*. Discourse IV is entitled 'De la première cause du mouvement'.
[2] *Treatise*, I. iii. 2, Everyman, p. 80, Fontana, p. 123.

granted that we feel a necessity; once *a* hits *b*, *b* must move. Yet this is no apprehension of a necessary relation in the objective world; it is a subjective necessity, an inner disposition to expect that *b* will move as we see *a* moving down upon it. Such subjective necessity he holds to be the outcome of our continued experience of the constant conjunction and the regular sequence. Now Kant, needless to say, rejects this theory, since it will not, in his opinion, provide the necessity and the universality which are a condition of an orderly and certain experience of the world. But it is to be noticed that when Kant in the Second and Third Analogies of the *Critique of Pure Reason* does make explicit the knowledge which thus conditions the very possibility of our understanding the world, it is not a knowledge of efficient causation. It is rather the knowledge that, first, any alteration in anything must necessarily take place in conformity with the law of the connection of cause and effect and that, secondly, things in space are in thoroughgoing reciprocity. The question arises however whether the argument of the Analogies can be understood without first taking efficient causation for granted. Thus in the well-known passage in the Second Analogy[1] Kant restates the regular-sequence theory, which he describes as 'the accepted view' in his day, and rejects it on the ground that it cannot explain the knowledge of *objective* necessity which he claims we possess. We know that everything that happens *must* have had a cause and this we can only know *a priori*, since experiences could not give necessary knowledge. But in this case how do we come to understand what 'having a cause' or 'being caused' signifies? Have we *a priori* knowledge of efficient cause? Kant does not say so. He perhaps comes nearest to discussing our knowledge of efficient cause in the passage about the power or force of substances in action[2] to which I have already referred.[3] Unfortunately this discussion is very brief and cryptic, but it does at least make clear that in Kant's view such knowledge is empirical. Is this then the source of our knowledge of efficient causation, and is such knowledge being assumed in the discussion of

---

[1] A 195–6, B 240–1.   [2] A 204, B 249–50.   [3] End of § 78 above.

causality in Kant's analogies? But what then of the objections of Cordemoy?

81. The constant-conjunction or regular-sequence theory at least respects Cordemoy. As a consequence, it has no room for efficient causation. Its procedure is strictly empiricist; whatever is in any way occult is to be avoided, only that which is manifest to experience is to be accepted. Now efficient causation, the power, the *vis a tergo*, is not manifest, so the constant-conjunction theory ignores it. Let us now see how it then fares.

On a strict empiricist basis when we say that *A* causes *B*, we mean at least this much: that *A* and *B* are contiguous in both space and time and that *B* follows *A* in time. Admittedly, there are remote causes and remote effects, as when the wireless signal broadcast in London affects the apparatus in Sydney. But in such a case, it is supposed, *A* causes *B* through a series of intervening causal relations. It must be understood too that when we speak of *A* causing *B*, we do not necessarily understand by *A* an isolated, simple occurrence. It may well be a complex or set of occurrences after which *B*, possibly itself complex, follows. Finally, the theory usually assumes temporal precedence. *A* precedes *B* in time and *B* never precedes *A*. None the less it would appear necessary to admit co-temporaneous causality. The engine pulls the railway coaches throughout the time taken by the journey, cause and effect being co-temporaneous.

But generally speaking when I say that *A* causes *B* I mean that *A* and *B* are contiguous and that *B* follows *A* in the chronological sense. Yet this obviously is not enough. It is easy to imagine a case in which *A* and *B* are contiguous in space and time and *B* follows after *A* and yet *A* is not the cause of *B*. The sound I heard a short time ago and the sound I heard a moment later seemed to come from the same quarter and were successive, and yet the first sound was not the cause of the second. Something else needs to be attended to, and this, we are told, is the regularity of the sequence. In my experience it is manifest that *B*s regularly follow *A*s. To say that *A*s cause *B*s is more, on this theory, than to say that *B*s follows *A*s; one is also saying that *B*s always follows *A*s.

But 'always' in this context may be a source of misunderstanding. All it ought to mean, if the theorist adheres strictly to his empiricist principles, is 'always in my experience and the experience of my informants'. The two sentences '*B*s always follow *A*s in my (and my informants') experience' and '*B*s always follow *A*s' are not identical, and the first is the only one the theorist has a right to assert in view of his determination to interpret the generalization '*A* causes *B*', i.e. events of the type *A* cause events of the type *B*, in manifest terms solely. For what is always the case is not manifest.

Yet it is at this point that most empiricists become a little uneasy. After all, to say that events of the type *A* cause events of the type *B* is surely to say that *B*s always follow *A*s, and not merely that they have followed *A*s in my experience up to date. Moritz Schlick did attempt on one occasion to put forward the regular-sequence theory in terms of the manifest solely.[1] But the consequence was that he found it most difficult to speak significantly of regularity, and so of cause in his sense of the term. How many times do we need to see *B*s following *A*s to enable us to make the generalization that *B* regularly follows *A*? He asks this question, but confesses that he cannot answer it.

It must be added, too, that when one says '*B* always follows *A*' one often means that *A* necessitates *B*. True, one may not always mean this. It may be that, if, after observing many regular sequences, one says '*B* always follows *A*', all one means is that this serves as a good working hypothesis or conceptual scheme without assuming any necessary connection. Even so, one would still be asserting complete regularity. Most often, however, necessary connection is assumed; it is assumed that *A* is not merely contiguous to *B* and prior to it but also necessarily connected with *B*. As Hume said: 'An object may be

---

[1] Cf. 'Causality in Everyday Life and in Recent Science', particularly p. 357, in *Contemporary Philosophic Problems*, ed. Y. H. Krikorian and A. Edel (New York, 1959). The original paper appeared in 1932.

contiguous and prior to another, without being considered as its cause. There is a necessary connection to be taken into consideration; and that relation is of much greater importance than any of the other two above mentioned.'[1] But if our empiricist in stating that B always follows A means even by implication that A necessitates B he is certainly proceeding further than the regular-sequence theory permits him to proceed. For the necessity, on this theory, is not manifested in experience. Nor is it a logical necessity independent of experience which an empiricist could assert on logical grounds alone. The proposition 'B always follows A' is not a logically necessary proposition. The reference is to a factual necessity which on the regular-sequence theory is something of a mystery, being beyond the regularity observed. The empiricist has ruled out the occult, but something very much like it has taken its place, namely, necessity. Hume saw the fundamental difficulty and tried to meet it by the ingenious suggestion that causal necessity is of a subjective order. Yet this does not save strict empiricism, since subjective necessity is at one with objective necessity in involving non-manifest elements.

The empiricist theory of causation, then, in so far as it is identified with the regular-sequence theory, is unconvincing. Its insistence on the need for eliminating non-manifest elements from explanation is obviously crucial; yet its theory in terms of regularities seems to break down, as in Schlick's case, unless it itself is permitted to bring in a non-manifest element, in asserting either that B is necessarily connected with A, or, at least, that B *always* follows A.[2]

82. The upholder of the regular-sequence theory has other difficulties to contend with. Perhaps the greatest is that he works, as it were, against the grain of ordinary language. This is not decisive evidence against the theory, but it must be

[1] *Treatise*, I. iii. 2, Everyman, p. 80, Fontana, p. 123.
[2] This is not to deny that the theory has pragmatic value. In some circumstances, in order to postulate a causal relationship all one needs to discover is a sequence that, as far as one's experience goes, is regular. The apparently regular sequence may suggest a useful working hypothesis.

taken into account. Consider a few sentences: 'The water forced the door open'; 'The released air drove the piston forward'; 'The cup of coffee refreshed me.' The verbs here are causal verbs, but what they are used to express is not a mere sequence. We are not merely saying that water came in contact with the door and that this was followed by the opening of the door. The water *forced* the door open, it did something to it. So with the released air; it *drives* the piston forward. The coffee *affects* my nervous system. These sentences were never intended to express mere sequence; rightly or wrongly ordinary language, illustrated in such sentences as these, points to something else. It points directly to the theory that the effect occurs *because of* the cause, and not merely that it follows *after* the cause. The water, the air, and the coffee bring about a change.

It is surprising how all-pervading the expression of the causal relation is in language. It has frequently been pointed out that this relation is not the sole relation in the natural world, and that knowledge of the causal law is not the only knowledge which makes prediction possible. There are, for instance, laws about the coexistence of qualities. Yet, admitting this, one must also add that both in ordinary speech and in science the causal relation colours the whole in a remarkable way. It is in the speaker's mind not merely when he uses verbs expressing activity or passivity, such as 'force', 'drives', 'breaks', 'pulls', and the like, but equally in his nouns and adjectives. Sometimes, its presence there is obvious as when I talk of a solvent or a leveller, a cutter, a mower, and so on. But when, too, I talk of water or of wood, their causal properties are constantly in my mind, as the sentences in which these words appear show. Further, adjectives ending in -able, -ible, and -uble, sometimes termed the dispositional adjectives, obviously refer to causal situations. But some adjectives which do not end in these suffixes, such as poisonous, burdensome, brittle, and so on, are dispositional adjectives too. As Nelson Goodman said of them, they are 'full of threats and promises'.

I do not wish to discuss this point here, but merely to remark, in recognizing the pervasiveness of the causal relation, that the language 'of threats and promises' is not the language of regular sequence. But, now, is the regular-sequence theory the only empiricist theory in the field? Or, if we reject the regular-sequence theory, have we to fall back on traditional rationalist theories and on *a priori* theories of the Kantian kind? There is always too the third alternative, namely, the denial of the very possibility of a *theory* of causality, that is to say, we may assert that causation is a mystery not to be comprehended by human minds. But this is a counsel of despair only to be accepted in the last extreme.

There is in fact another theory which deserves our attention. It is not an *a priori* theory and not an empiricist theory in the ordinary sense of that word. It argues from one's consciousness of one's own activity. I am conscious of my own efforts to make a change or to bring something about. Frequently, I succeed in making the change, and I am then conscious of my effort and of the change. What I have described as 'my effort' may be something very slight. I may be able to bring about the change almost without effort. On the other hand it may involve considerable striving over possibly a long period of time. I am certainly conscious of it. This means that I do *experience* the causing in at least one case of causation, namely, when I effect a change. Thus it is argued that even though it be granted that, strictly speaking, one cannot see one billiard ball causing a second ball to move, one is conscious of oneself causing a billiard ball to move. Now here, it is said, is a basis for a theory of causality which does not fall back on the occult and which does not appeal to the *a priori* but is empiricist, and yet does provide an account of efficient causation. I am directly aware of efficient causation in my own experience as an agent causing change. On the other hand, when I see someone get up and close a door I cannot be said to *see* a causing. None the less the sentence: 'He closed the door'—meaning not only that before the occurrence the door was open and now it is closed, but that he caused it to be closed—is significant for me because of my consciousness of efficient causation in my own actions. On this basis a theory of causation in general may be possible; it would rest on one's consciousness of one's own efficient causation together with a projection of efficient causation elsewhere.

One's first reaction on meeting this theory might well be that Hume has refuted it once and for all. If this be the case one need go no further. But, in my view, though a hasty reading of Hume might suggest this, a more careful reading leaves one uncertain. I must now explain why I think this to be so.

When Hume first published Book I of the *Treatise* in 1739 there was no reference in it to this projection theory. He confines himself to knowledge of causal relations in the external world and argues that in this case we have no 'impression' of *A*'s causing *B*. Accordingly, he thinks the regular-sequence theory, suitably modified to account for necessity, is the only possible theory. But when Book III of the *Treatise* was published in 1740 he added an appendix giving some of his second thoughts on matters dealt with in the earlier volumes, and it is only in this appendix that he refers to the projection theory. By this time he had realized that the charge might be made against him that he had not fully considered all the possibilities in dealing with knowledge of causal relations. He accordingly added a paragraph in the appendix. Its purpose was to dispose of an objection that might be made to the argument of i. iii. 14 of the *Treatise*, and to dispose of it as quickly as possible.

He sets out the projection theory in the first sentence: 'Some have asserted that we feel an energy or power in our own mind; and that, having in this manner acquired the idea of power, we transfer that quality to matter where we are not able immediately to discover it.'[1] He then proceeds to treat the relationship between the agent that moves and the physical object which is moved as one between the will and the physical object, and he argues that we no more experience the causal relation between the will and the physical object than we experience the causal relation between two physical objects.

[1] Cf. i. iii. 14, the addition is inserted in the text in Everyman, p. 159, and Fontana, p. 211. The Selby-Bigge edition of the *Treatise* retains it in the appendix.

As he says: 'So far from perceiving the connection betwixt an act of volition and a motion of the body, it is allowed that no effect is more inexplicable from the powers and essence of thought and matter.' On this basis, he concludes: 'We should in vain hope to attain an idea of force by consulting our own minds.'

It is, in the main, the same argument which we find in the *Enquiries*. But it is interesting to note that, whereas on other matters the *Enquiries* usually offers a much less detailed argument than the *Treatise*, on this point the reverse is the case. Whereas the *Treatise* devotes one paragraph to the matter, and that in an appendix, the *Enquiries* devotes in all twelve paragraphs to it in three sections (51–3). Obviously Hume feels that there is a case which needs answering and which had not been properly answered in the *Treatise*. I have no space here to consider these twelve paragraphs in detail, but I find them unconvincing, and this essentially because Hume adopts the same argument in them as in the appendix to the *Treatise*, that the relationship being considered is one between the will and the physical object. The question at issue is whether I have direct experience of attempting or striving to bring about a change when being conscious of my own activity. Hume changes the problem into quite a different one: whether I am aware of a causal relationship between two entities, namely, the will and the object affected. He concludes that this relationship is no more manifest to me than is that between two billiard balls when one ball makes the other move. But Hume is then surely ignoring the real issue. His argument against the possibility of understanding the relation between will and the object is irrelevant; what matters is whether we are ever conscious when we act of striving to bring about a change, and whether the concept of causing which we project elsewhere is derived from this source. Hume does not show either in the *Treatise* or in the *Enquiries* that we lack this consciousness.

Indeed, it could be argued that his final position is itself an admission that there is just such a consciousness. I refer to the footnote to section 52 of the *Enquiries*. (Was it added to the text on re-reading it, and is it further proof of his uneasiness about his position?) This footnote concludes: 'It must, however, be confessed that the animal *nisus* which we experience, though it can afford no accurate, precise idea of power, enters very much into that vulgar, inaccurate idea which is formed of it.' This is Hume's last word on the subject. We experience a *nisus*, an endeavouring, which 'enters into' the 'idea of power', although somewhat inaccurately. This is obscure and it is not clear how much Hume is admitting. Yet an argument with this as its last word surely cannot be held to be the classical refutation of the projection theory.

83. But though the projection theory would appear to survive any criticism of it to be found in Hume this should not be taken to mean that it is free from difficulties. On the contrary, difficulties and ambiguities abound both in its statement and in the arguments used to support it. It is usually stated in some such form as the following. When I bring about a change, I am conscious of, or feel, the effort involved. From this source, and from no other, is derived my concept of effort. But having once derived it I am then able to project effort into other situations, for instance, the situation in which a physical object is said to bring about a change in another physical object. Here, and here alone, lies the explanation of how I can speak significantly of one thing causing or bringing about a change in another thing.

On examination this statement turns out to be ambiguous. The phrases 'consciousness of effort' and 'projection' certainly require further clarification. A good deal of attention has been given to the analysis of statements about action recently and many of the results gained from this analysis are applicable here. When I now close the door I am the agent. It would be misleading to say that my volition brings about the change or is the cause of the change, since it may suggest that my volition is an entity in itself which can act as the cause. But what brings about the change when I close the door is myself, the person, who wills or wants or wishes to close the door. If this be accepted, the question that then arises is how I know that I do close the door if I do know this. Now it is obvious that I do know that I have closed the door. I felt a draught and I was conscious of wanting to close the door. The door was old and heavy and I had to use considerable energy to close it. I was certainly conscious of the effort involved. Presumably this is what Hume means in speaking of 'the feeling of energy or power'. It is not feeling in the sense of feeling a surface of an object, nor of feeling anger, nor again of feeling sick. It is more like that experience which Samuel Alexander used to term an 'enjoyment' of one's activities. A man does something and is at the same time conscious of the effort involved in doing it; he feels the effort involved.

Now is this consciousness of effort a consciousness of bringing about the change, a consciousness of a causal act? I am conscious of the striving to close the door. Am I conscious as well of myself as causing the door to be closed. When I look at one billiard ball hit another and cause it to move away Cordemoy's account of the matter is right, I see the first billiard ball move towards the second and touch it, I see the second move away, but I do not see the first ball cause the second to move. Is it so here? I see my arm stretch forth and my hand encircle the knob of the door, and then I see the door moved and it is closed. Am I conscious of the act of closing? Am I directly aware of the causing? Or is it that what I intended has now come about? Is this one more instance of an experienced correlation, namely between what I intend and what subsequently occurs? Is my awareness of the existence of a causal relation in this case identical in character with my awareness of a causal relationship between two inanimate bodies, namely an awareness of a regular correlation or constant conjunction? In that case, of course, my knowledge of my own causal activity would be explicable in terms of the constant-conjunction theory and could not be said to throw any special light on the nature of our knowledge of causal relations.

But does this account of the matter do full justice to the facts? Is there no difference between my consciousness of the relation between myself intending, willing, and striving to close the door on the one hand, and the closing of the door on the other, and my consciousness of the relations between the movements of the first billiard ball and the second? Consider another case: I am thinking about a problem and setting my thoughts on paper. But I remember that I have to prepare a lecture. Quite consciously I stop thinking about the problem and turn to consider the material for the lecture. I am conscious of the switching as my own act; I am directly conscious of bringing about this change. It would be foolish to try to explain this in terms of (i) my intending the change, (ii) my finding myself at the other task, and so (iii) my becoming aware of that conjunction of intention and occurrence which, on the constant-conjunction theory, betokens a causal relationship. This theory, it would appear, simply does not work in this case, because I am directly conscious not only of my intending but also of my carrying out the switching from the first task to the second. Now the case of my closing the door is more complicated. I am conscious of my wanting to close it and of my moving my arm. I am conscious of the strain in trying to close it. But there are elements involved, for instance, many of the muscular and physiological movements, of which I am not conscious at the time. I am consequently not conscious of all that is occurring. Can I be said to be conscious of an act of efficient causation? In the former case I do seem to be fully conscious of bringing about the change, but this case is more complex and I am not conscious of all the steps involved. None the less, I should say I am conscious of my bringing about the change in the second case as well and not merely of my desiring and of my striving to bring it about. The latter could occur without the change taking place. But the change in this case does take place and I am directly conscious of my self bringing it about. Now this is all that the supporter of the projectionist theory needs to establish in order to get his theory off the ground. He wants to argue that there exists a fundamental difference between (i) seeing the one billiard ball move towards the other and watching the second move away and (ii) my giving the ball a push with my hand and so causing it to move. For in the second case, he argues, I am conscious of my own act of bringing about a change, I am conscious of efficient causation. The evidence would seem to justify this statement of his, and if it does so, it does give him the starting-point for the theory. If, for instance, it be admitted that I am conscious of switching my thought from what I am now thinking about to the preparation of the lecture this would be enough; the projection theory could proceed.

So much for 'consciousness of effort'. What now of 'projection'? The advocate of the projection theory holds that the word 'causes' in 'The first billiard ball causes the second to move' is significant in the sense to be now explained and only in this sense. I do not *see* the first billiard ball cause the second to move, so there is a gap in my knowledge and I find it necessary in this case (as in so many others) to interpolate. I fill the gap by introducing effort, the source of my concept of effort being my experience of my own effort. So when I say the first billiard ball causes the second to move I say that something like the effort with which I bring about a change is present here too. This is what I mean when talking of causing and it explains the use of the word 'causes' in the above sentence.

Now the supporter of the projection theory not only thinks that he has here provided an explanation of our significant use of the word in this context, but it is also part of his thesis that it is the only possible explanation. The regular-sequence theory does not provide an explanation; for it does not begin to explain efficient causation. The sceptic may admit this but yet shake his head over the projection of effort into the physical world. How can anything like the effort I experience be there? This surely puts too great a strain on credulity. To ease the shock the supporter of the projection theory might feel that it would be helpful to refer to certain intervening cases between *my* bringing about an effect, on the one hand, and the first billiard ball causing the second to move, on the other. Consider, for instance, the case in which another person brings about a change. I say: 'He pushes the door open.' I see my companion put his shoulder to the door and I see it open, I observe the sequence of events. But there is a gap and, on the projection theory, I fill it by assuming that this person enjoys much the same sort of experience as I do when I push open a door. What I mean when I say: 'He pushed the door open' is not merely that the door did open, or that it opened after he put his shoulder to it—both being things that I observe—but also that he exerted himself and used force as I should do on a like occasion; and I know what this means, since I myself have frequently had that sort of experience. Now this seems not unreasonable. It is at least as reasonable and as justifiable as supposing that another feels pain or is angry. Moreover, when my friend describes his experience in pushing the door open, his description confirms my assumption that it is an experience like mine, and nothing that he says leads me to think the assumption unjustified. Finally, I have no logical grounds for rejecting the assumption. If I had grounds for thinking that nothing like my experience occurs elsewhere, or if again the evidence forced me to a solipsism, the assumption I now make would be refuted on logical grounds—but there are no such grounds. I conclude that it is logically possible that his experience is like mine.

This is reasonable. But now the theorist has to extend the scope and application of his theory. When we speak of animals and of plants as producing changes we can only do so significantly, he argues, by projecting into the occurrence an effort analogous to that which we ourselves experience. There are obvious difficulties here, but we need not stay to consider them, for the theory meets with still greater difficulties as it develops. Surely, the sceptic will say, the projection theory breaks down completely when we pass from the organic to the inorganic. In this case, the proposed interpolation of effort, analogous to the effort I experience when I bring something about, cannot possibly be justified. Consider for a moment what we are being asked to do. Whenever we expand the knowledge gained in sense-experience by interpolation we should expect that the gap we fill is to be filled with something that belongs to the same category of things as that which is experienced. But in the case under discussion, where one billiard ball causes another to move, what I fill the gap with on this theory is nothing belonging to the physical world, but something belonging to my inner world. The theory claims that it is possible to project into the material world that which *ex hypothesi* never has been and never can be a part of it, nor can it ever be experienced as a part of it.

The supporter of the projection theory may demur; his theory, he will say, is being misunderstood in some important particulars. To begin with, it in no way asserts that I project *my* effort into the gap. This would certainly be an absurdity. Nor does it assert that the first billiard ball *intends* to bring about the change which would be equally absurd. Nor, finally, does it assert that the billiard ball is conscious of its effort, feels it, or 'enjoys' it as I 'enjoy' mine. The projection theory is difficult enough to defend without supposing that these theses are contained within it. Moreover, the critic makes the argument much easier for himself by adopting a metaphysic which he has not established, according to which there is an absolute distinction between the inner world and the outer, the mental and the physical, even the organic and the inorganic. The projectionist, on the other hand, might wish to argue that, whatever the true mind–body metaphysic may turn out to be, the agent which he is considering, the I which moves the table and shuts the door, is not a mind as opposed to a body (and certainly not a volition) but rather a self which is body as well as mind. If this view be taken the sceptic's criticism may lose some of its force.

The advocate of the projection theory may indeed at this point turn upon his critic. He may ask: What other theory is being offered which explains our continued assumption of efficient causation throughout the organic and the inorganic world? The projection theory does provide an explanation; it argues that our consciousness of effort when we ourselves bring about a change is the key to the assumption, and it holds that this consciousness is the ultimate basis of our significant use of the term 'effort'. How are we to reply to this challenge? It seems to me that his theory cannot be ignored in any complete study of our knowledge of the causal relationship; it contains a germ of truth, to say the least, and is not to be written off as basically irrelevant. Possibly the theory, as normally stated, is too narrowly expounded and could have greater relevance in the scientific as well as the ordinary field if its scope were widened. It gives too much prominence to the concept of effort, and to the consciousness of bringing about a change. What of the consciousness of *suffering* a change? I feel the resistance of others and of other things and I feel them affecting me. My experience is not one of effort only, it is of giving way to pressure, of meeting resistance, of opposing, of co-operating, of adapting, and so on. Actions, reactions, oppositions, obstructions, resistances, stresses, and strains—such is the language in which I speak of my private individual life. But it is the language, too, in which I speak of the world around me. These words are part of the vocabulary of the scientist as well as of the individual describing his own inner experience. If we are to take the projection theory seriously, therefore, as the one theory that can begin to justify the way we speak and think of the causal relationship and of the interaction between things, it would be wise to widen it in the way suggested so as to cover the experience of suffering a change as well as of bringing one about.

84. But to return now to the question asked at the beginning of this chapter. The question was: Assuming that substance and the causal relationship are categorial features forming part of the framework of all our thought, what is the source of our knowledge of them? We now see that the assumption present in this question, namely that substance and cause are parts of the general framework of *all* thinking, needs to be questioned. It seems to be a justifiable assumption in the case of everyday thinking; our world then is a world of substances having attributes and between these substances causal interaction is

possible. But is it justified in the case of more precise thinking? For instance, it would be difficult to argue that it is a necessary condition of the physicist's thinking that he should think of the physical world as made up of substances which have attributes. To attempt to impose such a condition upon him would be to hinder the free development of his thought. Yet, if we deny that the condition is necessary, do we not give up the doctrine of categories, as the Kantians teach it? A category, such as substance, cannot be a category if it holds for thinking at one level and not at another; it holds for all thinking. The Kantian theory demands a single system of thought, having its twelve basic categories, and in respect of them no variations are possible; each and every individual human being must, and can only, think within this framework. This is presupposed in the possibility of a unity of experience.

Now the Kantian defence of rationalism rests on our acceptance of this unchangeable scheme. It is because the categories are necessary and universal that their source must be pure reason; they must be known *a priori*. 'Necessity and strict universality are sure criteria of *a priori* knowledge.'[1] Substance is such a category and the scientist must think in terms of it. So is causality. Experience may give us an inductively established rule, but it does not give us the necessary relation. The necessity of this relation points to another source. 'Appearances do indeed present cases from which a rule can be obtained according to which something usually happens, but they never prove the sequence to be *necessary*. To the synthesis of cause and effect there belongs a dignity (*Dignität*) which cannot be empirically expressed.'[2] The sequence in the causal relationship is necessary, and, since it is so, the knowledge of the sequence cannot be empirical knowledge. It has higher dignity. It is not purely logical, for the necessity in question here is not a logical necessity. It is a factual necessity, but since it is what must be it cannot be known empirically. It is the *a priori* knowledge that must be granted in order to explain the occurrence of synthetic *a priori* knowledge.

---

[1] *Critique of Pure Reason*, B 4.   [2] A 91, B 124.

Yet at the close of this chapter we find ourselves doubting the universality and necessity of the two categories we have examined. It seems clear that the category of substance is not part of the essential framework within which all thinking is carried out; the most precise thinking seems to be able to dispense with it. So too the scientist does not assume that alterations take place necessarily in conformity with a law, known *a priori*, of the connection of cause and effect. He does not need these categories, and his laws are not laws of this order.

In the case of substance and causality there is no compulsion upon us to accept the rationalist account of the framework of our knowledge. It is too inflexible. At any moment our thinking, it is true, does have its framework. What seems to be wrong, however, is to suppose that this must be a permanent framework which is universal and necessary. To insist on such a framework is to be dogmatic—an insistence in earlier rationalist schools which Kant himself attacked, but from which he did not altogether free himself. It would be wiser to think in terms of a multiplicity of frameworks. Such and such a framework may be needed at this moment; it could even be described as a necessary condition of our thought at this moment. But it need not be part of the framework for all our thinking, and it certainly need not be considered as an element conditioning all possible human thinking. In respect of substance and causality, at least, examination shows that these are highly complex and highly ambiguous concepts. We have no warrant for holding that they are universal and necessary categories for thought; the rationalist attempt to prove this fails. If this be granted it follows that we are not compelled to go on affirming the existence of pure reason as the source of our knowledge of substance and cause. These concepts are gained in another way, and it is not incumbent upon philosophers to teach that pure reason is needed to provide them. As for dignity, it is in no way clear why knowledge gained by pure reason, if such occurred, would be more dignified than knowledge acquired in any other way.

XII

CONSISTENCY AND THE LAWS
OF THOUGHT

85. To admit, as we must, that we normally think of our world in terms of substance and cause is not to admit that reason provides us with *a priori* knowledge of these concepts, nor that such *a priori* provision is a condition of thought. Thinking which has this categorial framework is rational, but rational in this sense only that it proceeds and develops against the background of the knowledge and experience of the world already gained. It is a characteristic of rational procedure, in this sense of the term, that we are permitted later to change the categorial framework if the circumstances demand it and to set out new conceptual foundations for thought. The theory that categorial features necessary for thought are determined once and for all by *a priori* reason does not stand close scrutiny. At least it does not do so in the case of the two categories of substance and cause.

The *a priori* rationalist, however, has still his trump card. Suppose, he will say, that it be granted for the moment that our knowledge of the categories of substance and cause could possibly be explained without reference to *a priori* knowledge by pure reason, there remains one demand on the thinker which must be conceded to be a directive proceeding from pure reason *a priori* and which could not originate from any other source. This is the demand for consistency. We know *a priori*, he contends, that any piece of thinking must be consistent with itself; if it fails in consistency it fails in rationality. We know too, and in the same way, that the general structure of the world is such that any thinking which turns out to be inconsistent with itself, is inapplicable to that world. The consciousness of the need for consistency is the most powerful determinant of thought; it is a criterion whose authority is universal.

In this chapter I want to examine this thesis. The *a priori* rationalist here uses these words 'consistency' and 'consistent' in a special sense. In ordinary speech we use it in other senses, for instance, we speak of a mixture in which the parts persist in roughly the same proportions throughout as consistent; in a slightly different sense, as meaning congruent, we speak of the colours in a painting as consistent, they do not clash but are compatible; again we speak of a person as being 'consistent in his wickedness' meaning that he adheres to the same evil principles throughout. The sense in which the *a priori* rationalist uses the word is not unrelated to these other senses, but is yet different. If I say that *a* is *x* then I should be inconsistent if I went on to say that *a* is not *x*. A person is inconsistent when his statements contradict one another. If he persists in his inconsistency then, as Aristotle points out, it is difficult to talk with him and quite impossible to argue with him. For everything he says may at the next moment be contradicted. Rational conversation and logical thought cannot take place in such circumstances, for at one and the same time he is both saying something and not saying it.

Now it is admitted that such inconsistency would at once stop all argument and severely limit communication between people. But the *a priori* rationalist, if I properly understand his position, says more than this. Inconsistency is condemned not because it makes communication between persons difficult— though that would be a sufficient reason for condemning it— but because it involves the breaking of laws or principles which men know *a priori*. These are logical laws, but also laws of being. There are logical laws which hold within constructed logical systems and which may have no application outside the system. But the laws now under consideration are laws setting out the (*a priori* known) nature of what exists, and are not merely formal (if we grant that we can sensibly talk of the 'merely formal'). Reason on this view provides man with intuitive insight into the structure of what is and so gives him

R

knowledge of the principles of being, and what the *a priori* rationalist condemns, when he condemns inconsistency, is the failure to obey these principles.

Now if this position is true it makes the account of the function of reason given in this book erroneous. For we deny that reason is a source of knowledge and, in particular, a source of *a priori* knowledge. But we then have to explain the demand for consistency, supposing it does not rest on *a priori* insight. This demand, as interpreted in the previous paragraph, is in effect a demand for complete obedience to the law of non-contradiction. If I say that *a* is *x* I must not at the same time say that *a* is not *x*. So the question becomes one as to our knowledge of the law of non-contradiction. This law is one of the three traditional 'laws of thought', the other two being the law of identity and the law of excluded middle. It is difficult to justify the limitation of laws of thought to these three. Any established principle in any branch of science is, within that branch, a law of thought, and even if we think of laws applying universally there are laws of thought other than contradiction, identity, and excluded middle which apply universally. Consider the principle that, if the statement *p* implies the statement *q* and *p* is true, then *q* is true. This obviously is a universal law of thought, but it did not appear to be as basic to logicians as non-contradiction did. The laws of identity and excluded middle, however, were given the same status as non-contradiction. Indeed it has been argued that these three so-called laws of thought are one—we shall shortly consider this point— but whether they are one or three it can be assumed that when the *a priori* rationalists spoke of insight into non-contradiction as the basic factor of human reasoning they were thereby claiming insight into the principles of identity and excluded middle as well. Consistent thinking requires, as a minimum, that our thinking be in accordance with these three laws and our problem, as thus interpreted, becomes one of accounting for our knowledge of these laws. The rationalist view is that they are known *a priori*. Can we accept this view? If not, what other view do we propose?

86. Our problem is now more definite: Can the claim that we have *a priori* knowledge of the three laws of thought be justified? The first, the law of identity, is usully formulated $x = x$, and in formulating it thus it is assumed that the values of x would be individual things. The fact that we normally think of this law in connection with individual things does not, however, rule out the recognition that qualities (and relations) can be spoken of as identical. So too can propositions, and in this case it has been found convenient in formal logic to formulate the principle of identity as $p \supset p$. The second law, the law of non-contradiction (sometimes spoken of as the law of contradiction), states that if a is a thing and f is an attribute then it cannot be that both a is f and a is not f. Applied to propositions the law is formulated $\sim(p.\sim p)$. The third, the law of excluded middle, affirms that if a is a thing and f an attribute then either a is f or it is not the case that a is f, a middle is excluded. Applied to propositions the law is formulated $p \vee \sim p$.

As has been mentioned, it has been argued that these three laws are not different from one another but are three ways of stating the same basic law. Leibniz, for instance, refers to the first as 'the axiom of identity or (what is the same thing) contradiction'.[1] Certainly, to say that a thing is itself is to say by implication that it is not anything else, that it is different from anything else. Again, speaking of propositions, if we say 'either p or not-p' (the law of excluded middle) then 'not both p and not-p' (the law of non-contradiction) seems to be implied. These laws are, to say the least, closely related in thought; admittedly this of itself does not permit us to speak of them as one law.

W. F. Bednarowski has used De Morgan's Theorems to make out the case that the three laws 'state the same'. The principle of identity, as has been said, is formulated in modern logic as $p \supset p$, the principle of excluded middle as $p \vee \sim p$, and the principle of non-contradiction as $\sim(p.\sim p)$. Now $p \supset p$, says Bednarowski, 'is equivalent to $\sim(p.\sim p)$, from which we can get by De Morgan's transformation: $\sim p \vee p$. Thus there seems

---

[1] Erdmann, *Opera* (1840), p. 136; Langley, *New Essays* (1896), pp. 13–14.

to be no difference between these three principles as far as what is stated is concerned: they all seem to state the same. The only difference is in the logical constants which are used for their formulation.'[1]

This argument shows, I believe, that the three laws as formulated are logically equivalent. But identity is formulated as $p \supset p$ and the question arises whether the principle $p \supset p$ is the same as $x = x$.[2] Further, if one and only one law is involved here rather than three, ought it not to be possible to formulate the one law, and so cease to speak of three laws? The retention of the three suggests that there are differences, which cannot be eliminated. Indeed there is evidence to suggest that the present tendency is not to the reduction of these laws to one but rather to their multiplication. For instance, the traditional law of identity, as we shall see, turns out, on more careful analysis, to be not one law but at least two and possibly more laws.

For the moment, however, we may make the following assumptions: first, that basic to our thinking are these three laws of thought, and secondly, that when we demand that our thinking be consistent we mean by consistent thinking a thinking which is in accordance with these laws. The problem that faces us then is whether these laws are known *a priori*. It is said they must be known *a priori*, since knowledge of them is necessary, universal, and independent of experience, but this is what we have to examine.

87. We may first consider the law of excluded middle, and we shall find that the necessity and universal applicability of this law is now frequently questioned. It is true that both philosophers and logicians desire exactness and decisiveness in thought and this the law helps to provide; they therefore set it down as basic to all thought. But are they justified? Is the subject-matter of thought sometimes such that this law cannot apply to it?

A thing can have an attribute or property or not have it.

---

[1] *Proc. Arist. Soc.*, Supp. 30 (1956), p. 80.					[2] Cf. p. 264 below.

No middle is possible; a either is f or it is not the case that it is f, and this holds for any a. Of two propositions, the one of which is the contradictory of the other, one is true and the other false, $p \vee \sim p$. Now within restricted limits the truth of this principle is not denied, but its universal truth in all inquiries is denied. For instance, it has been quite explicitly denied by the advocates of the intuitionist theory of mathematics. On this theory mathematical thinking is a species of creative thought that differs from ordinary thinking and to a certain extent requires a different logic. 'The reason is', says Heyting, a member of this school,[1] 'that in mathematics from the very beginning we deal with the infinite, whereas ordinary logic is made for reasoning about finite collections.' In particular, thinking that proceeds in accordance with the law of excluded middle cannot be the adequate instrument for creative mathematics; sooner or later it will impede its progress.

Again, to take another example, reflection upon paradoxes, it is argued, decreases our confidence in this law. We find ourselves sometimes driven to conclusions which are significant but which appear to be true and false at one and the same time. This is particularly so in the case of those paradoxes which are termed antinomies, for instance, the paradox of the Cretan, Grelling's paradox (the 'Heterological' paradox), and Russell's paradox of the class of all classes that are not members of themselves. In such cases we find ourselves being compelled to admit that a particular statement is true if, and only if, it is false. F. B. Fitch takes the statement 'This proposition itself is false' and argues that this statement 'cannot be assumed true without also being assumed false, nor can it be assumed false without also being assumed true. If such a proposition is regarded as satisfying the principle of excluded middle, then it must be treated as either true or false, and hence as both true and false. So we do not assert that it satisfies the principle of excluded middle.'[2] Fitch holds that it is 'an indefinite proposition', neither true nor false, as opposed to definite propositions

---

[1] A. Heyting, *Intuitionism*, p. 1.
[2] *Symbolic Logic* (1952), 2. 14, cf. further 10. 16 to 10. 20.

which are true or false, and in respect of indefinite propositions the law of excluded middle does not hold.

If we widen this distinction between definite and indefinite statements then many statements which may at first appear to be definite turn out to possess a streak of indefiniteness. The following example comes to mind. An acquaintance was recently asked to fill in a questionnaire about a candidate applying for a post. One of the questions asked was 'Is the candidate married?', and my acquaintance created some scandal by replying 'Yes and no'. He defended himself later by saying that this was the only answer he could truthfully give. He thus broke the law of excluded middle in the interests of what he took to be the truth. (He also broke the law of non-contradiction.)

It is reflecting on instances of this sort that has most frequently led thinkers to question the universality of the principle of excluded middle. The concept of being married is so vague a concept that the statement, 'He is married, but he also is not married' could in certain contexts be sensibly uttered. Yet to the question 'Is SP?', where 'S' is a subject-term and 'P' a predicate-term, we can, according to the principle of excluded middle, answer 'Yes' or we can answer 'No', but we cannot answer 'Yes and no'. Nevertheless the vagueness of the predicate frequently invites this answer. 'Is he bald?' 'Well, yes and no.' A simple unqualified 'Yes' or 'No' will not do as an answer. A way of saving the principle would be to define the word 'bald' so as to make it completely precise. (We may agree, for instance, that anyone with n hairs or more on his head is not bald.) Yet, a large number of empirical predicate-terms share in this sort of vagueness, and we could hardly hope to define each and all of them precisely. For the purpose of ordinary life of course we do not need to do so; we are content to be vague, as our speech reveals. We speak loosely of something being 'approximately so-and-so' or 'roughly so-and-so'. As we have seen, precision and exactitude are not the only desiderata when we communicate with one another; there is also the need for economy. Our conversations with one another would be greatly impeded if every concept-term had to be precisely defined before we used it. Our ordinary speech is fluid, indefinite, and indecisive, and so too is our ordinary thinking; the need for economy and speed are usually greater than the need for precision. But this means that in ordinary talk and in ordinary thinking the principle of excluded middle does not dominate our thought.

Such are some of the reflections which have led philosophers to doubt the rationalist assumption that the law of excluded middle holds universally.

88. We may next consider the law of identity. One of the underlying concepts in this consideration is Plato's concept of identity and difference; a thing is itself and it is not another thing. Now it may be felt that to say that a thing is itself is to say very little about it—$x - x$ is vacuous. This same criticism of course could be made of non-contradiction and excluded middle, but it is not a very serious criticism; the fact that these principles appear vacuous takes nothing away from their value in the attempt to set out the framework of thought and being. The question of importance is whether they do set out that framework. Is the element of identity, for instance, laid bare in the insight that a thing is itself, or $x = x$?

It is disturbing to be told that $x = x$ is a law of identity and that there are other laws of identity. If it is one law amongst others, then, presumably, it does not give the full truth about identity but has to be supplemented. There is considerable discussion of another law of identity, namely, Leibniz's law, and we may ask how this law is related to the law that a thing is itself. Consider the case in which someone describes x to me and later someone describes y. As I listen to the description of y I realize that it is like the x described earlier, and as the description proceeds I begin to suspect that identically the same thing is being described. I ask for further information to see whether x and y differ in respect of any quality they possess or in respect of any relationship with other things and find they do not. I therefore conclude that the two speakers were in fact describing one and the same thing. What now is the logical principle in this procedure? It is the law that when x is identical with y then whatever can be predicated of x can also be predicated of y, which may be formulated $(x = y) \supset (f)(fx = fy)$. The law may also be interpreted as signifying that x is identical with y if, and only if, every property which x has is a property which y has and conversely, $x = y \equiv (f)(fx \equiv fy)$.

Now in whichever way we formulate Leibniz's law it is obviously a different principle of identity from $x = x$—unless we suppose that $x = x$ needs revision and that a more correct formulation of identity would be one of the two formulations of Leibniz's law. But there is a difference between saying that a thing is itself and saying that if it is the case that whatever can be predicated of x can be predicated of y then x and y are one and the same thing. For instance, supposing we followed the traditional analysis of a thing and its predicates in which it was not supposed that the substantival thing was just the sum of that thing's predicates; in that case, even if we knew that whatever could be predicated of x could be predicated of y, it would not follow that x and y were identical. In other words, on this account of an individual thing Leibniz's law could not be a substitute for $x = x$ without loss of meaning.

Further, what are we to say of, and in what contexts can we speak of, identical qualities rather than identical things? We say 'x is the same as y in respect of f', where f is a quality, that is 'x is f' and 'y is f'. Common to the two statements is the type phrase '. . . is f'. Does this mean that the f that belongs to x is identical with the f which belongs to y? We should expect this to be so, but it is not always the case. Though I say, 'The table is brown and the book is brown' it does not follow that the brown of the table is identically the same colour as the brown of the book. There are different shades of brown. The table and the book are obviously not one and the same thing, but neither are the shades b_1 (of the table) and b_2 (of the book). These shades are sufficiently alike for me to speak of them as brown, but by so speaking of them I do not wish to imply that they are identical. In this case the colours of the two objects resemble one another, but they are not identical. Though we use the one word 'brown' to describe the two colours, it does not follow that the qualities are identical. Are we ever in a position to say that two qualities are identical? One's answer would depend on the view one took of the conflict between supporters of the resemblance and the identity theories. In the above example the two colours referred to by the word 'brown' resemble one another but are not identical. If we accept the resemblance theory this would be true in all cases in which we say 'x is the same as y in respect of f'; f in the case of x is f would be like but not the same as f in the case of y is f. The only possible qualitative identity here would be f's (in 'x is f') identity with itself, that is to say, b_1 in the above illustration is identical with itself, $b_1 = b_1$. On the other hand, if we adopt the identity theory then we could have a shade of brown which would be identical in table and book. Identically the same shade of colour could be present at the same time in different places. In such a case we could say that x and y are identical in respect of their colour, though they may differ from one another in other respects; but if we rejected the identity theory, we could only say that x and y resemble one another in colour.[1] In my view the truth in this matter of resemblance and identity theories is that there are resembling qualities on the one hand and identical qualities on the other and neither kind can be ruled out. Yet of course even when an identical quality is common to x and y it does not follow that x and y are identical, for they may differ in respect of other qualities. It should be added too that what has been said in this paragraph of qualities may also be said of relations.

Up to the present we have ignored the time factor in speaking of identity. The principle of identity as formulated $x = x$ is timeless; so is Leibniz's law. But, to return once again to individual things, we have the problem on our hands of what

---

[1] It is admitted that we speak loosely of x and y being identical in colour when both are brown, though the one is b_1 and the other b_2 and they are not strictly speaking identical in colour.

account to give of the individual thing (or person) that changes over the years and yet remains itself. Leibniz's law might appear to be the more helpful here, for certainly $x = x$ can be of little help. But does even Leibniz's law apply? We may consider an example. This man is identically the same individual as the boy who lived here thirty years ago, yet the man has now few of the properties that the boy possessed. At the present moment if x is the same individual as y then whatever can be said of x can be said of y; but this does not hold if x signifies the boy of thirty years ago and y the man as he is now—and yet they are the same individual. The boy who was three foot high, who could lift a few pounds only, who talked as a child, is now the six-footer, able to lift a hundredweight and to engage in sophisticated talk. No doubt it would be easier to accommodate temporal changes of this kind if a satisfactory tense logic were worked out. Still, an adequate account for instance of the identity of a human being, who is one though continually changing, whose continuity is conceived in terms of two apparently wholly different sets of criteria, the one the perceptual spatiotemporal criteria of all physical body continuance, the other the memory criteria—such an account would be difficult to achieve with any logic. We are here considering the normal human being. What of abnormal cases, such as split personality or changes of personality after, say, brain surgery? If we claim that it is one and the same individual being who persists in spite of such radical changes we can hardly then be thinking within the framework of Leibniz's law.

The difficulty is not confined to the discussion of the human person; it arises in the study of many natural phenomena. Consider natural fissions and fusions, for instance cell fission. Here is one cell but it divides into two. We say loosely that the same life goes on. Can we say that one and the same cell goes on? And if it does go on does it go on in one or other of the cells, or in both? Or should we say that the original cell is identical with neither? In that case it has ceased to be, and yet we say that it continues to be. But if it does continue to be, and if the division is real so that there are two cells rather than one, then Leibniz's law, in so far as it is claimed to be universal, is false. A. N. Prior, in discussing this and other problems,[1] is prepared to conclude that we must contemplate 'the abandonment or at least the modification of Leibniz's law'.[2]

We need not pursue the examination of the principle of identity any further. The present uncertainty about the principle is in itself very clear evidence against the theory that the principle is intuited by reason *a priori*. Clearly the principle is not yet fully thought out; we seem to have at least two principles of identity on our hands and we require both. Added to this it might be argued that at least the first formulation of Leibniz's law given above would necessitate two further principles of identity to cover the notions of symmetry and transitivity present in the Leibnizian concept of identity. Finally, one is conscious that in dealing with the concept of identity one is dealing with the same fundamental problems as face us in connection with the concept of substance, and as our thoughts on substance change so also do those on identity.

89. There remains what is generally assumed to be the supreme principle of reasoning, namely, the law of non-contradiction. It cannot be the case that something both is f and is not f; or, if we speak of propositions, it cannot be the case that both p is true and not-p is true, $\sim(p.\sim p)$.

About this law a reservation that Kant makes is interesting and highly significant, and we may begin by considering it. Plato, in the *Republic*, had set out the law as follows: 'It is clear that the same thing cannot act in two opposite ways or be in two opposite states at the same time, with respect to the same part of itself, and in relation to the same object.'[3] So too Aristotle in the *Metaphysics* asserts that 'it is impossible for any one to believe the same thing to be and not to be'. But his interest in statements led him to formulate the law also in terms of a subject and its attribute. 'The same attribute cannot at the same time belong and not belong to the same subject in

---

[1] 'Time, Existence and Identity', *Proc. Arist. Soc.*, 1965–6, 183 ff.
[2] Ibid. 192.   [3] *Republic* 436, Cornford's translation.

the same respect.'¹ There is, however, no suggestion in Aristotle that the law applies to statements only. It is a law about things that is binding on all thought about things.

We may contrast Kant's position. He regards the law of non-contradiction as universal in application within its field. But 'it belongs only to logic . . . irrespective of content . . . The *principle of contradiction* must therefore be recognised as being the universal and completely sufficient *principle of all analytic knowledge*; but beyond the sphere of analytic knowledge it has, as a *sufficient* criterion of truth, no authority and no field of application.'² Analytic knowledge on this view is a timeless, *a priori* knowledge, dominated by the principle of non-contradiction, but the principle applies to synthetic knowledge only in a negative sense. It there provides the negative criterion that a synthetic statement which contradicts itself cannot be true, but it provides no positive criterion as to what synthetic statements are true. Furthermore, since the principle is timeless, irrespective of content, and purely formal, Kant adds that its formulation in earlier times needs to be corrected. The phrase 'at the same time' in the traditional formulation shows carelessness and can mislead, for it turns non-contradiction into a principle of synthetic judgement, so that it ceases to be a solely formal principle. 'If I say', Kant explains, 'that a man, who is unlearned, is not learned, the condition, *at one and the same time*, must be added; for he who is at one time unlearned can very well at another be learned. But if I say, no unlearned man is learned, the proposition is analytic, since the property unlearnedness, now goes to make up the concept of the subject, and the truth of the negative judgement then becomes evident as an immediate consequence of the principle of contradiction, without requiring the supplementary condition, *at one and the same time*.'³ Kant did not foresee experiments to enable the logician to introduce tense inflections into logic, but what comes out clearly in this passage is his insistence that the principle of non-contradiction is a principle of analytic knowledge.

---

¹ *Metaphysics* 1005ᵇ18–25. ² *Critique of Pure Reason*, A 151, B 190–1.
³ A 153, B 192.

There are frequent echoes of this theory, that non-contradiction has 'no authority and no field of application' beyond the analytic, in subsequent thinking. It is taken for granted that non-contradiction is a merely formal principle determining 'pure' thinking, and guaranteeing validity in such thinking. At any point in the construction of a pure logical system the principle may be explicitly appealed to, but even when not explicit it is implicit throughout the construction. Within this field it holds universally and necessarily, but it is not therefore assumed that it must apply beyond the field. It is necessary only in a context, only within a conceptual scheme, but the scheme may be modified and the law may be revised, or even abrogated, in a new context. Outside the proper context we should not be surprised to find exceptions to the law.

It is usually supposed that the study of paradoxes and antinomies comes within analytic thinking, and it is noteworthy that we do not allow the occurrence of such paradoxes and antinomies to shake our faith in the authority of the law of non-contradiction. Thus, in the case of antinomies, strict adherence to the rules of right reasoning leads the thinker to conclusions which appear to be self-contradictory, to conclusions which are true if and only if they are false. But when we find that this is so, we do not reject the principle of non-contradiction, we rather regard the occurrence of such antinomies as a challenge and look to our other procedures in reasoning to save us from them. The authority of the principle of non-contradiction remains unaffected.

It is agreed, however, that the principle does not hold with equal force in our reasoning about the natural world. For, in the first place, some of the arguments already brought forward against the application of the principle of excluded middle to this world could be turned against the principle of non-contradiction. Consider, for instance, the argument from vague predicates. Because of the ambiguity of the predicate phrase '. . . is bald' it becomes possible to say significantly of someone: 'He is and he is not bald.' As has been suggested earlier, more precise definition of concepts might make these predicates less vague, yet we are not free to conceive and define them as we choose since they are concepts of natural phenomena. There may indeed be a relativity in nature which makes the principle of non-contradiction inapplicable. But, it may be argued too that contradiction in nature is not merely possible but essential. The discussion of this topic is complicated by the fact that the term 'contradiction' is being used loosely within it. Strictly speaking, only statements can contradict one another; yet the practice of speaking of qualities contradicting each other and again of things contradicting each other is general. Perhaps it would be safer to speak of incompatibilities in nature rather than of contradictions; for instance, two qualities are incompatible in the sense that if one of these qualities belongs to an object the other cannot belong to it. If that were the case then we should be contradicting ourselves if we said that the object a has at one and the same time and in the same respect the qualities q_1 and q_2 where q_1 and q_2 are incompatible qualities. Now the relativist theory mentioned above denies that incompatibilities in nature are absolute. The natural world is one of change, growth, and development: incompatibilities are relative only, consequently non-contradiction cannot be a basic principle of such a world. To return to the example of cell fission, the cell is now one (for it has not divided) but it is equally true that it is potentially two. Yet to say both of these things is to go some way towards contradicting oneself, or perhaps it would be better to say that the situation is one in which the principle of non-contradiction is not dominant. The process of growth is not one to which this principle applies unequivocally. Consequently, it is in no way surprising that the dialectical philosophers of the nineteenth and early twentieth centuries give little place to the principle of non-contradiction; their thought sometimes seems to be dominated rather by the opposite principle, namely, that contradiction is the key to the understanding of life. Hegel puts the point succinctly: 'Contradiction is the very moving principle of the world: and it is ridiculous to say that contradiction is unthinkable. The only thing correct in that statement is that contradiction is not the end of the matter, but cancels itself. But contradiction, when cancelled, does not leave abstract identity; for that is itself only one side of the contrariety.'[1]

The point is stated in more modern terms by F. H. Bradley in *Principles of Logic* and *Appearance and Reality*. One finds in these books a marked coolness towards the principle of non-contradiction. The principle is recognized as a logical law and incompatibilities in nature and life are admitted. But 'the real question', it is added,[2] 'is as to the limits within which, and the conditions under which, incompatibles are found and can be justified. How far in other words is the truth of contradiction, as such, only relative and more or less of an appearance? What, as I understand it, the Dialectical Method is concerned to deny is merely the absolute, utter and final, truth of fixed incompatibles.' This statement is made in the second edition of the *Principles*, but the same coolness to non-contradiction is evident in the first edition as well—indeed the principle is there written off as of little significance to human thinking. 'Its claims, if we consider them, are so absurdly feeble, it is itself so weak and perfectly inoffensive, that it can not quarrel, for it has not a tooth with which to bite any one.'[3] The law, in so far as it does apply, is strictly limited in its field and is relative to that field. Its relativity is further emphasized in Bradley's *Appearance and Reality*. Truth—absolute truth—is nowhere concerned with the law of non-contradiction; it is relevant only to conditional truths. We must rid ourselves of the idea that non-contradiction is the supreme principle of validity, as the formalists say. 'What is self-contradictory', Bradley declares, 'may also for me be valid.'[4]

This is strange doctrine for what Bradley would surely have regarded as our over-formal, mid-twentieth-century philosophy. But it is implicit in all evolutionary and process thinking, even though it is rarely stated in so blunt a fashion. It denies the universality of the principle of non-contradiction and

---

[1] *Logic* (*Encyclopaedia*) § 119. Wallace's translation (1892), p. 223.
[2] *Principles of Logic*, 2nd edn., 1922, p. 165.
[3] Ibid., p. 151.
[4] *Appearance and Reality*, 2nd edn., p. 565 n.

refuses to give it absolute status either in the world of nature or even in logic.

90. It is well to bear in mind that these are exceptional statements and that over against them stands the body of conviction that logical reasoning is reasoning in accordance with certain fundamental laws of thought. The exceptions however lead to doubt whether the fundamental laws in question are to be identified with the traditional 'laws of thought'. They lead one to question whether these traditional laws are adequately formulated and they confirm the belief that in any case they are not the only laws involved. But we do not doubt that there are principles regulating our thought and that the traditional laws (modified, if modification is necessary) are part of these principles. Not all our thinking is in fact strictly regulated by these principles, for ordinary thinking is rarely precise enough to be so regulated, though this of course does not deprive it of its usefulness. Yet precise thinking and valid thinking is thinking in accordance with the body of such principles, and it is the existence of the latter which gives meaning to the demand for consistency.

What account now is to be given at the end of this chapter of the source of our knowledge of these principles? In the first place, we reject the view that they are known by the mind *a priori* and that to provide such knowledge is part of the function of reason. It would be pleasant if we could know by reason (independently of unreliable sensory experience) the universal and necessary features of the framework and structure of being. It would be pleasant if the so-called 'laws of thought' set out those features once and for all. Yet the evidence brought forward in this chapter provokes doubt about the necessity, the universal application, and the absoluteness, of the 'laws of thought'. Thus identity, in the sense of $x = x$, does not formulate precisely what we have in mind when we speak of the identity of an individual. Leibniz's law would suit us better, but it too would appear to need modification. The law of non-contradiction, we may safely say, does hold of all *statement*. But is the knowledge of it truly a knowledge of the structure of being? Or are evolutionary and developmental theorists justified in doubting this? Excluded middle gives the logician the decisiveness he needs, but it does not help him to deal with Fitch's problem nor with mathematical intuitionism. It is consequently not the case that we know 'laws of thought' as the structural principles of being and know them by reason *a priori* in such a way that we have no uncertainty and no doubt about the necessity and the universal applicability of these principles. It may happen that logicians will some time in the future construct a logic that can take care of the exceptions which we have considered, but what clearly emerges from the present discussion of the 'laws of thought' is that they are not known by infallible reason *a priori*, nor are they known as applying universally throughout being.

It is frequently assumed that if we reject the view that these principles are acquired *a priori* we have only one alternative theory, namely that they are acquired in the course of experience. Yet there is clearly one other alternative to be considered and there may be more. The alternative that I have in mind is the conventionalist theory, and we may examine it briefly. In doing so, I need not discuss again[1] the conventionalism of the account of necessity according to which, for instance, a bachelor is necessarily for me an unmarried man once I have decided to treat 'bachelor' as the exact synonym of 'unmarried man'. If absolute synonymy is possible then a necessity of this kind must be conceded. But the necessity of the laws of thought does not rest on synonymy. When I say that a thing cannot have and not have a property I am not saying that the locution 'thing' is synonymous with the locution 'that which cannot have and not have a property' and find in this an explanation of the necessity pertaining to the law of non-contradiction. This would obviously be a false interpretation of that necessity.

The conventionalist case is more powerfully presented when it is argued that necessity rests not on a synonymy of locutions,

[1] Cf. § 70 above.

but on the stipulation of principles. The principles we are now considering are called 'laws of *thought*' and if we concentrate on thinking, in contrast to knowing, a case may certainly be made for the view that the principles on which thinking (and this the most precise thinking) rests may be freely stipulated by the thinker. We have seen how thinking can be axiomatic and how the axioms may be chosen by the thinker. The question whether the principles apply to the world of things, or do not apply, does not then arise; in this sense they need not be interpreted, all that matters is that the system should have its own internal truth. The thinker clearly would need to stipulate more than the three traditional laws of thought; he must set down all that is necessary for him to work out his system; for instance, the use of certain logical constants or again of additional principles of deduction not already covered by the principles of identity, non-contradiction, and excluded middle. Further, he must be able to handle subject-matter in such a way that it does not interfere with his argument. For instance, 'John is or is not at home' is true for him whoever John is and wherever his home is.

Systems may be set up in thought, for instance, in logic or in mathematics, on principles which the thinker arbitrarily chooses. He may admittedly take some of the principles that he uses for granted and some of these may never have been consciously chosen by him; but the principles or axioms of which he is conscious may all be freely chosen for the purposes of his system-building. The question before us is whether the principles of identity, non-contradiction, and excluded middle are conventionalist in this sense. Now every statement made by us has some conventional features, for language itself is a convention, and the three principles, being statements, are conventionalist in the sense in which every other statement is. But are they conventionalist in the further sense of being arbitrarily chosen by the thinker? If we take the view that they are not immune to revision but that they can be modified, we thereby concede that the thinker is to that extent free to change them. But this does not justify us in saying that he changes them as he chooses, or that he freely stipulates them. Most often they are implicit in his thought; on the rare occasions on which he consciously makes appeal to them there is no suggestion that he has arbitrarily chosen them as principles of his system and that he could have refrained from doing so if he had wished. He never thinks of them as principles formulated to provide a foundation for a thought-system he wishes to build. Though they are called 'laws of thought' they are regarded as applying outside axiomatized thought-systems as well as within. The fact that he may also use them in building his thought-systems does not make them conventionalist. They are principles applying to being; for instance, $x = x$ applies to whatever exists. As long as this is the case these principles are not to be conceived as mere adjuncts to system-construction in thought and cannot be mere conventions.

That a thing is itself and not another thing is a principle which the thinker affirms (using conventional language to do so), but what is affirmed is no invention of his nor is it any convention which he himself has made or one he has accepted from others. He knows that the principle is not his creation and he knows too that it is not a convention he has accepted from others. He is conscious that it is a discovery of some kind. He sets out the discovery in as precise terms as he can, setting down the three principles of identity, non-contradiction, and excluded middle. In doing so he makes use of linguistic conventions and is free to bring into being and use new linguistic conventions. But the laws of thought are not principles of syntax. What the thinker affirms in language is something discovered. Having discovered them, he may use these principles consciously as axioms of a thought-system involving the greatest possible abstraction from non-logical elements, or he may simply take them for granted in constructing such a system; yet never are they his creation. This is the case—and it is a strong case—against the theory that the 'laws of thought' are conventions.

91. The principles are not conventional creations. In some very

important sense not yet determined they are discovered, but they are not discovered by reason *a priori*. The only remaining possibility, it is said, is that they are discovered 'by experience'. This statement is not particularly illuminating, however, in view of the ambiguity of the term 'experience'. For instance, if it were said that the principles are discovered *in* experience, they might still be discovered *a priori* in the course of experience. To say that they are discovered *by* experience presumably implies that they are not discovered *a priori*. Experience itself reveals them. But what then is 'experience itself'? Sometimes it is the term used for the actual gaining of information—of the external world through sense-perception and of ourselves in self-consciousness—but more often for the body of information so gained. It is of experience in the latter sense that a-priorists speak when they use the celebrated argument that experience presupposes the principles, and since this is so the principles cannot themselves be known by experience. The body of information is a body of ordered material, the material in the case of our experience of the external world is the sensory manifold, the ordering is done by the mind, it is said, in accordance with its own *a priori* principles. But the argument rests on the supposition that 'experience' is this body of information, whose very existence presupposes a knowledge of principles which could not have been provided empirically.

Another account of experience, stressing the actual gaining of the information, and not abstracting from it to concentrate on the body of information itself, is however possible, and this in its turn makes possible a very different account of our knowledge of the ordering principles. For the gaining of information is a process in time, 'experience' does not emanate fully formed. If in any experience I find myself making use of principles, spatial, temporal, ontological, or logical, it does not follow that these principles must have been acquired outside experience. They may have been acquired in earlier experience. What is obvious is that I come to this new experience with principles that may be used by me in ordering and recognizing, and that the principles consequently are not acquired in this present experience. Nevertheless this is not my first experience. The principles could be the outcome of earlier experiences of mine. If it is argued that they cannot be derived from experience since they are necessary and universal, we have seen grounds for doubting this absolute necessity and universality. They have the relative necessity and universality which can be features of principles so described. If further it is argued that none of these principles, say that of identity, could be directly experienced, as a patch of colour is directly seen, this can be granted. Obviously the principle of identity is not 'directly experienced' in this sense of the phrase; the most that can be claimed is that it is derived from experience; that what we do directly experience suggests it.

But now can even this be claimed? Is there anything in experience that suggests these principles to us in the first place, and leads to our isolating and formulating them later? What is the primitive discovery? The most helpful answer would seem to be that it is the same sort of discovery as is made when we discover substances and causes. It is becoming clearer as we proceed, and it is a point that needs emphasis, that our thought is regulated by a web of related concepts, namely, substance, causality, individual thing, entity, identity, non-contradiction, and excluded middle; and the insights which lie behind the conceiving of these concepts are themselves related. These insights are part of our experience. We do not speak here of experience in traditional empiricist terms, the sensing of 'simples' and the combining of them into 'complexes', but rather of our full trafficking with the external world as it affects us.[1] Nor should 'experience' be thought of solely in terms of our knowledge of the natural world; it includes too our knowledge of other human beings, and, most important of all, of our own selves.

Our experience of the physical world around us and of ourselves leaves us with a sense of thinghood, of individuation, and substantiality. The example of seeing the Matterhorn may be recalled; we experience it as an entity standing out, separate from the other mountains around it. It is true that on reflection

---

[1] Cf. Chapters IV and X above.

we realize that we do not know the exact line of demarcation between mountain and valley, but this does not weaken the impression left upon us of a thing that is separate, an individual. Our experience of the physical world is an experience of individual things; the pen, the paper, the inkpot, the desk before me are all experienced as being separate entities. They are found too to last through time and though some of their qualities change they themselves remain the same. My most forceful experience of such identity, however, is my consciousness of myself. I am aware of myself as an entity, having many experiences but being myself one, as changing but lasting through changes. I remember my own past; I remember myself taking a walk yesterday. This consciousness of myself is the profoundest knowledge I have of an abiding unity, an entity, a continuant, an agent.

The main thesis of our present argument is that in such experiences as these we find the suggestion of concepts later to be explicitly conceived and elaborated by us. It is not being maintained that we know that $x = x$ in experience, but we do experience individual things. In particular, I am conscious of my own identity. I concentrate on this identity, abstracting it from the other features of my being of which I am conscious. I generalize and say of any such individual that it is identical with itself, and generalize still more widely so as to say of anything whatsoever that it is itself. If we have a variable x then whichever value of that variable we consider it will still be the case that it is itself, $(x)(x = x)$. This is the thesis. It does not seem to me to be an entirely impossible one to maintain and if it can be maintained it provides an origin in cognition for the principle of identity other than that which either the *a priori* rationalist or the conventionalist provides. It would be strengthened if it were further acknowledged that we usually arrive at the principle of identity not by starting from the conscious recognition of an individual thing's identity with itself, but rather from taking it for granted, in view of frequent experience of individuals. We are disposed to think in this way, but are so disposed, we should add, as the consequence of our experience.

The a-priorist might object at this point that whatever we make of this argument as it applies to the principle of identity, none of it applies to the principle of non-contradiction. It is still necessary to derive the latter principle, he will say, from an *a priori* source, and if this is necessary we may as well derive the other principles too from the same source. It may make some sort of sense to speak of experiencing a thing to be itself, but does it make sense to experience a negation, not to mention a contradiction? One may open a drawer and see a book inside, but one cannot open a drawer and find no-book inside. One sees a red patch; one cannot see a non-red patch. Now to consider this argument fully it would be necessary to propound a theory of negation and this would be out of place here. One may admit that one cannot see a non-book or non-red, still it does make sense to say that one may open a drawer and find no book inside, though it is also true to say that one does not then find amongst the individual things present a non-book. But is it the case that, in order to derive this concept of negation from experience, it is necessary to experience directly a non-thing or a non-quality? Consider once again what it is to have an experience of an individual thing. One is aware of it as that which is itself *and* other than all else. I experience myself as one being and as different from all others. Spinoza's principle that determination is negation is implicit in the experience of any entity, whether it be a thing or a person. The conscious experience of boundaries is an experience of negation; to be conscious that a thing is itself is to be conscious that it is not any other thing. In this sense one may sensibly talk of an experience of negation, and the experience contains too the very clear suggestion of what is afterwards formulated as the principle of non-contradiction. It cannot be both that x is f and x is not f. The same experience suggests the third principle that either x is f or it is not the case that x is f. Just as these three principles in one sense 'say the same thing' so too all three may be suggested by one and the same experience, that of a particular individual.

All that can be meant by 'suggestion' in this account is that the first insight is present, the insight that a thing is itself and not any other thing. It requires reflection to formulate the insight in the statement: 'A thing is itself, and not another thing'; and in the further statements: '$x = x$', 'If a is a thing and f is a quality then it cannot be that both a is f and a is not f'; and lastly: 'If a is a thing and f a quality then either a is f or it is not the case that a is f.' The claim is simply that becoming aware of an individual thing is to have an insight that, developed in reflection, may lead to the formulation of these statements. Moreover, statements themselves, these and all others, are objects of possible study and objects to which the above principles can apply. A statement, for instance 'Tom is tall', is on the one hand a token sentence, a series of sounds uttered in speech or of written words. Even so, it is itself, and the principles apply. On the other hand, it is also a significant statement, a proposition, which is true or false, and it is itself in this case not as being one and the same set of token words but as being a truth which if true *is* true. The formulation of token sentence identity would be $x = x$, but this will not do as the formulation of the identity of the significant statement. The usual formulation in its case, as we have seen, is the following: if any statement is true, then it is true, or $p \supset p$. Both $x = x$ and $p \supset p$ are formulations of laws of identity, but they are not themselves identical any more than $x = x$ is identical with Leibniz's law. This is why it is a serious mistake to argue on the assumption that $x = x$ is identical with $p \supset p$.

The ultimates of abstraction and reflective refinement appear tautologous. The degree of abstraction is so great as to produce statements that are almost vacuous of subject-matter, and one may be easily tempted as a consequence to suppose that these are merely conventional stipulations. But this would be to forget that the set of concepts in question in these last two chapters make up the framework within which we not merely think, but also know, the world of being. If they were mere stipulations they could serve as basic axioms for uninterpreted thought-systems, but then there would be no guarantee that they could apply to being. Yet they do so apply. On the other hand they are not intellectual intuitions by *a priori* reason of the structure of being, for then they would hold necessarily and universally. There would be no room for exceptions, and modifications could not be made. It seems clear, however, that this framework needs to be modified and is modified by us, and that the formulation even of the three laws of thought is not final and not immune to revision. In this situation *a priori* rationalism is to be rejected along with conventionalism. The case in fact is strong for the thesis that our knowledge of this framework is derived from our consciousness of the world, on the one hand, and of our own self on the other; so that what tend to regulate our thinking in the attempt to extend our knowledge are principles derived from the knowledge of the world we already possess. We face the world with strong dispositions, and again with consciously accepted principles; we face it with a conceptual framework which is not *given* now in our present experience of the world but is that in terms of which we make sense of what is given. Yet the source of our knowledge of this framework is our prior experience of the world around us and of ourselves.[1]

[1] I am grateful to my colleague, Mr. J. M. B. Moss, for discussing the contents of this chapter with me and for his helpful comments.

CONCLUSION

IN concluding this book its underlying purpose may be re-asserted. It is to analyse and to relate three features of cognition, namely, knowing, thought, and reason.

The analysis of knowing deals primarily with certain knowledge. We claim to know with certainty, though we also acknowledge that much of our knowledge is probable only. But the fundamental difficulty has to do with the claim to certain knowledge; for I can be certain or sure and yet be in error and in that case though I am certain I do not know. I have to admit that sometimes when I have been quite certain that p, I have subsequently found that I was in error, and this is the crux of the problem. The realization that such a state of affairs is possible leads to two reactions, first, that we cease to speak of certainty in human knowledge and speak only of probability. But this in effect is to refuse to face the difficulty. For we *are* certain at times, just as at other times we are not certain but merely judge or believe or opine that, say, p is probably true. The second reaction is to accept that we are certain, but to add that being certain or being sure is not enough. Being sure, it is argued, is only one condition of three that must be satisfied; it is also necessary that the certainty should be backed by adequate evidence, that is to say, evidence that is objective and universally acceptable, and it is further necessary that what one is certain of should be true. Unless these conditions are met there is no knowledge that p even though we are completely certain that p.

We find however that this latter theory is harassed by a circularity in its argument which makes it impossible for its demands to be met, for the final appeal both on adequacy of evidence and on truth is to that very assurance which is all along suspect. We become conscious too of the oversimplification in the traditional division into knowledge and opinion. Traditionally, the former is taken to be infallible and the latter fallible, yet we see that the true state of affairs is different from this. A more correct analysis of cognition in general provides a threefold division: (1) opining or believing, a state in which one is not sure, (ii) being sure but yet being fallible, (iii) being sure and being infallible. The conclusion to which the first part of this book points is that the human condition is (i) or (ii) but never (iii), at least no instance of infallible knowledge can be adduced by us. This may be thought to be a sceptical conclusion, but it is to be emphasized that the scepticism in this case is one side of the coin only, for though fallible we are capable of knowing with a certainty which is complete. The issue is completely settled; we are constrained to accept and there is no doubt; yet our knowledge is still fallible. The absolute, infallible knowledge that the intellectual intuitionist speaks of is an ideal which can be conceived but not attained by us. Thus the conclusion about certain knowledge at which we finally arrive is that we do gain such knowledge, but that it is primal; the assurance itself is absolute but the knowledge is not absolute since it is fallible.

Next a firm distinction needs to be made between knowing and thinking. Thinking is frequently spoken of as if it were knowing and this is not difficult to understand in view of the close interrelationship between the two. Thinking may help us to know, and so in a loose sense may be thought to be knowing. Moreover, given certain metaphysical assumptions it could be argued that thinking is knowing in a precise sense. For it might be held that what is real is Idea or Spirit, whose essential feature is thought, so that the development of a piece of thinking in accordance with the strict laws of thought would inevitably be a revelation and knowledge of the world that exists. But if this metaphysic be rejected there appears to be no other that permits us to assume that our thinking is a knowing.

We can think out thought-systems which are not meant to be applicable to the existing world, and no claim is made that they do apply. This may be true even though we then use past knowledge as subject-matter in our thinking, or again imagery derived from such past knowledge. As our thinking becomes more abstract it will contain less and less subject-matter of this kind, but even when we consciously use such subject-matter in our system-building we need not be using it in order to apply our system of thought to the existing world. Thinking is thus something fundamentally different in character from knowing; it is a creativity and a making, whereas knowing is a discovery or even a constraint to accept.

The creativity of thought is revealed in its invention of symbols and in their use, particularly those symbols which man uses in speaking and writing. Phonemes are used to frame utterances which are significant to the speaker himself and to his listener. Language, this most splendid of human inventions, greatly improved communication between man and man and also helped in the further development of thought, although language was not, and is not, a perfect instrument either for communication or for thought. Yet, to speak of the latter, human thinking gained greatly in scope and power through man's use of language which lent itself to abstraction, generalization, and analysis. More than all, the invention of the general word made easier the grouping and classifying of things on the basis of the observation of resembling or identical qualities. It helped man to frame concepts and to think in universal terms, it helped him to use a word as a nucleus around which would be gathered empirical and linguistic dispositions so that a concept could be attributed to a subject. It enabled him to make general statements which were eternal.

The inventiveness and spontaneity of thought which mark the high intelligence of man are found throughout human life, from the rude interpolation and extrapolation of everyday life onward. They are seen at their best in inductive ampliation together with hypothesis-making in the natural sciences, and in deduction both in the natural sciences and in mathematics and logic. In the system-construction of mathematics and logic thought is at its freest; through abstraction the reference to subject-matter is almost wholly eliminated, so that a situation of near vacuousness is reached, and in this situation the thinker finds himself most free to create his systems. He sets down his own principles and builds as he chooses; everything is tolerated, except only inconsistency.

This qualification leads us to our final problem. A thinker, it is said, must think in accordance with the principles of reason, but if these are extraneous to his thinking how then is his thinking free? This is the problem of the function of reason. Are there immutable principles supplied by reason *a priori* and do these regulate thought even at its most abstract? In that case thought is not free; there are elements in it which are imposed on the thinker by pure reason. We have found grounds however for doubting the traditional rationalist doctrine of the *a priori*. But we have further seen that the opposing doctrine, conventionalism, whereby the thinker is supposed to be at each moment wholly free to create whatever principles he needs in his system-building, is also unsatisfactory. The conclusion that seems best to fit the evidence is that, while it is neither the case that pure reason supplies the principles nor that the thinker himself brings them into being as is convenient for him, the principles are partly extraneous but yet not wholly so. They are suggested in experience, and this is why we may entertain the hope that they can apply to our world and not merely to logical systems which we ourselves have created in thought. Just as the real world, with its resembling and identical qualities and its natural recurrences, lends itself to grouping and classifying and to the thinking of it in general terms, so too does it lend itself to the application to it of such fundamental principles as the laws of thought. On the other hand, the thinker formulates these principles or accepts another's formulation, and he is free to modify his or another's formulation of them whenever he chooses. He goes forward to meet fresh experiences with these principles in mind, but not because they are innate and *a priori*. Fundamentally he is in no different position from the scientist who approaches experience with the principles of his own science in mind. These are principles which have been acquired by him, or by others from whom he has learnt them, in past experience. The principles we now consider are more general and apply on a wider scale; none the less they too have been known in the same way. If they were given absolutely and necessarily our knowledge of them would be infallible and not open to revision. But logicians today are revising these laws and philosophers are revising their concepts of entity, identity, substance, and cause, and they do so in the light of further reflection on the information, both old and new, which is to hand. In doing this they are proceeding rationally, in the sense in which 'reason' is being used in this book, since they bring what is known to bear upon their present thinking; and it is in this sense that the principles they use are rational.

Finally, two things should be said about truth. In the first place it follows, if our argument is accepted, that there is one truth and one truth only, that is to say, there are not two truths, factual (ontological, metaphysical, epistemological) truth and logical truth. We can and do distinguish between different sorts of statements, between, for instance, 'man has landed on the moon' and 'if a is f then a is either f or g'. But when we say that the first statement is true and the second is true we mean the same by '. . . is true'; we do not mean that the first is 'factually true' and the second is 'logically true'. In this sense there are no sorts of truth, though there exist many different kinds of true statements.

In the second place, there is much to suggest that the concept of truth presupposes the concept of knowledge and not vice versa. The truth is what is known. From many angles the argument of this book points to this conclusion. If it be accepted it then follows that just because there is a distinction between fallible and infallible knowledge so there is a distinction between primal and absolute truth, not however as between two sorts of truth but as one and the same truth viewed by a fallible and again an infallible being. If our knowledge were infallible then whatever was known would be true absolutely. But we rest in doubt whether any of our knowledge is infallible. Consequently we do not know absolute truth. None the less we may *think* it, for it would be that which would be known if our knowledge were infallible. The absoluteness of truth is therefore something we think. None the less we are conscious of the difference between the true and the false, for we know in a primal sense and know then with certainty that this statement is true and that one false. It is admitted that when we are most sure we may be in error; this is the human situation. Yet this assurance is sufficient to make the concept of the true and the false significant for us and without it we should not have the concept. It would seem therefore not to be the case that we first have the concept of truth and then use it as a test of knowledge.

INDEX OF PERSONS

Anscombe, G. E. M., 95 n.
Aristotle, 30, 33–6, 45, 211–13, 241, 251
Augustine, 31
Austin, J. L., 5
Ayer, A. J., 4 n., 18 n. 1

Dain, A., 134 5
Bednarowski, W. F., 243–4
Bentham, J., 105 n.
Bergson, H., 195
Berkeley, George, 58, 83, 213
Black, Max, 151, 221 n.
Blanshard, B., 175–6
Bloomfield, L., 110 n., 111, 114
Bradley, F. H., 163–5, 255–6
Braithwaite, R. B., 153–4
Brentano, F., 92–5
Bridges, Robert, 117, 119 and n. 2, 122

Carnap, R., 160, 167
Champawat, N., 53 n.
Chisholm, R. M., 18–22, 92, 93 n., 95 n.
Chomsky, N., 109 n., 115
Clark, Michael, 53 n.
Cohen, L. J., 18 n., 95 n.
Cordemoy, G. de, 222, 224, 232
Croce, B., 195

De Morgan, A., 243
Descartes, R., 30–2, 39, 40, 42, 61, 131

Einstein, A., 161
Euclid, 40–1

Fitch, F. B., 245
Frege, G., 128

Gettier, E. L., 53 n.
Gibson, J. J., 84 n.
Goodman, N., 227
Griss, G. F. C., 169 n.
Groenewold, H. J., 152–3

Hampshire, Stuart, 115 n. 2
Heath, T. L., 41 n.
Hegel, G. W. F., 47, 254

Heyting, A., 169 n., 245
Hume, D., 78, 158, 189, 207, 215, 222, 226, 229–31
Humphrey, G., 99 n.
Husserl, E., 93

Jean Paul, 192
Jespersen, O., 135
Jones, Owen R., 88 n.

Kant, Immanuel, 7–9, 23, 24, 36, 64, 133, 147, 176, 182, 192–3, 213–20, 222–3, 238–9, 251–2
Keynes, J. N., 134–5
Kneale, William, 95 n., 195
Köhler, 97–8
Kraus, Oscar, 93 n.

Lehrer, Keith, 53 n.
Leibniz, G. W., 30, 37 9, 138, 169, 215, 243, 247–51
Locke, John, 31, 36–7, 105, 138, 213
Louch, A. R., 221 n.

Malcolm, Norman, 18 n., 59 n.
Martinet, André, 112, 114
Marty, Anton, 93
Medawar, P. B., 162 n.
Meinong, A., 93
Mill, J. S., 105, 156–8, 210
Mises, L. von, 158
Moore, G. E., 51
Moss, J. M. B., 265

Newcastle, Marquis of, 31

Oxford Realists, 51, 54

Peetz, D. W., 162 n.
Peirce, C. S., 156
Piaget, J., 96, 124 n.
Plato, ix, 30, 36, 210, 212, 216, 247, 251
Popper, K., 159–61
Price, H. H., 74, 101 n.
Prior, A. N., 95 n., 251

Quine, W. V., 135

Radford, Colin, 10 n.
Ramus, 137
Reichenbach, H., 158
Rozeboom, W. W., 53 and n. 2
Russell, Bertrand, 42, 120 n., 138 n.,
 162, 216–17, 245
Rutherford, Lord, 152

Sapir, E., 124
Saunders, J., 53 n.
Schlick, Moritz, 225–6
Sosa, Ernest, 53 n.
Spinoza, B. de, 211, 215, 263

Swinburne, R. G., 162 n.

Thomas, L. E., 18 n.

Ullmann, S., 112 n., 119, 126
Urmson, J. O., 95 n.

Warnock, G. J., 12, 18 n.
Whitehead, A. N., 120 n.
Whorf, Lee, 124
Wilson, J. Cook, 73–4
Wittgenstein, L., 183
Woozley, A. D., 10, 18 n.

INDEX OF SUBJECTS

A priori knowledge, 181–8, 196, 201, 212–20, 237–9, 256–7, 269
Absolute knowledge, Ch. 3, 86–8
Absolute truth, 63–5
Abstract and concrete, 203–4
Accepting, 19–20
Action, 231–4
Ampliation (inductive), 157–61
Analogy, 147, 149–57, 179
Analytic and synthetic, 37–8, 129–34
Analyticity of language, 120–2, 129–34
Articulation, double, 112–15
Axiomatic theory, 44–5

Basic truths, 34–6, 45
Behaviourism, 69–70
Being sure, viii, 9–12, 19, 20, 25–6, 29, 50–63, Ch. 4, 266–7
Belief, viii, 3, 7–9, 21, 60–1
Body and Mind, 66–72, 92

Categories, 209 ff., 237–9
Cause, 220–37
Certainty, 61–3, 88, 266–7
Communication, 123–6, 144
Concepts, 139–43, 198–208, 268
Consistency, 168–70, 201, 240–65
Constraint in knowledge, 57–9, 87–8
Conventionalism, 45, 119–20, 127–9, 147, 257–9
Conviction, 8, 9–12, 14–15

Decision, 56–7, 147
Deduction, 32, 43, 145, 149–50, 162–6
Descriptions, theory of, 138
Disengagement, 95–8
Dreaming, constraint theory of, 58–9
Dualist theory of Sense-perception, 77–86

Efficient cause, 220–4, 231–7
Empiricism, ix, 36–40, 180, 186–7, 195, 213, 220, 238, 257, 263–5
Epistemology, vii, 43, 52
Error, 10–11, 22, 29, 40
Evidence, 12–14, 19–21
Excluded Middle, 244–7

Experience, 36–40, 180, 186–7, 195, 213, 220, 238, 257, 260–5

Fallibility, human, 10–11, Ch. 2, 266–8
Freedom to think, 148–9

General, existence of the, 195–208
Generalization techniques, 99–102, 134–43
Grammar, universal, 109, 114–15, 154–5

Homonymy, 118, 126

Idealism, 81, 182–3, 201–2, 267
Identity, Law of, 247–51, 264
Illumination, 31
Imagining, 123, 140–3, 197–8
Induction, 34–5, 37, 145, 150, 157–62, 178
Infallibility, Ch. 2, 270–1
Inference, 43, 162–6
Intentional inexistence, 92–5
Intuition, 3, 30–48, 50, 161, 163–5, 176, 180, 182, 195–6
Inventiveness, 98–9

'Knowing that' and 'Knowing how', 5, 9
Knowledge, certain and probable, viii, 3, 7–9, 11, 18–21, 49–50, 266–7; (in the strict sense) personal, 55–6, issue settling, 56–7, and constrained, 57, primal and absolute, 60–3, 270, of self, 66–72, 190–4, of other minds, 72–7, 194–5, of things, 77–86, 188–90

Language, viii, 6, 44, Chs. 6 and 7, 200–1, 209, 268
Logic, 43, 209
'Logically' true, 17–18, 270

Mathematics, 40–2
Memory, 96–7, 206–8
Mental activity and passivity, 31
Minds, other, 72–7, 194–5
Models, 147, 150–4
Morpheme, 112–15

Multiple meaning, 118–19

Necessity, 17–18, 44, 183–4
Non-contradiction, Law of, 35–6, 45, 251–6

Opinion, 3, 7–9, 22

Paradoxes, 42, 245–6, 253
Particulars, 187, 188–208
Permanence of substance, 214–15
Phonemes, 110–14, 118
Physical bodies, 77–82, 188–90
Polysemy, 118, 125
Postulate of parallels, 41
Power, 216, 231
Primal knowledge, 60–3
Probabilism, 52–4, 60
Projection Theory, 228–37
Psi-sentences, 68–72

Rationalism, ix, 49, 59–60, 177, 180, 237–9, 240–65
Reason, ix, Ch. 9, 208, 240–2, 269–70
Regular Sequence Theory, 222–8
Relative frequencies, 158
Religious knowledge, 28
Resemblances and identities, 202–8

Scepticism, 11, 63, 266–7

Science, 33–4, 36–9, 46, 187, 216–17
Self, knowledge of, 29, 38–9, 66–72, 190–5
Self-evident, 43
Sensa, 77–86
Sense-perception, 33, 77–86, 213
Sensing ('bare'), 28–9
Sign Theory, 105–7
Signs, 99–102
Singular and general, 134–8
Speech, 110–15, Ch. 7
Spontaneity, 147–71
Subjectivism, 20, 70–1
Substance, 210–20
Synonymy, 119, 126, 257
System-construction, 147, 166–70, 202

Tense logic, 249–51
Thinking, viii, Ch. 5, Ch. 7, 267–9
Thought, Laws of, 240–65
Three Condition Theory, 4–26, 50–4, 63, 66, 180
Toleration, principle of (Carnap), 167
Truth, 23–4, 37–8, 50, 63–5, 270–1

Universals, 198–208, 249, 269

Words, performative use of, 6; as free forms, 111–13, and as concepts, 140–3